A Q U A V I T

A Q U

AND THE NEW

WITH A PREFACE BY HÅKAN SWAHN

PHOTOGRAPHS BY SHIMON & TAMMAR

A V I T

MARCUS SAMUELSSON

HOUGHTON MIFFLIN COMPANY

BOSTON   NEW YORK   2003

For information about permission to reproduce selections from
this book, write to Permissions, Houghton Mifflin Company,
215 Park Avenue South, New York, New York, 10003.

Visit our Web site: www.houghtonmifflinbooks.com.

LIBRARY OF CONGRESS CATALOGING-IN-PUBLICATION DATA

Samuelsson, Marcus.

Aquavit and the new Scandinavian cuisine / Marcus Samuelsson ; with
a foreword by Håkan Swahn ; photographs by Shimon & Tammar.

p. cm.

Includes bibliographical references and index.

ISBN 0-618-10941-2

1. Cookery, Scandinavian.   2. Aquavit (restaurant)   I. Title.

TX722.A1S22 2003

641.5948—dc21   2003042018

Book design by Anne Chalmers
Food styling by Rori Spinelli-Trovato
Prop styling by Robyn Glaser
Typefaces: HTF Requiem, The Sans

Printed in China

CAC 10 9 8 7 6 5 4 3 2 1

TO MY GRANDMOTHER,

HELGA JÖNSSON,

AND MY FATHER,

LENNART,

AND MOTHER,

ANN MARIE

ACKNOWLEDGMENTS

Working on this book has been a great experience — and one that would not have been possible without many other people. I am deeply grateful for their dedication, commitment, and support.

First, I'd like to thank the entire staff of Aquavit for their hard work and their commitment to quality — especially the key members of the kitchen crew, who always inspire me with their ideas and their passion: Nils Norén, Tomas Bengtsson, Adrienne Odom, Roger Johnsson, Vinny Chirico, and Kingsley John.

Of the others who were a big part of the book, I'd particularly like to thank Angela Miller, Rux Martin and the entire team at Houghton Mifflin, Judith Sutton, Shimon and Tammar Rothstein, Maria Robbins, Rori Trovato, Sharon Bowers, Christina Skogly, and Christine Ziccardi.

I am also grateful to the many people who have inspired me and helped me along the way, from the chefs and restaurateurs who provided me with so many different opportunities to my fellow chefs and colleagues.

I'd especially like to thank my good friend Richard Lavin, who took me under his wing when I first came to America, introduced me to the cooking community, and taught me about the history of American food and the restaurant industry.

And, of course, special thanks to Håkan Swahn, who took a big chance in making me executive chef when I was only twenty-four years old. He not only gave me the job but then stepped back and let me have my way. He has taught me everything I know about the business side of running a restaurant. I will be forever grateful for the break he gave me, but, most valuable of all, he has also become my very good friend.   —M. S.

CONTENTS

FOREWORD

When I conceived of opening Aquavit in New York City in the early 1980s, most people thought the plan was plagued by the ignorance and wishful thinking that doom so many restaurant startups. Their skepticism was natural: Americans did not associate Scandinavia with fine dining.

My idea was born partly of frustration. Even though the restaurant scene in Stockholm was evolving rapidly, contemporary Swedish food could not be found in New York City—or anywhere in the United States, for that matter. Even gravlax, the most famous Swedish dish, was all but unknown.

Most Americans, if they thought of Scandinavian food at all, associated it with the smorgasbords that had flourished throughout the Midwest in the 1950s. These restaurants were usually opened by Scandinavians who had worked on cruise ships and prepared the food the way they had learned to make it there, and the chefs often had little training or imagination.

While Swedish food in America was becoming increasingly stodgy and clichéd, however, a new generation of cosmopolitan chefs was creating an innovative cuisine in Stockholm's popular restaurants. Most of these chefs had been trained in France, where they were influenced by nouvelle cuisine, and their culinary horizons had been further expanded by travels around the globe.

In opening Aquavit, I wanted to present the emerging cuisine of Scandinavia without compromising the integrity of its classic dishes. For inspiration, I turned to Tore Wretman, the father of modern Swedish cooking. Tore was one of the first Swedish chefs to train in France, and his education there shaped his culinary journey—and that of the many young chefs who emulated him—when he returned to Sweden. His Stockholm restaurant was a driving force in contemporary Scandinavian cuisine, and he became the first gastronomic counselor to King Gustaf Adolf VI—a position on the same level as that of a military general. Tore and I began crisscrossing the United States in the 1980s to promote Swedish food, and he gave me many ideas about what a modern Swedish restaurant in New York City should be.

In 1987, Aquavit opened in the beautiful and historic Rockefeller Townhouses. Today, more than 100,000 guests walk through our wrought iron doors each year. Our food has drawn visitors not only from New York but from all over the United States and the rest of the world.

Much of our success is due to chef Marcus Samuelsson, who has done more than anybody I know to improve the reputation of our food. Like Tore Wretman, Marcus understands that Scandinavia's culinary foundation is as much about flavors as it is about individual dishes, and this knowledge allows him to incorporate new dishes inspired by discoveries he has made on his travels while staying true to the Scandinavian spirit.

The curing and preserving methods that are the basis of many Scandinavian classics have given rise to innumerable variations. Other traditional dishes never change, except in their presentation. And the ingredients that have always identified Swedish food—fish from the sea and our thousands of lakes, berries and game from our forests, and herbs and spices such as dill, fennel, and cardamom—remain an essential part of Marcus's repertoire. The result is a cuisine that, like any living tradition, is in motion, looking back and ahead at the same time.

—HÅKAN SWAHN, OWNER, RESTAURANT AQUAVIT

I was born in Ethiopia, but my roots are in Sweden. I was adopted when I was three years old, and I grew up on the southwestern coast of Sweden in Göteborg, the largest city after Stockholm and the largest seaport in Scandinavia. I had a very happy childhood there, living in a city whose harbor hosted trading ships from all over the world. My grandmother, Helga, lived just a short walk from our house. I started cooking with her when I was no more than five or six years old, and I spent many hours in her kitchen. Much of the soul and spirit of my food comes from her.

Before moving to Göteborg, my grandmother had lived most of her life just outside Helsingborg, in the province of Skåne. To say a person comes from Skåne carries a lot of meaning for a Swede. At the southernmost tip of the country, Skåne is in many ways like Provence. With the mildest climate and the most fertile soil in Sweden, it is the country's chief agricultural region. Not surprisingly, Skåne has always been known for its great food and great cooks, and my grandmother was no exception. Her world revolved completely around food — so much so that in my memory I almost always see her from the back, because she usually stood facing the stove. She never sat down if friends or family were there to be served.

For my grandmother, each year was a cycle of gardening, preserving, and cooking. Preparations for Christmas began in October. First she would make 1-2-3 vinegar, the unique, sweet-tart Swedish vinegar used for pickling everything from fish to mushrooms. There were jams of all kinds to be put up and homemade mustards to add to the pantry. Near the end of November, it was time to pickle the herring and the cabbage.

2 AQUAVIT

Next she set aside aquavits, clear liquors served before or after a meal, to infuse for several weeks or more. These were traditionally flavored with caraway, cardamom, and/or fennel, and she also prepared sweeter versions with lingonberries or black currants, but she never drank them. As in many households, these strong spirits were reserved for the men. Finally, she would make batches of dough for ginger cookies and other Christmas cookies and freeze them. By the time she was finished, it was already December.

My grandmother's food was rustic — the recipes for some of the traditional Swedish dishes she cooked are in this book. Every Sunday she roasted a chicken seasoned with cardamom, star anise, cloves, and other spices for dinner. Nothing was ever wasted in her kitchen; frugality was one of the most important lessons I learned from her. She would turn the leftover chicken into another dish and use the carcass as the basis for her delicious chicken soup.

She made many other soups as well, such as a potato soup flavored with chives and the yellow split pea soup called *ärtsoppa*. (*Ärtsoppa* is so much a part of Swedish culture that when winter arrives, even the most sophisticated Swede craves a bowl of it.) Simple pork dishes were also one of my grandmother's mainstays, often served with cabbage, or, in a classic Swedish pairing of meat and fruit, with plums. Respect for ingredients was another important lesson I learned from her. Other people might buy canned fish balls, the seafood equivalent of Swedish meatballs, but she always made hers from scratch, starting with fresh local cod, and served them with mashed potatoes and lingonberries. And we often

baked together, making cookies, flatbreads and other peasant breads, or cinnamon buns.

My grandmother always had projects that needed to be done, so whenever I popped over to her house — which was often, because I loved her food — she would say, "Ah, there you are. Come, I have a job for you." And she would set me up to string rhubarb or shell peas or pluck a chicken. That was how I was inducted into the pleasures and pains of kitchen work and gardening.

When we weren't doing chores around the house, we were out foraging in the countryside, picking mushrooms and whatever berries might be in season. There was a forest just minutes away from Göteborg, and although I often found it a little scary, because I might encounter a snake or accidentally pick a poisonous mushroom, I always went along to help my grandmother carry the wooden baskets and learn as much as I could from her. My father, a geologist, spent most of his time outdoors, and he was an expert mushroom hunter. Our house was always filled with baskets of fresh mushrooms, strings of mushrooms hanging to dry, and pickled and preserved mushrooms in jars for another day.

In the summer my family went to Hasselesund, a tiny fishing village just north of Göteborg, to stay at what had been my paternal grandfather's house. There we lived like every other fishing family on the west coast. We caught and ate fresh fish and shellfish every day, feasting on mackerel, shrimp, cod, salmon, and crab, none of it more than a few hours out of the water. And there was no need to buy groceries — everyone bartered with the neighbors to get whatever was needed.

I had my first summer job in Hasselesund, working in a fish factory, sorting the many different varieties of seafood the boats brought in. When I wasn't working, I might bicycle to Smögen, another small village, which is known particularly for its shrimp. Its famous auctions were held three times a day — at eight in the morning and at five in the afternoon to sell the day's catch, and then at seven in the evening for the shrimp. My uncle worked there, and I learned from him how the complicated auctions worked and how to choose the freshest fish. Those were exciting days, and my friends and I would watch as buyers from all

over competed for the best seafood for the shops and restaurants they represented. I think of those summers every time I visit a fish market or breathe the salt air of a seaside town.

Freshwater and saltwater fish, not surprisingly, are a cornerstone of Swedish cooking, for the country is not only surrounded by the sea but is dotted with lakes, ponds, and rivers. Most people live along the seacoast, and the taste for seafood dates back to well before the Vikings. (Kitchen middens filled with herring bones, dating from Neolithic times, have been found in coastal areas all over Scandinavia.)

But Sweden is also a land of ancient forests and mountains. Hunting for game and foraging for wild berries and mushrooms are time-honored traditions that are still very much a part of Swedish life. Wild boar, venison, rabbit, quail, and pheasant, as well as an amazing variety of wild mushrooms, appear with great regularity on Swedish tables. The seasons for wild strawberries, lingonberries, cloudberries, and other berries are eagerly awaited.

Geography is not the only thing that affects a country's cuisine; climate plays an important role as well. Long, cold winters and very brief summers are a fact of life in Sweden, so traditionally people spent the summer days on activities that would ensure survival through the harsh winter. Meats and fish were dried, salted, smoked, brined, or pickled. Vegetables—potatoes, beets, rutabaga, and parsnips are Scandinavian staples—were pickled or stored in root cellars, and fruits and berries were turned into preserves. Just as the sweet-salty or sweet-tart balance that characterizes many pickled and preserved foods is a national taste, sweet and savory combinations are also popular, such as game served with lingonberries and pork served with apples or other fruit.

Dill is a principal seasoning—it is the traditional flavoring for both gravlax and aquavit—and chives, fennel, and other herbs and spices are also important. For those unfamiliar with Scandinavian food, the appearance of curry and garam masala in my recipes may seem to be an example of fusion cuisine. But in fact Indian spices have formed part of the Swedish pantry for hundreds of years. In the seventeenth century, Dutch and English merchants made Göteborg a flourishing commercial center,

and the Swedish East India Company was established there in 1731. My grandmother often roasted a pork shoulder rubbed with garam masala, and glögg, that most Swedish of holiday drinks, more often than not includes garam masala or a similar combination of spices.

When I was fourteen, I began working part-time at a bakery and then in restaurants in Göteborg, and I entered the Culinary Institute there when I was sixteen. Shortly after graduating, I landed a job at the top restaurant in the city, Belle Avenue. Like all the best restaurants at the time, it served classic French food, and I spent a year and a half working in every position and learning the fundamental techniques of that cuisine. With Göteborg's bustling harbor at hand, the restaurant naturally served a lot of seafood,

and although I'd absorbed a great deal during my summer job at the fish factory, it seemed as if I had to learn the name of a new kind of fish every day. The chef became one of my first mentors, and he helped me get my next job, at one of the most famous hotels in Interlaken, Switzerland. There too the cuisine was classic French, but the atmosphere was far more formal than that in the relaxed Swedish kitchens I was accustomed to (I had to retire my turquoise Converse high-tops). The hours were long and the work demanding. My first job was preparing the fish, and every morning I came in to face a wall of it — stacked, literally, from floor to ceiling — waiting to be cleaned, scaled, and filleted. As I moved among the different stations in the kitchen, I also learned more about luxury ingredients such as foie gras, truffles, and caviar.

When I arrived in New York City in 1993 for a six-month apprenticeship at Aquavit, I discovered a completely new world, both in the city, with its cultural richness and its mix of races and ethnicities, and in the restaurant kitchen, where there was a range of ingredients that I could never have imagined. When I left New York at the end of my apprenticeship, I knew I wanted to return someday.

The world began to open up for me. I took a position with an international cruise ship line and cooked my way around the globe. Traveling from Asia to the Caribbean to South America and countries in between, I discovered an incredible number of new and exotic cuisines, an experience that, together with my earlier stay in New York, changed my perspective. I became more and more curious about different cultures, reading whatever I could get my hands on, and I kept copious journals filled with notes on ingredients and recipes and ideas for new dishes. When my international tour ended, I jumped at the chance to work in France — an apprenticeship at Georges Blanc's three-star restaurant outside Lyon was not something any aspiring chef would turn down!

Yet New York City was where I longed to be, so I wrote to Aquavit's owner, Håkan Swahn, and asked him for a job. After a year in France, I reported for work at Aquavit as a sous-chef under the executive chef, Jan Sendel. Then fate intervened. Two months later, Sendel died unexpectedly. In a great leap of faith, Håkan put me, then just twenty-four years old, in charge of the kitchen.

At first, one of our main goals was to educate Americans about

Swedish cuisine, and though I wanted to make a lot of changes to the menu, I was determined to hold on to the essence of Swedish cooking: seafood, game, and pickled and preserved dishes. But America was educating me as well. After working in different kitchens and traveling around the world, I was amazed to find many of the spices, condiments, and food combinations of far-flung parts of the globe on nearly every corner of New York. Within just a few blocks of my apartment or the restaurant were Asian and Italian markets, Japanese sushi bars, and restaurants serving Korean or Turkish or Caribbean food — and I was working as a Swedish chef in a Swedish restaurant! It was a total sensory overload. But as my vocabulary of tastes and flavors continued to grow, I realized that I might be able to draw on these different cuisines and incorporate them into my cooking, keeping in mind the guiding principles we had set for the restaurant.

All my early training had centered on technique, the foundation of classic French cuisine. But a palette of flavors is just as essential to a creative chef, and I was starting to develop an international repertoire. For example, although coriander seeds have been used in Scandinavian cooking for centuries, fresh coriander (cilantro) is very much a new thing there, and I eagerly added it to my kit of ingredients. After tasting miso, the fermented soybean paste that is a mainstay of the Japanese culinary tradition, I decided to try it as a marinade for tuna — not such a great leap, since both Scandinavia and Japan are fish-eating cultures, and both peoples have a taste for salty, pickled, and fermented foods. Gradually, my approach to creating new dishes became driven less by technique and more by flavor.

In the process, I began to pay more attention to texture, temperature, and aesthetics, focusing on elements of contrast. For a salad, I might combine a mix of crisp and soft greens, creamy blue cheese, and crunchy toasted hazelnuts, with some toasted garlic chips. My riff on wild mushroom salad incorporates mushrooms with three different textures — pickled, sautéed, and raw — and my otherwise classic cauliflower and potato puree is offset by crisp accents of sautéed potatoes and artichokes.

Contrasting temperatures also give dishes a distinctive identity. I serve pan-seared fish fillets, hot from the skillet, in a chilled tomato soup

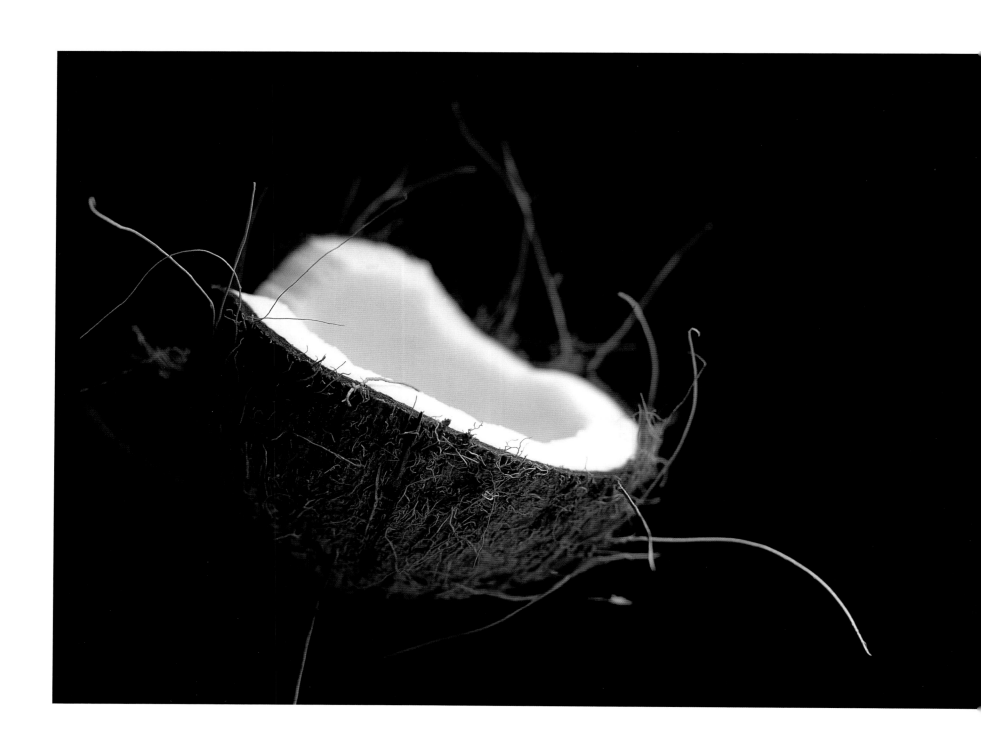

and play off icy-cold sorbet against a hot, spicy dish. Cucumber sorbet with rare grilled tuna and curry sorbet with hot-smoked salmon are favorite pairings.

Since an appreciation of aesthetics is deeply ingrained in Swedish culture, it was natural that dramatic composition was part of my approach from the start. My grandmother might be surprised to see the bright paintings I create on the plate, but the homemade mustards I make them with are the same ones she taught me.

The essence of Swedish traditional cuisine, classic techniques, familiar and exotic flavors, and contrasting flavors, textures, and temperatures are all reflected in the new Scandinavian cuisine that I am proud to present in this book.

THE

RAW

AND

THE

CURED

GRAVLAX WITH MUSTARD SAUCE

SERVES 10 TO 12 AS AN APPETIZER, MORE AS PART OF A BUFFET

Gravlax, salmon cured to a velvety, silky-smooth texture in a sugar-salt-dill mixture, is one of the great traditional Scandinavian dishes. An essential part of any smorgasbord table, it also makes an elegant appetizer for a dinner party, perhaps a New Year's Eve celebration. Although it is a special-occasion dish, it is simple to prepare. I like to start the cure at room temperature, so that the sugar and salt slowly dissolve, penetrating the flesh of the fish, then finish with a longer stint in the refrigerator. (The word *gravlax* comes from *gravad lax*, literally, "buried salmon," because in the days before refrigeration, the salmon was buried in the ground to keep it cold as it cured.) ✣ As gravlax has become popular in the United States, chefs have experimented with all sorts of cures — using tequila and cilantro, for example, or gin and juniper berries. But of all the fresh herbs used in Sweden, dill is the most popular, particularly in fish preparations, and I offer the classic version here, with the traditional mustard-dill sauce as an accompaniment. I do add a little coffee to the sauce to give it a touch of earthiness. ✣ On a smorgasbord table, present the cured fish whole, with a sharp slicing knife so guests can serve themselves. If you're not sure about your guests' knife skills, slice the gravlax and arrange the paper-thin slices on a platter, with the mustard sauce alongside.

1   cup sugar

¹/₂ cup kosher salt

2   tablespoons cracked white peppercorns

2¹/₂–3 pounds skin-on salmon fillet, in one piece, any pin bones removed

2–3 large bunches fresh dill, coarsely chopped (including stems)

FOR THE MUSTARD SAUCE

2   tablespoons honey mustard

1   teaspoon Dijon mustard

2   teaspoons sugar

1¹/₂ tablespoons white wine vinegar

1   tablespoon cold strong coffee

Pinch of salt

Pinch of freshly ground black pepper

³/₄ cup grapeseed oil or canola oil

¹/₂ cup chopped fresh dill

Thin slices Potato Mustard Bread (page 204) or whole-grain bread

1. **PREPARE THE GRAVLAX:** Combine the sugar, salt, and peppercorns in a small bowl and mix well. Place the salmon in a shallow dish and rub a handful of the salt mixture into both sides of the fish. Sprinkle the salmon with the remaining mixture and cover with the dill. Cover the dish and let stand for 6 hours in a cool spot.

2. Transfer the salmon to the refrigerator and let cure for 36 hours.

3. **UP TO 1 DAY AHEAD, PREPARE THE MUSTARD SAUCE:** Combine both mustards, the sugar, vinegar, coffee, salt, and pepper in a blender. With the machine running, add the oil in a slow, steady stream, blending until the sauce is thick and creamy. Transfer to a bowl and stir in the dill. Cover and refrigerate for at least 4 hours, or overnight, to allow the flavors to marry.

4. Scrape the seasonings off the gravlax. Slice the gravlax on the bias into thin slices, or leave whole so your guests can slice it themselves. Serve with the mustard sauce and bread.

Buy only the freshest salmon for gravlax; ask the fish market for sushi-quality fish. If wild salmon from the Pacific Northwest or Alaska is in season, so much the better; wild salmon has more flavor and a better texture than the farm-raised fish. There are several different varieties of salmon, most of which are in season in the late spring or in the summer. Look for wild salmon at good fish markets.

Gravlax will keep in the refrigerator, well wrapped, for at least 7 days. Leftovers can also be frozen, wrapped in plastic and then in foil, for up to 2 months.

Be sure to save the salmon skin to make Crispy Salmon Skin (page 20). If you serve only part of the salmon, cut off the exposed skin and reserve it. When you are ready to serve the remainder of the gravlax, crisp the skin as directed in the recipe, then break it up and use it as a garnish for the fish.

CRISPY SALMON SKIN

**MAKES 1 CRISPY SALMON SKIN OR ABOUT 1½ CUPS BROKEN-UP PIECES
IF MADE WITH THE SKIN FROM A WHOLE SIDE OF SALMON, LESS IF USING THE SKIN FROM GRAVLAX**

½ cup water

¼ cup sugar

2 tablespoons soy sauce

2 tablespoons freshly squeezed lemon juice

Skin from one side raw salmon or from Gravlax (page 18)

It is important to scrape away every bit of meat and fat from the skin, or it may burn while crisping in the oven.

If you leave the skin in one piece, you can use it as an edible platter for other seafood.

1. Combine the water, sugar, soy sauce, and lemon juice in a small saucepan and bring to a boil, stirring to dissolve the sugar. Remove from the heat and let cool.

2. Lay the salmon skin on a cutting board and use a very sharp knife to scrape away any bits of meat and fat. Transfer the skin to a shallow dish (or a zipper-lock plastic bag). Pour the marinade over the skin and cover with plastic wrap (or pour the marinade into the bag and seal the bag). Transfer to the refrigerator and let marinate for at least 3 hours, or as long as overnight.

3. Preheat the oven to 300°F. Line a baking sheet with aluminum foil or parchment paper.

4. Drain the salmon skin and lay it on the baking sheet. Bake for 20 minutes. Increase the oven temperature to 400°F and bake for 5 more minutes, or until the skin is very crisp. Remove from the oven and let cool.

5. Break the salmon skin into cracker-sized or smaller pieces, or leave it whole (see Note). Serve or use the same day.

One of the best parts of salmon is the skin. Cooked until crisp, it is as tasty as bacon or roasted chicken skin. Broken up into large or small pieces, it can be used as a garnish for Gravlax (page 18), nibbled as a snack on its own, tossed into a salad, or served instead of chips with a dip. Although this might seem like a chef's creation, it is actually an instance of economy in the kitchen, a tradition handed down to me by my grandmother. ✣ Use the skin the same day you make it, and don't refrigerate it, or it will lose its crispness. And, of course, if you don't have the skin from a whole side of salmon, you can certainly do this with a smaller piece.

PICKLED HERRING SUSHI-STYLE

¾ pound fingerling or Yukon Gold potatoes

1 tablespoon mustard oil (see Pantry, page 282) or olive oil

1 teaspoon Dijon mustard

1 teaspoon rice vinegar

½ teaspoon wasabi powder

½ teaspoon kosher salt

4 whole pickled herring fillets or one 12-ounce jar (or two 6-ounce jars) pickled herring (home-style or in wine sauce, not in sour cream), drained

Purple Mustard (page 267)

At Aquavit, we use a sushi mat to prepare these, but the potato mixture can also be simply shaped into logs on a cutting board, as described here.

1. Put the potatoes in a medium saucepan, add salted water to cover by 1 inch, and bring to a boil. Cook for 20 minutes, or until tender. Drain and let stand until cool enough to handle.

2. Peel the potatoes, put them in a medium bowl, and mash well with a fork. Add the mustard oil, Dijon mustard, rice vinegar, wasabi, and salt, and mix well.

3. Divide the potato mixture into quarters. On a board or other work surface, roll each portion under your palms into a log about 1 inch in diameter and 9 inches long.

4. If using whole herring fillets, slice them on the diagonal into ½-inch-wide strips. If necessary, cut any larger pieces of jarred herring in half, or trim them to fit the potatoes. Cut the mashed potato logs into 1½-inch lengths. Stand them on end and top each one with a piece of herring. Serve at room temperature, or refrigerate and serve chilled.

5. Just before serving, garnish each piece of "sushi" with a dollop of purple mustard.

The similar textures of pickled herring and the raw fish used in sushi inspired this recipe. Because herring is almost always served with potatoes in Scandinavia, I replaced the traditional sushi rice with mashed potatoes. These "sushi" make an unusual hors d'oeuvre for a party, or you can serve several pieces per person as an appetizer. ✣ Whole pickled herring fillets can be found in some gourmet markets and delis. If you cannot locate them, jars of pickled herring pieces are available in most supermarkets; look for them in the refrigerated section.

GRAVLAX-CURED TUNA WITH PAPAYA SALAD

SERVES 4 TO 6 AS AN APPETIZER

FOR THE CURED TUNA

- 1 cup sugar
- ½ cup kosher salt
- 1 tablespoon crushed white peppercorns
- ½ cup finely chopped fresh dill
- 1 2-inch piece ginger, peeled and finely chopped
- ¾ teaspoon ground ginger
- ½ pound sushi-quality tuna

FOR THE PAPAYA SALAD

- ½ cup olive oil
- 2 ripe but fairly firm papayas, peeled, seeded, and cut into ½-inch cubes
- 2 tablespoons pine nuts
- 1 2-inch piece ginger, peeled and grated
- 2 garlic cloves, grated on the fine holes of a grater or finely minced
- 1 jalapeño pepper, seeded and finely chopped
- 2 scallions, trimmed and finely chopped
- 4 mint leaves, finely chopped
- 4 cilantro leaves, finely chopped
- 1 teaspoon sambal oelek (see Pantry, page 283)
  Juice of 2 limes
- 2 tablespoons sherry vinegar
- 2 tablespoons soy sauce

When fully ripe, papayas are bright golden yellow and quite soft to the touch. These are great for purees and desserts. But for salsas like this one or for salads or other accompaniments to savory dishes, slightly less ripe fruit works best. Look for papayas that are still slightly firm when pressed.

1. PREPARE THE TUNA: Combine the sugar, salt, peppercorns, dill, and the chopped and ground ginger in a small deep bowl, mixing well. Add the tuna, turning it in the mixture to coat; make sure it is completely covered by the mix. (Or combine the ingredients in a zipper-lock bag, tossing to mix well, then add the tuna, "burying" it in the mixture.) Cover and let stand at cool room temperature for 4 hours, then refrigerate overnight.

2. PREPARE THE PAPAYA SALAD: Heat 1 tablespoon of the oil in a large skillet over medium heat. Add the papaya and pine nuts and sauté for 1 to 2 minutes, or until the pine nuts are golden brown and the papaya has softened. Remove from the heat and let cool.

3. Combine the ginger, garlic, jalapeño, scallions, mint, and cilantro in a medium bowl. Add the sambal oelek. Add the remaining 7 tablespoons oil, the lime juice, sherry vinegar, and soy sauce, and mix well. Add the papaya and pine nuts, tossing to coat.

4. Scrape the seasonings from the tuna and slice it very thin. Serve with the papaya salad.

Fresh tuna was unknown in northern Europe until about a decade ago, so when I was growing up, we had only canned tuna. But once I'd discovered the great taste and texture of the fresh, I wondered why salmon should be the only fish to benefit from the type of cure used for gravlax — and tuna prepared in this way proved delicious. Although tuna doesn't require the 2-day cure used for salmon, you do need to start marinating it the day before serving.

BASS CEVICHE WITH PINE NUTS

SERVES 4 AS AN APPETIZER

3 shallots, thinly sliced

³/₄ cup freshly squeezed lime juice

1 tablespoon olive oil

8 garlic cloves, very thinly sliced

1 tablespoon pine nuts

1 tablespoon chopped fresh cilantro

2 teaspoons chopped fresh basil

¹/₂ pound sushi-quality black bass fillets

Buy the highest-quality, freshest fish possible for ceviche.

You can substitute Chilean sea bass, Spanish mackerel, salmon, or tuna for the black bass. Or use the same marinade to make a ceviche of fresh oysters.

1. Combine the shallots and lime juice in a small bowl. Set aside to marinate for 6 to 8 hours.

2. About a half hour before serving the ceviche, heat the olive oil in a small skillet over medium heat. Add the garlic and pine nuts and cook, stirring, for 2 to 3 minutes, until they just start to color. Transfer to a small bowl and let cool.

3. Stir the cilantro and basil into the garlic and pine nuts, then stir in the shallots and lime juice.

4. Thinly slice the bass on the diagonal in pieces about ¹/₄ inch thick. Arrange the fish on a deep platter and pour the marinade over the top. Set the platter in a large bowl filled with ice cubes (or in the coldest part of the refrigerator) and marinate the fish for 15 to 20 minutes, until it becomes slightly opaque.

5. Leave the platter on the ice cubes, if you used them, and serve, letting people help themselves to the fish and some of the juices.

Ceviche, which originated in Peru but is also a specialty of Ecuador and Chile as well as other South American countries, is a simple method of quick-pickling fish. The flavors and texture remind me of the many varieties of pickled fish we eat in Sweden, but because the marinating time is so much shorter and the pickling solution replaces the vinegar with citrus juices, the taste is much fresher. Unlike our pickled fish, however, ceviche must be eaten soon after it is made. ✤ While the bass is cured for only 15 to 20 minutes, the shallots that go into the mix are macerated in the lime juice for 6 to 8 hours, transforming their flavor from sharp to soft and sweet.

TANDOORI-SMOKED SALMON WITH GOAT CHEESE PARFAIT

SERVES 6 TO 8 AS AN APPETIZER, MORE AS PART OF A BUFFET

FOR THE CURE

- ½ cup packed light brown sugar
- ½ cup kosher salt
- 1 tablespoon tandoori spices (see Pantry, page 283)
- ½ cup chopped fresh dill
- 1½ pounds salmon fillet, in one piece, skin and any pin bones removed (if desired, save the skin to make Crispy Salmon Skin, page 20)

FOR THE GOAT CHEESE PARFAIT

- ½ cup milk
- 1½ teaspoons powdered gelatin
- ½ pound fresh goat cheese, crumbled

FOR THE SMOKER

- 1 cup applewood chips
- 2 teaspoons tandoori spices

Generous 1 tablespoon tandoori spices

1. PREPARE THE CURED SALMON: Combine the brown sugar, salt, tandoori spices, and dill in a small baking dish. Add the salmon and rub this mixture all over both sides of the fish. Cover and let sit for 6 hours at room temperature, turning the salmon once after 3 hours.

2. MEANWHILE, PREPARE THE GOAT CHEESE PARFAIT: Put the milk in a small saucepan, sprinkle the gelatin over it, and let stand for 5 minutes to soften the gelatin. Then stir over low heat until the gelatin has completely dissolved. Remove from the heat and whisk in the goat cheese. Pour the mixture into an 8-inch square baking pan. Cover and refrigerate for at least 3 hours, or until the parfait is set. (The parfait can be made 1 day in advance.)

Instead of the tandoori spices, experiment with other seasonings, such as berberé spices (see Pantry, page 279), curry powder, or Pastrami Spices (page 268).

For information about stovetop smokers, see page 287. Or, use a disposable roasting pan to improvise a smoker: put the wood chips in the bottom of the pan, lay the fish on a roasting rack set over the chips, and cover the pan tightly with aluminum foil. Proceed as directed in the recipe.

3. SMOKE THE SALMON: Scrape the seasonings off the salmon with the back of a knife, then wipe it with a damp kitchen towel. Put the wood chips in the bottom of a stovetop smoker and sprinkle with the 2 teaspoons tandoori spices. Lightly moisten the wood chips with a few teaspoons of water. Cover with the rack and lay the salmon on top. Cover the smoker and place over low heat. Cook for 5 minutes after you see the first wisps of smoke, then turn off the heat, turn the salmon over, cover, and let stand for 10 minutes to absorb the smoke. (The salmon will be very rare—if you prefer your salmon cooked a little more, increase the initial cooking time by 5 to 10 minutes.) Transfer the salmon to a plate and let cool, then rub the remaining tandoori spices on top of the salmon.

4. Meanwhile, using a 1-inch round cookie cutter, cut rounds from the goat cheese parfait. Place on a plate, cover, and refrigerate until ready to serve.

5. To serve the salmon as part of a buffet, leave the fish whole and let your guests slice it themselves, or slice it on the bias into $1/4$-inch-thick slices and arrange on a platter; garnish the platter with the goat cheese parfait. To serve as an appetizer, slice the salmon, transfer to individual plates, and garnish with the parfait.

Most smoked salmon is cold-smoked, but I like this hot-smoked version best of all. Two curing techniques are used here: first, a salt-and-sugar cure, similar to the one used for gravlax, then a brief stay in the smoker to add flavor and texture to the fish. At the restaurant we serve this salmon quite rare, smoking it just to flavor it. (If you don't have a stovetop smoker, you can easily improvise one using a foil roasting pan; see the Note on facing page.) ✤ Tandoori spices are an aromatic mixture used in India to season food cooked in clay tandoor ovens. The pungent spices are wonderful paired with rich salmon, and here I use them both in the cure and as a finishing touch—as well as in the smoker itself. The goat cheese parfait provides a cool balance to the salty, spicy fish. We cut the parfait into rounds or other shapes with small cookie cutters, but you could simply scoop the parfait into ovals with a small spoon.

HOT-SMOKED CHAR WITH SPICY LEMON BROTH
SERVES 4 AS A MAIN COURSE

Arctic char is very popular in Scandinavia. It is called *röding* in Sweden, meaning "The Red," because of the rosy color of its flesh, but other varieties are much paler. In Sweden, the fish is always harvested from the wild, but most of the char we get in this country comes from Iceland, where it is farm-raised. The wild fish usually has more flavor and better texture. With that in mind, I came up with the idea of lightly smoking the farm-raised char over applewood chips, just until cooked to slightly rare, to enhance its taste. ✤ The Duck Confit Risotto provides a rich bed for the fish, but for a simpler dish, you could substitute steamed or boiled rice. Or, for a lighter dish, just serve the char and the flavorful broth.

2   cups Chicken Stock (page 263)

Juice of 4 lemons

1   2-inch piece ginger, chopped

1   shallot, minced

1   garlic clove, minced

1   tablespoon light brown sugar

½   teaspoon berberé spices (see Pantry, page 279; optional)

FOR THE SMOKER

1   cup applewood chips

FOR THE CHAR

4   6-ounce Arctic char fillets, skin removed

½   teaspoon berberé spices (optional)

Kosher salt to taste

Duck Confit Risotto (page 198)

4   sprigs mint

1.   **PREPARE THE BROTH:** Combine the stock, lemon juice, ginger, shallot, garlic, brown sugar, and berberé spices (if using) in a small saucepan and bring to a boil. Reduce the heat and simmer for 20 minutes, or until reduced to 1 cup. Strain the broth through a fine sieve into another small saucepan, and set aside.

2.   **PREPARE THE CHAR:** Put the wood chips in the bottom of a stovetop smoker. Lightly moisten the chips with a few teaspoons of water and cover with the rack. Sprinkle the char fillets with the berberé spices (if using) and salt, and place on the rack. Cover the smoker and place over low heat. Cook for 7 to 10 minutes after you see the first wisps of smoke; the fillets should be beginning to turn opaque but still be rare in the center.

3.   Meanwhile, reheat the broth.

4.   Spoon the risotto into large shallow soup plates and place the char on top. Ladle the broth over and around the fish, garnish with the mint sprigs, and serve.

For information about stovetop smokers, see page 287. Or, use a disposable roasting pan to improvise a smoker: put the wood chips in the bottom of the pan, lay the fish on a roasting rack set over the chips, and cover the pan tightly with aluminum foil. Proceed as directed in the recipe.

Salmon or tilefish can be substituted for the char.

MARINATED TUNA WITH PARMESAN BROTH
SERVES 4 TO 6 AS A MAIN COURSE

FOR THE TUNA

- 1/2 cup rice wine vinegar
- 1/2 cup soy sauce
- 1/2 cup sugar
- 1 1 1/2-inch piece ginger, peeled and finely chopped
- 1 1/2 pounds tuna steak, cut 1 inch thick
- 4 slices bacon
- 1/4 cup white miso (see Pantry, page 282)
- 1 tablespoon water

FOR THE PARMESAN BROTH

- 2 tablespoons unsalted butter
- 1 tablespoon olive oil
- 2 shallots, finely chopped
- 2 garlic cloves, finely chopped
- 2 cups Chicken Stock (page 263)
- 1/2 cup heavy cream
- 2 sprigs fresh thyme
- 1/2 cup freshly grated Parmigiano-Reggiano
- 1 tablespoon brandy
- 1 tablespoon Madeira
  Kosher salt and freshly ground black pepper

  Lime Risotto (page 195)

This dish is all about contrasting textures and flavors: the smooth texture of the tuna, the salty crunch of the bacon crumbs, the chewiness and tang of the lime risotto, and the rich, creamy Parmesan broth. The cubes of tuna are marinated in a mixture of rice vinegar, soy sauce, and sugar, so that the acidic vinegar "cooks" the fish as for ceviche, while the soy sauce and sugar, like the salt-sugar mixture used for gravlax, cure and season it.

1. **PREPARE THE TUNA:** Combine the vinegar, soy sauce, sugar, and ginger in a small saucepan and bring to a boil, stirring occasionally to dissolve the sugar. Remove from the heat and let cool.

2. Cut the tuna into 1-inch cubes and place in a medium bowl. Pour the cooled vinegar mixture over the fish, cover, and marinate at room temperature for 1 1/2 to 3 hours.

3. Meanwhile, cook the bacon in a large skillet until crisp. Drain on paper towels and let cool, then finely chop.

4. Remove the tuna cubes from the marinade and pat dry with paper towels. Combine the miso and water in a small bowl, and brush the tuna all over with this mixture. Roll the tuna in the chopped bacon, place on a plate, and set aside.

5. **PREPARE THE BROTH:** Melt the butter with the olive oil in a medium saucepan over medium-high heat. Add the shallots and garlic and sauté for 2 minutes, or until softened. Add the chicken stock, heavy cream, and thyme, and bring to a simmer, then reduce the heat slightly and simmer for 10 minutes to reduce the broth slightly and blend the flavors.

6. Whisk in the cheese, brandy, and Madeira, and bring to a boil, stirring, then remove from heat. Strain the broth and season with salt, if necessary, and pepper.

7. Divide the risotto among four to six shallow soup bowls, top with the tuna, and pour the broth around the risotto. Serve immediately.

For a simpler dish, serve the fish over rice instead of the risotto. Without the risotto, this dish makes a great appetizer; it will serve 6 to 8 as a first course.

Substitute salmon, sea bass, or black bass for the tuna.

LIGHTLY CURED COD WITH RED WINE SAUCE

SERVES 4 AS A MAIN COURSE

FOR THE RED WINE SAUCE

- 3 slices bacon, diced
- 2 cups dry red wine
- 1 6-ounce can tomato paste
- 2 teaspoons fresh thyme leaves
- 1 bay leaf
- ½ cup Fish Stock (page 264)
- 2 tablespoons unsalted butter

FOR THE COD

- 1 cup water
- ¼ cup beer
- 3 tablespoons kosher salt
- 2 tablespoons olive oil
- 4 6-ounce cod fillets

You can substitute monkfish, salmon, or trout for the cod.

1. **PREPARE THE SAUCE:** Cook the bacon in a small skillet until crisp, about 10 minutes. Transfer to paper towels to drain. Pour off the bacon fat and wipe out the skillet with a paper towel.

2. Add the red wine, tomato paste, thyme, and bay leaf to the skillet and bring to a boil over high heat, stirring occasionally. Reduce the heat to medium and simmer for 15 to 20 minutes, until reduced to 1 cup. Add the stock and bring to a simmer, then reduce the heat to low and simmer gently for 10 minutes to blend the flavors. Remove from the heat and set aside.

3. **MEANWHILE, PREPARE THE COD:** Combine the water, beer, salt, and 1 tablespoon of the olive oil in a large bowl. Add the cod, turning to coat, and set aside to marinate for 25 minutes.

4. Prepare a hot fire in a charcoal or gas grill, or preheat the broiler.

5. Lift the fish out of the curing liquid and pat thoroughly dry with paper towels. Brush the fillets with the remaining 1 tablespoon olive oil. Place the fillets on the grill, or place in the broiler pan and put it about 4 inches from the heat source. Cook the fish for 5 minutes, then turn and cook for 3 to 5 minutes longer, depending on thickness, until just opaque throughout.

6. While the fish cooks, reheat the sauce over medium-low heat. Remove from the heat and whisk in the butter. Set aside, covered to keep warm.

7. Spoon a little of the sauce onto each plate and top with the fish. Scatter the bacon over the fish, and pass the remaining sauce at the table.

Unlike the mix used for gravlax, the brine for this cod contains just salt, no sugar. For centuries, curing fish was a way to preserve perishable food without refrigeration. Today, brining is used primarily to impart flavor. In Sweden, we would use the beautiful white cod called *skrej*, caught in the icy northern waters off Norway throughout the fall and winter.

SALT-CURED DUCK BREASTS

SERVES 4 AS A MAIN COURSE

2 quarts warm water

1 cup kosher salt

4 boneless skin-on duck breasts (about 6 ounces each)

Serve the duck with Mango Risotto (page 196), Creamed Baby Bok Choy (page 152), or Mustard Greens with Bacon (page 174). Or, for a simpler meal, serve the sliced duck breasts on a bed of salad greens.

1. Combine the water and salt in a large bowl, stirring until most of the salt has dissolved. Let cool.

2. Meanwhile, trim away any excess fat from the duck breasts. Pierce the skin all over with a sharp kitchen fork.

3. Put the duck breasts into the brine and place a small plate on top of the duck to keep it submerged. Cover and refrigerate for 6 hours.

4. Preheat the oven to 400°F.

5. Heat a cast-iron skillet over medium heat until hot. Remove the duck breasts from the brine and pat dry with paper towels. Lay the duck breasts skin side down in the pan and cook for 6 minutes, or until the skin is crisp and browned. Drain most of the fat from the skillet, turn the breasts over, and transfer the skillet to the oven. Roast for 5 minutes. Remove the skillet from the oven and let the duck breasts sit in the hot skillet for 4 minutes to finish cooking.

6. Thinly slice each duck breast on the diagonal and serve.

I learned this salt cure from my grandmother, who never used standard measures when she cooked. She would do an "egg check" to determine when the brine for the duck was salty enough: she'd put an egg in the salted water and then add more salt until the egg floated to the top. When my grandmother was growing up, salt cures were necessary because there was no refrigeration, and I once thought of this as a very old-fashioned dish. I've since realized a short cure in salty brine both tenderizes the duck breasts and adds tremendous flavor. Crisping the skin in a hot skillet just before serving adds textural contrast. This is one of our most popular dishes at Aquavit, yet it's very easy to prepare—a perfect main course for a simple but elegant dinner.

RICE-SMOKED DUCK BREASTS WITH HONEY–ICE WINE SAUCE

SERVES 4 AS A MAIN COURSE

Duck and orange are a classic pairing, and here the duck is marinated in orange juice along with lime juice and fresh herbs. Tea leaves are also added to the mix, with enough salt to cure the meat slightly. Then the duck breasts are smoked over rice and more tea leaves, emerging moist, tender, and delicately scented with citrus juice and the mellow aroma of the tea. ✤ The sauce plays off the same sweet-savory combination of duck and fruit, but its sweetness comes from ice wine and honey. Most ice wine comes from Germany, where it is called *Eiswein*, although a few winemakers are now producing it in the United States. When I traveled in Ethiopia, I tasted the homemade fermented honey wine called *tej*, which has the same intense sweetness and gave me the idea for this sauce.

FOR THE DUCK

- 4 boneless skin-on duck breasts (about 6 ounces each)
- ½ cup kosher salt
- 1 tablespoon black tea leaves
- 1 cup freshly squeezed orange juice
- 2 tablespoons freshly squeezed lime juice
- 1 teaspoon chopped fresh rosemary
- ½ teaspoon fresh thyme leaves

FOR THE HONEY–ICE WINE SAUCE

- 2 tablespoons unsalted butter
- 2 tablespoons honey
- 2 3-inch pieces ginger, peeled and finely chopped
- 2 shallots, finely chopped
- 2 garlic cloves, finely chopped
- 1 tablespoon finely chopped fresh tarragon
- 2 cardamom pods
- 2 cups ice wine or Sauternes

FOR THE SMOKER

- 2 cups raw rice
- 4 sprigs fresh mint
- 1 cinnamon stick

For information about stovetop smokers (or an easy alternative), see pages 26 and 287.

Ice wine, or *Eiswein*, is a dessert wine made from late-harvest grapes, usually Riesling, that are left on the vine until the first frost. The grapes are then immediately picked and crushed gently to extract only the drops of juice that have not frozen. The result is a wine that is honey-sweet, comparable to nectar.

1. MARINATE THE DUCK: Trim the duck breasts of any excess fat. With a sharp knife, score the skin in a crisscross pattern. Put the duck breasts in a shallow baking dish. Combine the salt, tea leaves, orange juice, lime juice, rosemary, and thyme, and pour over the duck breasts. Cover and let stand for 2 hours at room temperature, turning the duck occasionally.

2. MEANWHILE, PREPARE THE SAUCE: Melt the butter in a small saucepan over medium heat. Add the honey, ginger, shallots, garlic, tarragon, and cardamom pods, and cook, stirring, for 1 minute. Add the wine, bring to a simmer, and simmer until the liquid is reduced to 1 cup, about 20 minutes. Strain the sauce and set aside.

3. PREPARE THE SMOKER: Place the rice, mint, and cinnamon stick in the bottom of a stovetop smoker, sprinkle with a few teaspoons of water, and cover with the rack. Lay the duck breasts skin side up on the rack, cover the smoker, and place over low heat. Cook for 10 minutes after you see the first wisps of smoke. Transfer the duck breasts to a plate.

4. Heat a large cast-iron or other heavy skillet over medium-high heat until hot. Add the duck breasts skin side down and cook for 6 minutes, or until the duck has rendered some of its fat and the skin is golden brown. Turn the duck and cook for 1 minute longer, just to sear the meat. Remove from the heat.

5. Cut the duck breasts into thick slices (or slice thinly if you prefer) and transfer to serving plates. Drizzle the duck with some of the sauce, and pass the remaining sauce at the table.

The duck breasts can also be served at room temperature, drizzled with the sauce. With a green salad on the side, they make a great buffet dish.

WARM BEEF CARPACCIO IN MUSHROOM TEA

SERVES 4

1   10-ounce center-cut beef tenderloin roast

FOR THE FILLING

2   tablespoons olive oil

4   shallots, finely chopped

2   garlic cloves, finely chopped

2   cups peeled and diced fingerling or Yukon Gold potatoes

1   cup peeled and diced taro root (see Pantry, page 284)

2   cups Chicken Stock (page 263)

2   cups heavy cream

2   cups milk

8   tablespoons (1 stick) unsalted butter, cut into chunks

2   fresh thyme sprigs, leaves only

1   teaspoon truffle peelings (see Sources, page 290; optional)

1   teaspoon truffle oil (see Sources, page 290; optional)
     Kosher salt and freshly ground black pepper

FOR THE GARNISH

     Juice of 1 lemon

1   tablespoon olive oil

1   teaspoon truffle oil (optional)

1   tablespoon grated fresh horseradish (see Pantry, page 281)
     Kosher salt and freshly ground black pepper

2   shallots, thinly sliced

2   shiitake mushrooms, stems removed, caps thinly sliced
     Mushroom Consommé (page 92)

If you omit the truffle peelings, you may want to use more truffle oil in the filling.

Substitute bottled horseradish for the fresh if necessary.

1. Wrap the meat in plastic wrap and freeze for about 30 minutes, or until partially frozen (this will make the meat easier to slice).

2. Using a very sharp knife, cut the beef into 12 thin slices. Pound each slice between two sheets of plastic wrap until very thin. Transfer the beef to a plate, cover, and refrigerate.

3. PREPARE THE FILLING: Heat the oil in a large deep skillet, preferably nonstick, over medium-high heat. Add the shallots and garlic and sauté for about 1 minute, just until lightly softened. Add the potatoes and taro and sauté until lightly golden brown. Add the stock, cream, and milk, and bring to a boil. Reduce the heat slightly and boil gently, stirring occasionally, for 15 minutes, or until the potatoes and taro are very soft.

4. MEANWHILE, PREPARE THE GARNISH: In a small bowl, whisk together the lemon juice, olive oil, truffle oil (if using), horseradish, and salt and pepper to taste. Add the shallots and mushrooms, toss well, and set aside.

5. Drain the potatoes and taro, reserving the cooking liquid, and return them to the pan. Add the butter, thyme, truffle peelings and oil (if using), and about half the reserved cooking liquid. Mash the potatoes and taro with a fork, adding additional cooking liquid as necessary until the potatoes are the consistency you like. Season with salt and pepper to taste.

6. Heat the consommé in a saucepan over medium heat until hot.

7. Meanwhile, lay out the slices of beef on a work surface, with a short end of each slice facing you. Place 1 to 2 tablespoons of the potato-taro filling toward the bottom of each slice, and roll up to enclose.

8. Arrange 2 or 3 rolls in each shallow soup plate. Arrange the mushroom garnish on top of the rolls, pour the hot consommé over and around the rolls, and serve immediately.

The idea for this dish came from a trip to Japan, where I saw people eating Kobe beef sushi or sukiyaki; for both these dishes, the meat was sliced extremely thin and then eaten raw, as sushi, or rare, as sukiyaki. For this "carpaccio," the beef is sliced very thin and pounded even thinner, then rolled up around a garlicky taro root–potato mash. It's served in shallow soup plates, two or three rolls per person, and the meat is cooked only by the hot broth that is poured over it, leaving it very rare. ✢ Kobe, the famous Japanese beef, has an amazing texture and flavor, and we use it at Aquavit for this dish. Unfortunately, it is expensive and difficult to find, so we call for regular beef tenderloin in this recipe; flavorful boneless rib-eye steak would also work well.

CURED TENDERLOIN OF BEEF

SERVES 6 TO 8 AS AN APPETIZER

This cured beef makes an unusual alternative to gravlax, and it is sure to appeal to anyone who likes cured fish. Laid out on a plate, the thinly sliced meat looks very much like the elegant Italian appetizer called carpaccio. The beef is served with Mango Ketchup, to provide a sweet, fruity accent.

2   cups sugar

2   cups kosher salt

8   black peppercorns, coarsely cracked

1   teaspoon crushed dried jalapeño or other hot chile

1   star anise

1   cup freshly squeezed orange juice

½   cup citrus-flavored vodka (such as Absolut Mandarin or Citron)

½   cup olive oil

1   tablespoon soy sauce

1   2-inch piece ginger, peeled and finely chopped

8   sprigs fresh mint

1   1-pound center-cut beef tenderloin roast
    Mango Ketchup (page 213)

Choose a pan that will hold the beef snugly—it must be buried in the sugar-salt mixture to cure properly.

For a more traditional presentation, serve the beef with Fruit and Berry Chutney (page 215) and a little horseradish. Or, for a more contemporary dish, serve it over a simple arugula salad.

Any leftover beef makes delicious sandwiches, with the Mango Ketchup.

1. Combine the sugar, salt, peppercorns, jalapeño, and star anise in a medium bowl and mix well. Add the orange juice, vodka, olive oil, soy sauce, ginger, and mint, and stir well. Pour into a nonreactive loaf pan or other pan or dish that will hold the beef snugly.

2. Place the beef in the loaf pan and turn it several times, rubbing the curing mixture into the meat; the beef should be buried in the curing mixture. Cover the beef with plastic wrap and weight it with a 28-ounce can, clean brick, or other heavy weight. Refrigerate for 6 to 8 hours.

3. Remove the beef from the pan, brushing off the curing mixture, and pat dry with paper towels. Wrap in plastic wrap and put in the freezer for about 30 minutes, or until partially frozen. (This will make the meat easier to slice.)

4. Slice the beef as thin as possible. Arrange the slices on a platter and let stand for 20 minutes, or until the beef has reached room temperature. Serve with the Mango Ketchup on the side.

BITES, SNACKS, AND LITTLE PLATES

These little nibbles, casual snack foods, and sophisticated dishes can be served as appetizers or hors d'oeuvres. But you could also prepare a variety and make them a whole meal as part of a nontraditional smorgasbord table. Serve several dishes for a supper for four, or add a few more for a larger group and arrange the plates or platters on a buffet table. Some of the recipes are designed to serve a crowd, and others can be doubled easily.

SWEET AND SALTY PINE NUTS

MAKES 1 CUP

1 cup pine nuts

2 tablespoons ketjap manis (see Pantry, page 281)

1 tablespoon Thai red chile dipping sauce or sweet chile sauce (see Pantry, page 284)

If you want to double the recipe, it's best to make it in two batches (or use two pans), so the nuts toast and glaze evenly.

Serve these crispy pine nuts with cocktails or beer — they make a nice change from peanuts. Of course, you could make these with any nut you like, such as pecans or walnuts. The nuts are lightly glazed with ketjap manis, a syrupy Indonesian sauce that is both salty and sweet, and sweet-hot Thai chile sauce.

1. Toast the nuts in a large skillet over medium heat, stirring frequently, until they start to turn golden brown, 3 to 4 minutes. Add the ketjap manis and chile sauce and heat, stirring, until most of the liquid has evaporated, about 2 minutes. Transfer to a bowl and let cool.

2. Transfer the nuts to a small bowl and serve.

ROOT VEGETABLE CHIPS

SERVES 4 TO 6

CHOOSE 2 OR 3 (OR ALL) OF THE FOLLOWING

- 1 medium (1–1½ pounds) taro root (see Pantry, page 284)
- 2 Yukon Gold potatoes or 4 fingerling potatoes
- 2 medium beets
- 1 yellow (medium-ripe) plantain

About 4 cups grapeseed oil or canola oil, for deep-frying

FOR GARNISH

Confectioners' sugar, for dusting

Kosher salt and freshly ground black pepper

Tandoori spices (see Pantry, page 283) or curry powder (optional)

Plantains are a type of banana, sometimes called cooking banana, since they aren't usually eaten raw. Available in Latin and specialty produce markets and in some supermarkets, plantains range in color from green to yellow to black, depending on ripeness. Green, underripe plantains and yellow ones are prepared in similar ways, often fried for chips. Choose medium-ripe yellow plantains (a few spots of brown are fine) for this recipe. Unless they are overripe, plantains are not as easy to peel as a banana. To peel an underripe or medium-ripe plantain, cut off both tips and cut the fruit crosswise in half. Make 4 lengthwise slits in each half, cutting through the peel to the flesh, then pull off the strips of peel.

Other vegetables to consider for chips are parsnips, yucca, and salsify. If you use salsify, slice it lengthwise.

If you don't have a mandoline or other vegetable slicer, use a very sharp knife to slice the vegetables, but try to make the slices no more than ¹⁄₁₆ inch thick.

The chips can stand for several hours if necessary, but the sooner you serve them, the better they taste.

1. Peel the vegetables. Slice the taro, potatoes, and/or beets as thin as possible — no more than ¹⁄₁₆ inch thick — on a mandoline or other vegetable slicer; if using the plantain, cut it lengthwise into slightly thicker slices. Put the slices in a bowl of cold water (if using beets, put them in a separate bowl or they will turn the other vegetables pink) and set aside to soak for 10 minutes. See Note for preparation of plantain.

2. Drain the sliced vegetables and pat thoroughly dry. Pour 3 inches of oil into a deep-fryer or a deep heavy saucepan and heat over medium-high heat to 350°F for taro, plantains, or beets, and 375°F for potatoes. Fry the vegetables separately in batches, a handful at a time, separating the slices as necessary when you add them to the oil, and cook until golden brown: 3 to 4 minutes for beets; 2 to 3 minutes for plantains or potatoes; 1 to 2 minutes for taro root. Lift out the chips with a skimmer or slotted spoon and drain on paper towels. Be sure to let the oil return to the proper temperature between batches.

3. Sift a little confectioners' sugar over the chips while they are still warm, and sprinkle with salt and pepper and the tandoori spices, if using. Serve immediately.

Everyone loves chips, but few people realize how easy it is to make them. You can season your own chips to your own taste as well. I like to use tandoori spices or good curry powder, but you might try other combinations of spices. ✤ Almost any root vegetable makes a good chip; deep-frying capitalizes on these vegetables' inherent sweetness. With the selection listed here, you will have not only a great mix of flavors — sweetness from the beets and plantain, nuttiness from the taro, and earthiness from the potatoes — but an assortment of colors ranging from yellow to purple to golden brown. Add other favorite vegetables as you like — see the Notes for additional suggestions.

CRISPY POTATOES
SERVES 4

The inspiration for this recipe goes back to my childhood, when I was fascinated with "junk food" culture. Before I knew how the English word was spelled, I used to write my own Swedish transliteration, *djunk*, all over my school notebooks. I still like good junk food. When you pop these crispy potatoes into your mouth, you'll fall instantly in love with their flavor and texture. ✣ Panko, Japanese bread crumbs, give fried foods a light, crisp coating; the corn flakes add more crunch and a slightly sweet undertone. A bowl of these potatoes quickly disappears at a cocktail party.

2 Idaho potatoes

About 4 cups grapeseed oil or canola oil, for deep-frying

2 cups corn flakes

1 cup panko (see Pantry, page 283)

1½ cups all-purpose flour

1 teaspoon kosher salt, plus more to taste

½ teaspoon cayenne pepper

3 large eggs

Freshly ground black pepper

The potatoes are fried twice, the same way the best french fries are made. The first time, they are "blanched" in the hot oil until almost cooked through; then they are fried a second time at a higher temperature to finish the cooking and turn them golden brown and crisp.

Serve the potatoes on their own as cocktail food or alongside Barbecued Boneless "Ribs" (page 54) or Slow-Roasted Turkey Wings (page 53).

1. Peel the potatoes. Cut them into sticks ½ inch thick and 4 inches long, dropping them into a bowl of cold water as you work to prevent them from discoloring.

2. Pour 3 inches of oil into a deep-fryer or deep heavy pot and heat over medium-high heat to 350°F. Meanwhile, drain the potatoes and pat thoroughly dry with paper towels. Add the potatoes, in batches if necessary, to the hot oil and fry, stirring occasionally, for 5 minutes, or until they start to turn golden brown. With tongs or a slotted spoon, transfer the potatoes to paper towels to drain. Carefully set the pot of oil aside.

3. Transfer the potatoes to a baking sheet, spreading them out in a single layer, and place in the freezer for about 1 hour, or until they are partially frozen.

4. Combine the corn flakes and panko in a blender or a food processor and process until fine. Transfer to a shallow bowl. Combine the flour, 1 teaspoon salt, and the cayenne in a second shallow bowl. In a third bowl, lightly beat the eggs. Roll the semi-frozen potato sticks in the flour, dip them in the eggs, letting the excess drip off, and roll them in the corn flake mixture. Repeat the process a second time, and place the potatoes in a single layer on a large plate.

5. Heat the oil over medium-high heat to 375°F. Fry the potatoes, a handful at a time, for 3 to 4 minutes, or until golden brown. Remove with a slotted spoon and drain on paper towels. Be sure to allow the oil to reheat between batches. Sprinkle the potatoes with salt and pepper and serve immediately.

CRISPY TEMPURA SEAFOOD WITH CITRUS AÏOLI

SERVES 4

FOR THE BATTER

1 cup pale beer (lager)

½ cup water

Juice of 5 limes

2 tablespoons soy sauce

6 drops Tabasco sauce

1 tablespoon finely chopped fresh dill

1½ teaspoons kosher salt

¼ teaspoon freshly ground black pepper

1¾ cups all-purpose flour

2 tablespoons cornstarch

1 teaspoon baking powder

FOR THE CITRUS AÏOLI

2 large egg yolks

¾ cup mashed potatoes

1½ teaspoons Dijon mustard

2 roasted garlic cloves

Finely chopped zest of 1 lemon

Finely chopped zest of 1 lime

2 tablespoons toasted sliced blanched almonds

1 tablespoon balsamic vinegar

1 cup olive oil

¾ cup water

Juice of 1–2 lemons, or to taste

Juice of 1 lime, or to taste

Kosher salt and freshly ground black pepper

About 4 cups grapeseed oil or canola oil, for deep-frying

1¼ pounds firm-fleshed fish, such as salmon or halibut fillets or tuna steaks, cut into bite-sized chunks, and/or scallops or shucked oysters or clams

All-purpose flour, for dredging

Lemon and lime wedges, for serving

1. PREPARE THE BATTER: In a medium bowl, combine the beer, water, lime juice, soy sauce, Tabasco, dill, salt, and pepper.

2. In another medium bowl, combine the flour, cornstarch, and baking powder. Add the beer mixture, stirring until combined. Cover the batter and refrigerate for 30 minutes.

3. MEANWHILE, PREPARE THE AÏOLI: Combine the egg yolks and potatoes in a blender and blend well. Add the mustard, garlic, citrus zest, and almonds, and blend well, then add the vinegar. With the machine running, add the olive oil in a slow, steady stream, blending until thoroughly incorporated. Gradually add the water. Transfer to a bowl and season with the lemon juice, lime juice, and salt and pepper. Cover and refrigerate until ready to serve.

4. Preheat the oven to 400°F.

5. Pour 3 inches of oil into a deep-fryer or deep heavy pot and heat over medium-high heat to 360°F. Pat the fish dry with paper towels and dredge lightly in flour. Working in small batches, dip each piece of seafood, one kind at a time, into the batter, letting the excess drip off, and add to the hot oil. Fry for 3 to 4 minutes, turning the pieces occasionally, until just golden and just cooked through; or, if using tuna, cook for just 2 to 3 minutes, to medium-rare. Remove with tongs and drain on paper towels.

6. Transfer the seafood to a small baking sheet, without crowding, and place in the oven for about 2 minutes, just to reheat. Drain briefly on paper towels, season with salt and pepper, and serve hot, with the aïoli and lemon and lime wedges.

We think of tempura as quintessentially Japanese, but the technique was actually brought to Japan by the Portuguese. When properly cooked—with the oil at the right temperature, and in small batches, to avoid crowding the pot—this fried seafood is crisp on the outside, moist on the inside, light, and not all greasy. At home, I like to serve tempura seafood informally. I spread the kitchen table with newspapers and drop the fried seafood onto the papers to drain. My guests sit around the table, drinking beer and dipping the tempura into bowls of garlicky citrus aïoli.

To roast garlic, rub the unpeeled cloves with a little olive oil and wrap in foil. Roast in a preheated 350°F oven (or a toaster oven) for 25 to 30 minutes, until the cloves are soft enough to squeeze out of their skins. Let cool, then squeeze out the soft garlic pulp.

For finely chopped citrus zest, remove the zest with a zester (or use the rasp-type grater called a Microplane), then finely chop. If you don't have a zester, remove the zest with a vegetable peeler (avoid the bitter white pith) and cut into thin strips, then chop. For a great version of fish 'n' chips, serve this with Crispy Potatoes (page 44).

STEAMED CRAB ROLLS

SERVES 6

1 cup (about 6 ounces) jumbo lump crabmeat, picked over for shells
   and cartilage
2 tablespoons finely chopped sun-dried tomatoes (see Note)
1 tablespoon finely chopped fresh cilantro leaves and tender stems
1 tablespoon finely chopped fresh mint
2 tablespoons Citrus Aïoli (page 46) or mayonnaise
2 tablespoons freshly squeezed lime juice
6 8- to 10-inch rice paper rounds
   Tomato Mustard Jam (page 212) or Mango Ketchup (page 213)

If you have only dry-packed sun-dried tomatoes rather than those in oil, soak them for 5 minutes in warm water to cover, or until softened. Drain and pat dry before chopping.

Cilantro stems (and sometimes the roots as well) are used along with the leaves in much of Southeast Asia and Latin America. The stems have even more flavor than the leaves.

Rice paper, called *banh trang* in Vietnamese, is a brittle edible paper made from rice flour, salt, and water. Sold in plastic packages containing rounds or triangles of various sizes, it is used to make summer rolls or Vietnamese spring rolls. You can find rice paper in Asian markets.

1. Combine the crabmeat, sun-dried tomatoes, cilantro, mint, aïoli or mayonnaise, and lime juice in a bowl, and gently mix until well combined.

2. Set a large bowl of warm water next to your work surface. Working with 2 or 3 sheets at a time, dip each sheet of rice paper into the water for about 10 seconds, until pliable, then lay on a clean kitchen towel. Place 2 tablespoons of the crab salad on the lower third of each rice paper sheet and spread it into a line about 3 inches long. Fold the bottom of the rice paper round up over the filling, fold over the sides, and roll up into a compact cylinder.

3. Put the rolls seam side down on the rack of a steamer, cover, and steam over boiling water for about 5 minutes, or until warmed through.

4. Cut each crab roll in half, and serve with Tomato Mustard Jam or Mango Ketchup in small bowls, for dipping.

Although these rice-paper-wrapped crab rolls look Asian, sun-dried tomatoes and aïoli, both delicious with the sweet crabmeat, give them quite another dimension. ✣ Rice paper, unlike spring roll or wonton wrappers, doesn't have to be cooked or heated before serving. Here the crab rolls are steamed and served warm, but in the summertime, you could simply assemble the rolls and serve them at room temperature or cold.

LOBSTER ROLLS WITH PICKLED ASIAN PEARS
SERVES 4

This is one of my favorite recipes. Succulent lobster stands up well to the hot spices, which in turn play off the sweetness of the shellfish. At the restaurant, we sometimes serve these rolls with spicy Ginger Ale Granita (page 225). The "wrapping" for the rolls is actually paper-thin slices of pickled Asian pears, softened and sweetened by a Swedish vinegar marinade. Serve this unusual and sophisticated appetizer at a dinner party with a bowl of Citrus Salsa (page 214) on the side for dipping.

2 Asian pears

1 cup Swedish 1-2-3 Vinegar (page 262)

2 teaspoons white miso (see Pantry, page 282)

1 tablespoon mayonnaise

¼ cup freshly squeezed lime juice

¼ teaspoon sambal oelek (see Pantry, page 283) or about 6 drops Tabasco sauce

1 tablespoon finely chopped fresh cilantro

1½–2 cups bite-sized chunks cooked lobster (from two 1½- to 2-pound lobsters; see Note)

2 medium tomatoes, peeled, seeded, and diced

FOR THE HERB SALAD

1 tablespoon olive oil

Juice of 1 lime

2 sprigs fresh mint, leaves only

2 sprigs fresh cilantro, leaves only

2 sprigs fresh basil, leaves only

1–2 garlic cloves, thinly sliced

2 teaspoons caviar, preferably from California farmed sturgeon (optional)

Asian pears, also called apple pears, are in season in from late summer through early fall. If you can't get them, substitute ripe Bosc pears.

You could also make these rolls with crabmeat, boiled shrimp, or even cooked salmon.

Instead of caviar from Russian or Iranian sturgeon, which are endangered or depleted, look for caviar from the new California farmed white sturgeon, which is of very high quality (see Sources, page 290).

1. PREPARE THE LOBSTER ROLLS: Using a mandoline or other vegetable slicer, cut the (unpeeled) pears into paper-thin slices: starting on one side, slice each pear lengthwise down to the core, then turn it around and slice the other half. Put the slices in a small bowl, pour the vinegar over them, and set aside to marinate for 20 minutes.

2. Combine the miso, mayonnaise, lime juice, sambal oelek, and cilantro in a medium bowl. Add the lobster and tomatoes and toss to mix.

3. Lay a piece of plastic wrap about 10 inches long on a work surface. Arrange 8 pear slices in two rows down the center of the plastic wrap, overlapping them as necessary, to make a 4x6-inch rectangle. Place a line of the lobster mixture — about 2 tablespoons — across the lower third of the rectangle. Using the plastic wrap to help you, roll up the pear slices around the filling as tightly as possible into a compact roll. Place on a plate, and repeat with the remaining pear slices and filling, to make a total of 4 rolls. Cover and refrigerate. (The rolls can be prepared up to 6 hours ahead. Serve chilled, or bring to cool room temperature before serving.)

4. JUST BEFORE SERVING, PREPARE THE HERB SALAD: Whisk the olive oil and lime juice together in a small bowl. Stir in the herbs and garlic.

5. Using a very sharp knife, cut each roll into 2 or 3 pieces. Place on plates. Arrange the salad next to the rolls, garnish with the optional caviar, and serve.

To cook lobsters, bring a large pot of water to a boil and throw in a couple of handfuls of salt; the water should be almost as salty as seawater. Plunge the lobsters headfirst into the water, cover the pot, and cook for 12 to 15 minutes after the water returns to a boil, depending on size. Remove the lobsters with tongs and let sit until cool enough to handle. Crack the tails and claws, and remove the meat.

SQUAB TOASTS

SERVES 4

1 teaspoon grapeseed oil or canola oil

4 boneless squab breasts (see Sources, page 289)
  Kosher salt and freshly ground black pepper

1 tablespoon light brown sugar

½ cup ruby port or Madeira

4 ripe figs, halved

4 narrow rectangles brioche (4 inches long, 1 inch wide, and ½ inch
  thick) (see Note)

2 tablespoons fresh goat cheese

2 tablespoons crème fraîche or sour cream

1 teaspoon garam masala, for garnish (see Pantry, page 281;
  optional)

Fresh figs are in season from June through October. They may be green, white, yellowish green, or purple, depending on the variety; the purplish black Mission, the green Calimyrna, and the yellow-green Kadota are among the most popular types. Ripe figs are soft, plump, and fragrant; those that have begun to shrivel slightly at the stem are at the height of ripeness and will be especially sweet. Figs are quite perishable and should be used as soon as possible, although they can be refrigerated for up to 2 days.

Brioche is a rich, buttery egg bread, sold at good bakeries. If you can't find it, substitute challah or another egg bread, or use high-quality white bread instead.

1. Preheat the oven to 400°F.

2. Heat the oil in a large heavy skillet over medium-high heat. Season the squab breasts on both sides with salt and pepper. Add the squab skin side down to the pan and cook for 3 minutes. Turn the breasts over and add the brown sugar, port or Madeira, and figs. Bring to a simmer and cook for 2 minutes. Remove from the heat and let sit for about 2 more minutes to finish the cooking.

3. Meanwhile, toast the bread on a small baking sheet in the oven for about 3 minutes, until lightly golden. Set aside on the baking sheet.

4. Combine the goat cheese and crème fraîche and spread over the toasted brioche. Remove the figs and squab from the skillet (set the pan aside), and thinly slice both the figs and squab. Lay the figs and squab on top of the goat cheese toasts, dividing them evenly. Drizzle the glaze from the skillet over the toasts, and return the baking sheet to the oven for about 2 minutes, just until the topping is warmed through.

5. Transfer the toasts to a serving platter or individual plates, and dust the rim(s) of the platter or plates with the garam masala, if using. Serve with knives and forks.

Squab is one of the tastiest birds there is. The tender dark red flesh has a rich, full-bodied flavor with just a hint of wildness. These elegant little toasts are quite easy to prepare. The crust is toasted sliced brioche, the cheese is goat cheese blended with crème fraîche, and the sauce is a rich, syrupy port glaze. Ripe figs add sweetness and a little crunch from their seeds.

SLOW-ROASTED TURKEY WINGS
SERVES 8

8 turkey wings (about 7 pounds), wing tips removed (reserved for stock, if desired)

1 tablespoon kosher salt

3 cups ketchup

3 cups orange juice, preferably freshly squeezed

2 teaspoons Tabasco sauce, or more to taste

1 large onion, finely chopped

12 garlic cloves, smashed

2 teaspoons fresh thyme leaves

Unlike chicken wings, which come as "three-part" wings, with two joints and the wing tips, turkey wings are sold as one meaty portion with the wing tip attached.

VARIATION

To make Slow-Roasted Chicken Wings: Substitute 6 to 7 pounds chicken wings for the turkey wings. Cut the wings apart at the joints, and discard the wing tips (or reserve for stock). Blanch for 2 minutes, and roast for 1½ hours at 300°F and then about 30 minutes at 375°F.

1. Preheat the oven to 300°F.

2. Bring a large pot of water to a boil. Add the turkey wings and salt and return to a boil, then reduce the heat slightly and simmer for 5 minutes. Drain the wings thoroughly and arrange them in a single layer in a roasting pan.

3. Combine the ketchup, orange juice, Tabasco, onion, garlic, and thyme in a bowl and mix well. Pour the sauce over the wings, turning to coat. Roast, stirring occasionally, for 2 hours.

4. Increase the oven temperature to 375°F and roast for 30 to 45 minutes longer, or until the wings are very tender and the sauce has thickened.

5. Serve the wings hot or at room temperature.

Now that turkey parts are readily available, there's no reason that turkey wings shouldn't be just as popular as chicken wings — they are inexpensive and tasty. The wings are quickly blanched to render some of their fat, then slowly roasted in a spicy tomato-orange sauce until tender. ✣ This is casual, fun food. I like to serve the wings in a large bowl with a big fork or chopsticks (and plenty of napkins).

BARBECUED BONELESS "RIBS"

FOR THE "RIBS"

- 1 3- to 4-pound boneless smoked pork shoulder butt roast
- 1 medium onion, coarsely chopped
- 1 carrot, coarsely chopped
- 3 bay leaves

FOR THE BARBECUE SAUCE

- 2 tablespoons olive oil
- 2 red onions, finely chopped
- 1 3-inch piece ginger, peeled and finely chopped
- 4 garlic cloves, finely chopped
- 2 tablespoons honey
- 2 tablespoons light brown sugar
- 1½ cups chopped drained canned tomatoes
- 2 tablespoons ketchup
- 2 tablespoons Thai red chile dipping sauce or sweet chile sauce (see Pantry, page 284)
- 2 tablespoons Worcestershire sauce
- ½ chipotle chile in adobo sauce, chopped
- 2 tablespoons tomato paste
- 1 teaspoon finely chopped fresh rosemary
- 1 teaspoon chopped fresh thyme
- 3 cups water
- 1 cup brewed coffee

Smoked pork shoulder can be found at specialty butchers and in some supermarkets.

Chipotle chiles are smoked dried jalapeños. Although sometimes available dried in bulk, they are usually canned in a spicy adobo sauce. They have a strong smoky flavor and are quite hot. You can find them in most supermarkets, with other Mexican and Latin American foods.

For a main course, serve the ribs with mashed potatoes (see pages 188–190) and braised kale or another sturdy green, or even spinach.

It wasn't until I came to this country that I discovered barbecue. Playing around with its sweet, salty, and smoky flavors, I created this dish: the "ribs" are not the usual spareribs but instead finger-sized pieces of slow-simmered smoked pork shoulder in a spicy barbecue sauce. ❖ Serve this easy dish hot or at room temperature. It's great for picnics or as part of a buffet dish, with a side of corn bread if you like. The pork also makes delicious sandwiches. ❖ Note that the meat needs to stand overnight after cooking.

1. **PREPARE THE "RIBS":** Put the pork in a large pot and add the onion, carrot, bay leaves, and cold water to cover. Bring to a boil over high heat, reduce the heat to medium-low, and simmer for $1^1/_2$ hours, or until the internal temperature reaches 160°F. Remove from the heat and let the meat cool in the liquid, then refrigerate, still in the liquid, overnight.

2. **PREPARE THE BARBECUE SAUCE:** Heat the olive oil in a large heavy saucepan over medium-high heat. Add the onions, ginger, and garlic, and cook, stirring, for about 5 minutes, until the onions are softened. Add the honey and brown sugar and cook, stirring, for about 10 minutes, until the sugar melts and caramelizes and the vegetables are a dark golden brown. Add the tomatoes, ketchup, chile sauce, Worcestershire sauce, chipotle chile, tomato paste, rosemary, thyme, water, and coffee, and bring to a brisk simmer. Reduce the heat to medium-low and simmer gently for 1 hour, or until the sauce is reduced by about half and thickened. Remove from the heat. (The sauce can be made a day ahead. Let cool, then cover and refrigerate; bring to room temperature before proceeding.)

3. If serving the ribs hot, preheat the oven to 350°F.

4. Remove the pork from the liquid and cut into pieces approximately $^1/_2$ inch thick and 2 to 3 inches long. Lay them in a single layer in a large baking dish.

5. Pour the barbecue sauce over the meat, tossing to coat. To serve hot, heat in the oven for 15 minutes. Transfer the ribs to a large platter or deep serving dish and serve.

GOAT CHEESE AND ARTICHOKE TART

SERVES 8 AS AN APPETIZER, 10 TO 12 AS PART OF A BUFFET

½ cup plus 2 tablespoons olive oil

2 cups thinly sliced artichoke hearts (see Note)

8 garlic cloves, cut lengthwise in half

¼ cup balsamic vinegar

8 oil-packed sun-dried tomatoes, cut lengthwise in half

6–12 anchovy fillets, coarsely chopped

About ⅓ cup pitted kalamata or niçoise olives, or a combination

1 teaspoon fresh thyme leaves, plus (optional) thyme sprigs for garnish

2 small or medium Idaho or other baking potatoes

1 10-inch Buttery Tart Shell (page 275, made with the herbs), prebaked

Kosher salt and freshly ground black pepper

½ pound fresh goat cheese

For the artichoke hearts, you will need 4 large artichokes. Fill a large bowl with water and squeeze the juice of 1 lemon into it; set the lemon halves aside. Bend back and snap off the outer green leaves from each artichoke until you get to the inner cone of tender yellowish green leaves; slice off the cone of leaves. Trim off the stem of each artichoke, cut the artichoke heart into quarters, and scrape out the fuzzy choke (a grapefruit spoon works well for this), then cut the artichoke quarters into thin slices. Rub the cut surfaces of the artichokes occasionally with the lemon halves as you work, and drop the sliced artichokes into the lemon water to prevent discoloration. Drain thoroughly and pat dry before using.

You can substitute one 9-ounce package frozen artichoke hearts, thawed, for the fresh. Thinly slice them and pat dry. Reduce the artichoke cooking time slightly, and proceed as directed.

1. Heat 2 tablespoons of the oil in a large skillet over medium-high heat. Add the artichokes and garlic and sauté for 10 to 15 minutes, lowering the heat slightly if necessary, until the artichokes start to soften and the garlic starts to turn golden brown. Remove from the heat.

2. Combine the remaining ½ cup oil, the vinegar, tomatoes, anchovies, olives, and thyme in a medium bowl. Add the artichokes and garlic and mix well. Cover and let marinate at room temperature for 2 hours.

3. After the artichokes have marinated for 1 hour, preheat the oven to 450°F.

4. Bake the potatoes for 40 minutes, or until they are mostly cooked through, with only a little resistance in the center when pierced with a thin-bladed knife. Remove from the oven and let cool slightly. Reduce the oven temperature to 375°F.

5. Peel the potatoes and slice into ½-inch-thick rounds. Layer them in the bottom of the tart shell, seasoning them generously with salt and pepper as you go. Drain the artichoke mixture, and spread the artichokes, tomatoes, anchovies, and olives over the potatoes. Crumble the goat cheese over the top.

6. Bake the tart for 20 to 25 minutes, until the cheese starts to turn golden. Transfer to a wire rack to cool, and serve warm or at room temperature garnished with thyme sprigs, if desired.

For this tasty and unusual tart, inspired by my love of Mediterranean flavors, artichoke hearts are first sautéed with garlic, then marinated with sun-dried tomatoes, anchovies, and olives in balsamic vinegar and olive oil for a subtly pickled effect. The buttery herbed tart shell is lined with a layer of baked potato slices, then topped with the artichoke hearts and crumbled fresh goat cheese. ✤ Serve as an appetizer or part of a buffet, or cut into thin slices and serve alongside Slow-Cooked Leg of Lamb (page 155), as we do at Aquavit.

NAPA CABBAGE DOLMAS

SERVES 6 TO 8, OR MORE AS PART OF A BUFFET

12–16 large napa cabbage leaves
¼ pound veal sweetbreads or chicken livers
¼ cup grapeseed oil or canola oil
¼ small red onion, finely chopped
1 small shallot, finely chopped
3 ounces chorizo sausage, diced
1 small apple, peeled, cored, and diced
½ teaspoon garam masala (see Pantry, page 281)
½ teaspoon fresh thyme leaves
2 cups Chicken Stock (page 263)
2 tablespoons soy sauce
1 tablespoon dark molasses

Chorizo is a spicy Spanish smoked sausage. It is available in Latin markets and in other specialty or gourmet markets.

VARIATION

These dolmas can be made with a variety of fillings: you could even use the Asparagus Potato "Risotto" (page 194) as a vegetarian filling. Or substitute the meat mixture for the Swedish Meatballs (page 142).

1. Bring a large pot of water to a boil. Add the cabbage leaves and simmer for 3 minutes, or until wilted. Drain and pat dry with paper towels. Set aside.

2. If using sweetbreads, bring a small pot of water to a boil. Add the sweetbreads and simmer for 2 minutes. Remove the sweetbreads with a slotted spoon and drain on paper towels. When they are cool enough to handle, pull the sweetbreads apart into 1-inch pieces. Set aside. If using chicken livers, rinse them, trim, and cut into 1-inch pieces.

3. Heat 1 tablespoon of the oil in a medium skillet over medium-low heat. Add the onion, shallot, chorizo, apple, garam masala, and thyme, and sauté for 2 minutes, or until the onions are beginning to soften. Add the chicken livers, if using, and sauté until browned on the outside but still pink inside, about 2 minutes. Remove from the heat. Add the sweetbreads, if using, and mix well.

4. Lay out half the cabbage leaves on a work surface. Place a heaping tablespoon of filling in the center of each leaf. Fold the bottom of the leaf up over the filling, fold over the sides, and roll up to form a neat packet. Repeat with the remaining leaves and filling, and secure each packet with a toothpick.

5. In a large skillet, preferably nonstick, heat the remaining 2 tablespoons oil over medium-high heat until hot. Add the dolmas and cook, turning occasionally, for about 8 minutes, or until browned on all sides. Transfer to a large serving dish and remove the toothpicks. Cover to keep warm.

6. Add the chicken stock to the skillet, bring to a boil, and boil until reduced by half. Add the soy sauce and molasses, stir well, reduce the heat slightly, and simmer until the sauce is reduced and thickened, about 5 minutes.

7. Pour the sauce over the dolmas and serve warm or at room temperature.

Although dolmas are of Middle Eastern origin, they have been popular in Sweden for a very long time. In fact, this recipe is based on one from a Swedish cookbook dating from 1822. Traditionally, dolmas consist of grape leaves stuffed with rice and lamb, but Swedish versions are more likely to use green cabbage and ground pork. I substitute napa cabbage for the sturdier green cabbage, and the filling varies with what I'm in the mood for or happen to have on hand. Sweetbreads (or chicken livers) add richness, chorizo sausages provide some spiciness, and a sauce that includes molasses and soy sauce rounds out the dish with the sweet-salty combination so beloved in Sweden.

Sweetbreads are the thymus gland of young animals such as calves or lambs; veal, or calf's, sweetbreads are considered the best, with the most delicate flavor. Available at specialty butchers, sweetbreads are very perishable and should be used as soon as possible after purchase, certainly within 24 hours.

Although it is not necessary, you can soak sweetbreads in water to which lemon juice has been added to whiten them before cooking. Put the sweetbreads in a bowl of cold water to cover, add a few squeezes of lemon juice, and refrigerate for 2 hours, changing the water several times; drain thoroughly. Remove the outer membranes and any noticeable fat or connective tissue, separating the sweetbreads into smaller clusters. Cover and refrigerate until ready to cook (some recipes call for blanching and weighting the sweetbreads before further cooking).

SERRANO-WRAPPED FIGS WITH MASCARPONE

SERVES 4

2 tablespoons mascarpone cheese

1 teaspoon balsamic vinegar

4 ripe figs, cut in half

½ cup pine nuts, toasted

8 very thin slices serrano ham or prosciutto

Fresh figs are in season from June through October. They may be green, white, yellowish green, or purple, depending on the variety; the purplish black Mission, the green Calimyrna, and the yellow-green Kadota are among the most popular types. Ripe figs are soft, plump, and fragrant; those that have begun to shrivel slightly at the stem are at the height of ripeness and will be especially sweet. Figs are quite perishable and should be used as soon as possible, although they can be refrigerated for up to 2 days.

You can prepare the figs early in the day; cover them with plastic wrap and refrigerate. Remove from the refrigerator half an hour before serving.

To toast pine nuts, heat them in a large skillet over medium heat, stirring with a wooden spoon, for 3 to 4 minutes, or until they start to turn golden brown. Watch carefully, as they can burn easily, and transfer them to a plate to cool as soon as they are done.

1. Combine the mascarpone and balsamic vinegar in a small bowl and mix well with a fork, or mash with the back of a spoon.

2. Spread ½ teaspoon of the mascarpone mixture on each fig half. Top each with a few pine nuts. Wrap each fig half in a slice of ham (the thinly sliced ham will stick to itself—no need for toothpicks). Arrange on a platter or on small plates and serve.

Ripe figs, green or purple, are essential for this irresistible appetizer, with its combination of salty, sweet, and tart flavors. The Mediterranean influences are obvious, with balsamic vinegar and mascarpone from Italy, luscious figs that are typical of much of the region, and serrano ham from Spain. The toasted pine nuts add a bit of crunch and smokiness. These figs are simple to prepare, and the recipe can be doubled easily—but you will probably find that no matter how many you make, there are never leftovers. They are especially good with port or sherry.

FOIE GRAS "SUSHI"

MAKES ABOUT 30 PIECES; SERVES 6 TO 10

FOR THE SUSHI RICE

1½ cups sticky rice

¼ cup mirin

1 tablespoon rice wine vinegar

1½ teaspoons sake

1 tablespoon freshly squeezed lemon juice

1½ teaspoons sugar

1 small sheet kombu (see Pantry, page 281; optional)

½ papaya, peeled, seeded, and cut into small dice (about ¾ cup)

FOR THE FOIE GRAS

½ pound Grade A duck foie gras (see Sources, page 289)

Kosher salt and freshly ground black pepper

Mango Ketchup (page 213)

Sticky rice, also called sweet rice or glutinous rice, is a short-grain Asian rice used for sushi and for some desserts. It can be found in Asian markets and some health food stores.

Mirin is Japanese sweet rice wine. It is available in some supermarkets, as well as Japanese and other Asian markets.

If not serving the sushi immediately, set aside at room temperature briefly rather than refrigerating it—both the flavor and texture of the rice are best if not chilled.

1. PREPARE THE RICE: Put the rice in a large bowl, cover with cold water, and let soak for 5 minutes; drain and rinse. Repeat at least three times, or until the soaking water is completely clear.

2. Combine the rice and 1½ cups water in a medium saucepan and bring to a boil. Turn off the heat, cover the pot tightly with a lid and then a heavy towel, and let the rice steam for 15 minutes.

3. Meanwhile, combine the mirin, vinegar, sake, lemon juice, and sugar in a small saucepan and bring to a boil, stirring to dissolve the sugar. Remove from the heat, add the kombu, and let stand for 10 minutes to soften the kombu. Strain the broth and set aside.

4. Transfer the rice to a bowl and sprinkle ¼ cup of the broth over it, tossing a few times. Let cool, stirring from time to time.

5. Stir the diced papaya into the rice. Using your hands, shape the rice into flattened ovals 1½ inches long and ½ inch wide.

6. PREPARE THE FOIE GRAS: Cut the foie gras into pieces 2 to 2½ inches long and about 1 inch wide; you should have the same number of pieces as rice ovals. Remove any noticeable veins from the foie gras. Heat a large nonstick skillet over high heat until hot enough to make a drop of water skitter across the surface. Add the foie gras, in batches, and sear for about 10 seconds on each side. Transfer to paper towels and season with salt and pepper to taste.

7. Lay a piece of foie gras across each oval of rice. Arrange the sushi on a large platter and serve, with a bowl of Mango Ketchup for dipping.

These elegant hor d'oeuvres are a sensational way to savor foie gras. The sushi-style rice, with diced papaya adding fruitiness, provides a contrasting base for the briefly seared, meltingly rich foie gras. Anyone who likes sushi and foie gras will love these—serve them for a special occasion, with Champagne.

FOIE GRAS "GANACHE"

SERVES 8

- ½ pound Grade A duck foie gras (see Sources, page 289)
- 1 cup plus 2 tablespoons white port
- 2 tablespoons brandy
- 2 shallots, finely chopped
- 1 teaspoon finely chopped fresh tarragon
- ¾ pound (3 sticks) unsalted butter, at room temperature
- ½ cup almond flour (see Pantry, page 279)
- Scant 1 tablespoon garam masala (see Pantry, page 281)
- ½ teaspoon kosher salt
- 2 large eggs
- 1 large egg yolk

FOR GARNISH

- Aged balsamic vinegar
- Fleur de sel (see Pantry, page 283)

This has become my signature dish, one that we can never take off the menu. At first glance, it doesn't look like much on the plate — it resembles a small chocolate cake — hence the name. But when you cut into it and the molten foie gras pours out and you taste the first divine bite, you will understand why some people become almost addicted. The "ganache" is cooked just until barely set around the edges, so that the center is almost like a very rich sauce — and in the bottom of the ramekin, you will discover a chunk of foie gras, marinated in port and brandy, that has not quite melted. ✤ This dish is not especially difficult to make, but the timing can be tricky — you may not think the ganache is cooked when you check it, but just follow the directions exactly and you will be rewarded with a truly luxurious treat.

You can substitute dry sherry for the port.

For an elegant meal, serve the ganache as an appetizer before Salt-Cured Duck Breasts (page 32), Coffee-Roasted Duck Breasts (page 139), or Crispy Duck with Glögg Sauce (page 140).

1. Preheat the oven to 400°F. Generously butter eight 4-ounce ramekins, dust with flour, and shake out the excess.

2. Cut 2 ounces of the foie gras into 8 equal pieces. Combine the port and brandy in a small bowl, add the pieces of foie gras, turning once or twice, and let marinate at room temperature for 20 minutes.

3. Meanwhile, combine the shallots, tarragon, and the remaining 1 cup port in a small saucepan and bring to a boil over medium-high heat. Reduce the heat slightly and boil gently for about 15 minutes, until the shallots are soft and all the liquid has cooked away. Remove from the heat and set aside.

4. Cut the remaining 6 ounces foie gras into 1/2-inch pieces. Put the butter and foie gras in the top of a double boiler or a heatproof bowl and heat over simmering water for 4 to 5 minutes, until the butter and most of the foie gras have melted. Turn off the heat and keep warm over the hot water.

5. Toast the almond flour and garam masala in a skillet over medium heat, stirring and shaking the pan frequently, for about 10 minutes, or until fragrant and golden brown. Transfer to a plate and let cool.

6. Puree the cooked shallots in a blender. Add the almond flour mixture and blend for 1 minute on high speed. Add the salt. With the blender on medium-low speed, gradually add the butter–foie gras mixture. Transfer to a bowl and whisk in the eggs and egg yolk.

7. Divide the mixture among the prepared ramekins. Drop a piece of the marinated foie gras into the center of each. Set the ramekins in a large baking pan and add enough boiling water to the pan to come two-thirds of the way up the sides of the ramekins.

8. Bake for exactly 8 minutes, until the ganache has pulled away from the sides of each ramekin, the edges are lightly browned and look firm, the center is still jiggly when shaken, and a pool of molten foie gras ganache remains in the center—the ganache may not look done at this point, but it is; do not overcook.

9. Carefully remove the ramekins from the water bath and wipe them dry. Gently invert onto plates, if desired. Drizzle a few drops of balsamic vinegar over each ganache, sprinkle with a few grains of fleur de sel, and serve immediately.

SANDWICHES

GRAVLAX CLUB SANDWICH

MAKES 4 SANDWICHES

FOR THE GUACAMOLE

- 2 ripe Hass avocados, halved, pitted, and peeled
  Juice of 2 limes
- ½ medium red onion, finely chopped
- 1 medium tomato, peeled, seeded, and finely chopped
- 1 jalapeño pepper, seeded, and finely chopped
- 1 tablespoon finely chopped fresh cilantro
  Kosher salt and freshly ground black pepper

- 8 thin slices Gravlax (page 18)
- 12 thin slices whole-grain bread, toasted
  Generous 1 cup torn or shredded iceberg lettuce

Substitute smoked salmon for the

gravlax for an equally tasty sandwich.

1. **PREPARE THE GUACAMOLE:** Mash the avocados with a fork in a medium bowl. Add the lime juice, onion, tomato, jalapeño, and cilantro, and mix well. Season with salt and pepper to taste.

2. Spread a layer of guacamole over 8 slices of the toast. Place a slice of gravlax on 4 of these slices and arrange half the lettuce on the gravlax. Top with the remaining guacamole toasts, gravlax, and lettuce. Place the remaining slices of toast on top. Secure each sandwich with toothpicks and cut into quarters. Serve.

The most popular sandwich in our café combines the velvety textures of guacamole and gravlax, set off by crisp iceberg lettuce and chewy whole-grain bread. Serve with crunchy Root Vegetable Chips (page 43), rather than ordinary potato chips.

TUNA BURGER WITH CABBAGE TZATZIKI

MAKES 4 SANDWICHES

½ pound tuna steak, cut into ¼-inch dice

6 large sea scallops, cut into ¼-inch dice

1 tablespoon finely chopped pickled ginger

2 garlic cloves, finely chopped

1 tablespoon finely chopped fresh cilantro

1 tablespoon Thai red chile dipping sauce or sweet chile sauce (see Pantry, page 284)

1 teaspoon wasabi powder (see Pantry, page 285)

¼ cup freshly squeezed lime juice

   Kosher salt and freshly ground black pepper

4 small squares focaccia or small soft rolls

2 tablespoons olive oil, plus extra for brushing

4 tomato slices

1 cup Cabbage Tzatziki (page 148)

You can substitute ½ pound skinned salmon fillet for the scallops.

1.   In a medium bowl, combine the tuna, scallops, pickled ginger, garlic, cilantro, chile sauce, wasabi, and lime juice, mixing well. Season with salt and pepper to taste. Let stand for 10 minutes, then transfer to a strainer set over a bowl to drain off any excess liquid.

2.   Split the focaccia in half and toast lightly. Brush the cut sides with a little of the olive oil.

3.   Shape the tuna mixture into 4 patties. Heat the 2 tablespoons olive oil in a large skillet over medium-high heat until hot. Add the tuna burgers, reduce the heat to medium, and cook, turning once, for 2 minutes on each side, or until golden brown; be careful not to overcook — the tuna should be medium-rare.

4.   Put a slice of tomato on the bottom half of each of four squares of focaccia and top with a tuna burger. Spread the tzatziki over the tuna, cover with the tops of the focaccia, and serve.

For these patties, diced tuna and scallops are flavored with sweet-hot pickled ginger, spicy chile sauce, and pungent wasabi, then cooked quickly so that the tuna remains medium-rare. Tzatziki, a Greek condiment or salad traditionally made with cucumbers and yogurt, has long been popular on Swedish tables. This cabbage version provides a crunchy, cooling contrast to the spicy burgers.

KIPPERS ON CRISPBREAD

MAKES 8 OPEN-FACED SANDWICHES

2 soft-cooked egg yolks

1 tablespoon Dijon mustard

1 tablespoon olive oil

2–3 kippers or smoked herring (to make about 1 cup flaked fish)

8 crispbread crackers or 8 pieces (about 2 by 5 inches) Crispy Flatbread (page 202)

1 small red onion, finely chopped, for garnish

2–3 tablespoons drained capers, for garnish

For the soft-cooked egg yolks, put 2 large eggs in a saucepan and cover with water. Bring to a boil, reduce the heat to a simmer, and cook for 2 minutes. Drain the eggs and cool them under cold running water. Crack each eggshell in half with a knife, carefully split the egg apart, and scoop out the yolk with a teaspoon.

Kippers are salted, dried, and cold-smoked herring. Look for them at delis and specialty markets.

You can find crispbread in the cracker section of any supermarket. Wasa and Ryvita, which are widely available, are both good.

1. Combine the egg yolks, mustard, and olive oil in a medium bowl and mash to a paste with a fork. Add the kippers and mash them into the egg yolks.

2. Spread the mixture on the crackers or flatbread and sprinkle with the red onion and capers. Serve.

One of my favorite excursions from Stockholm is the forty-five-minute boat ride to the island of Fjäderholmarna, where there is a wonderful little restaurant overlooking the harbor. The best thing to order there is a sandwich like this one, made with herring freshly smoked at the factory next door. Sitting outdoors and looking out at the water, you enjoy a perfect summer meal. ✣ Serve these quick, easy, and very tasty open-faced sandwiches for lunch, pack them for a picnic, or cut them into squares or triangles for an hors d'oeuvre. You could also substitute smoked trout or another smoked fish for the kippers.

SHELLFISH SAUSAGE SANDWICH

MAKES 4 SANDWICHES

1 teaspoon unsalted butter, plus 1 tablespoon softened butter

1 tablespoon corn kernels

4 large sea scallops

1 large egg

2 tablespoons heavy cream

About ³/₄ cup finely chopped cooked lobster (from one 1¹/₂-pound lobster; see Note)

1 teaspoon finely chopped fresh cilantro

3–6 drops Tabasco sauce

Kosher salt and freshly ground black pepper

¹/₂ cup fine dry bread crumbs

2 tablespoons grapeseed oil or canola oil

1 cup Corn Mashed Potatoes (page 189)

4 good-quality hamburger buns

To cook the lobster, bring a large pot of water to a boil and throw in a couple of handfuls of salt; the water should be almost as salty as seawater. Plunge the lobster headfirst into the water, cover the pot, and cook for 12 to 15 minutes after the water returns to a boil, depending on size. Remove the lobster with tongs and let sit until cool enough to handle. Crack the tail and claws, and remove the meat.

VARIATION

You could also use the seafood mixture to make sausage links if you're so inclined; sausage casings are available at specialty butchers (or see Sources, page 290). Pipe the mixture into the casings using a pastry bag with a plain tip, and prick the sausages in a few places before cooking, to prevent bursting.

1. Melt the 1 teaspoon butter in a small skillet over medium heat. Add the corn and sauté for about 3 minutes, just until tender. Remove from the heat and let cool.

2. Combine the corn, scallops, egg, and cream in a food processor or blender and process until smooth. Transfer to a medium bowl and fold in the lobster, cilantro, and Tabasco. Season to taste with salt and pepper.

3. Shape the lobster mixture into 4 patties. Spread the bread crumbs on a plate and coat the patties on both sides with the crumbs.

4. Heat the oil in a large skillet over medium heat until hot. Add the sausage patties and cook for 3 minutes on each side, or until golden brown and cooked through.

5. Meanwhile, reheat the mashed potatoes in a small saucepan over low heat, stirring occasionally (add a little cream or milk if necessary). Toast the hamburger buns. Spread each bun with some of the softened butter and ¹/₄ cup of the mashed potatoes.

6. Put the sausages in the buns and serve hot.

Although sausages of all kinds are very popular in Scandinavia, seafood sausages are fairly uncommon. You can prepare these as patties or stuff them into casings (see Note). You could also substitute crabmeat or shrimp for the lobster. Serve the patties in hamburger buns or the links in hot dog buns — just like a Maine lobster roll.

SCANDINAVIAN SHRIMP WRAP

½ pound fingerling or Yukon Gold potatoes

3 hard-cooked eggs, peeled and chopped

1 medium red onion, finely chopped

2 garlic cloves, finely chopped

1 teaspoon finely chopped fresh chives

¼ cup freshly squeezed lime juice

1 tablespoon bottled horseradish

1 tablespoon sour cream

1 tablespoon mayonnaise

3 cups (about 1 pound) cooked and peeled small shrimp
    Kosher salt and freshly ground black pepper

4 small sheets lavash, flour tortillas, or other soft flatbread

Sandwich-sized flatbreads are available in many supermarkets, as well as in Middle Eastern markets and other specialty markets. Look for Damascus flatbreads, also called soft lavash, or other soft flatbreads sold specifically for sandwich wraps.

1. Put the potatoes in a medium saucepan, add salted water to cover, and bring to a boil. Cook for 18 to 20 minutes, or just until tender. Drain and let cool, then peel and dice.

2. Combine the potatoes, eggs, onion, garlic, chives, lime juice, horseradish, sour cream, and mayonnaise in a medium bowl and mix well. Fold in the shrimp and season to taste with salt and pepper.

3. Divide the shrimp salad among the lavash or other flatbread, roll it up in the bread, and serve.

When I was a kid, I spent my summers at Smögen, a picturesque fishing village on a small island off Sweden's northwestern coast. Everything seems to taste of the sea in Smögen, and it is known particularly for its shrimp, which is as famous as Maine lobster. We usually just peel and eat the shrimp, but I also like them in this salad with potatoes, mayonnaise, and horseradish. The salad makes a great sandwich filling, but it could also be served on its own, with Crispy Flatbread (page 202) or crispbread on the side. ❧ I prefer to use small shrimp and keep them whole, not chop them up with the other ingredients, so that they have a real presence. The best shrimp to use here are small to medium Gulf shrimp or pink shrimp from Maine, which, like those from Smögen, are cold-water shrimp.

LAMB SAUSAGE WRAP

MAKES 4 SANDWICHES

2   tablespoons olive oil

1   roasted red bell pepper, peeled, seeded, and finely chopped

1   shallot, finely chopped

3   garlic cloves, finely chopped

½   pound ground lamb

¼   pound ground pork

1   teaspoon fresh marjoram, oregano, or thyme leaves

1   teaspoon kosher salt

Freshly ground black pepper

1   cup Garlic Mashed Potatoes (page 188)

4   sheets Norwegian lefse, small sheets lavash, or flour tortillas

¼   cup Spicy Sauerkraut (page 184)

Lefse, a traditional Norwegian flatbread made from potatoes, flour, butter, and cream, is available at markets specializing in Scandinavian ingredients and some bakeries, but you can use any soft flatbreads for these wraps. Sandwich-sized flatbreads are available in many supermarkets, as well as in Middle Eastern markets and other specialty markets. Look for Damascus flatbreads, also called soft lavash, or other soft flatbreads sold specifically for sandwich wraps.

1.   Heat 1 tablespoon of the oil in a small skillet over medium-high heat until hot. Add the roasted pepper, shallot, and garlic, and cook, stirring, for 2 to 3 minutes, until the shallots have softened. Transfer to a medium bowl.

2.   Add the lamb, the pork, marjoram, oregano, or thyme, salt, and pepper to taste, and mix well with your hands. Shape the mixture into 8 oval patties about 3 inches long by 1½ inches wide.

3.   Heat the remaining 1 tablespoon oil in a large skillet over medium heat. Add the sausages and cook, turning once, for 4 minutes on each side, or until cooked through. Remove from the heat.

4.   Meanwhile, reheat the mashed potatoes in a small saucepan over low heat, stirring occasionally (add a little cream or milk if necessary).

5.   Spread a layer of mashed potatoes over each flatbread. Top the potatoes with the sauerkraut. Put 2 sausages on each flatbread, roll up in the bread, and serve.

You can also grill the sausages on a charcoal or gas grill.

To roast bell peppers, grill them over a hot fire, or directly over a gas flame, turning occasionally, until blackened all over; do not allow the flesh to char. Transfer to a bowl and cover tightly with plastic wrap, or put them in a paper bag and seal tightly, and set aside to steam and cool for about 10 minutes. Then remove the core and seeds and slip off the skin; don't worry if a few little bits of skin are left. Don't rinse the peppers, or you will lose some of their flavor.

These sausages of ground lamb were inspired by the foods of the Turkish community in Sweden. The patties are rolled up in flatbreads that have been spread with garlicky mashed potatoes and sauerkraut.

SALADS

PICKLED BEET AND APPLE SALAD

SERVES 4 TO 6

2 tablespoons canola oil

1 medium red onion, halved and thinly sliced

2 Granny Smith apples, quartered, cored, and thinly sliced

¼ cup freshly squeezed lemon juice

4 Pickled Beets (page 181), thinly sliced

2 tablespoons drained capers

2 tablespoons mayonnaise

2 tablespoons sour cream

Kosher salt and freshly ground black pepper

2 tablespoons finely chopped fresh flat-leaf parsley

1 tablespoon finely chopped fresh chives

1. Heat the oil in a large skillet over medium-high heat. Add the onion and apples and sauté for 3 to 5 minutes, until the apples are softened. Transfer to a medium bowl and sprinkle with the lemon juice. Add the beets and capers and toss well.

2. Mix the mayonnaise and sour cream together, then add to the salad, tossing to coat. Season with salt and pepper to taste.

3. Transfer the salad to a serving bowl or individual plates, garnish with the parsley and chives, and serve.

Serve as a side dish for Swedish Meatballs (page 142) or as an accompaniment to Pickled Herring Sushi-Style (page 22) or Kippers on Crispbread (page 68).

This salad is best served at room temperature rather than chilled.

This is a very traditional salad — the combination of pickled beets, apples, and onions (or leeks) is familiar to every Swede — and a classic accompaniment to Swedish meatballs. Baby beets are an excellent choice for this recipe. You'll need up to a dozen, depending on size. Look for them at farmers' markets or specialty produce grocers.

FRUITS OF THE FOREST SALAD

SERVES 4 TO 6

FOR THE PICKLED MUSHROOMS

- 1 cup sliced chanterelles
- 1 cup Swedish 1-2-3 Vinegar (page 262)

FOR THE VINAIGRETTE

- 1 tablespoon Roasted Garlic Paste (page 269)
- 2 soft-cooked egg yolks
- 1 tablespoon freshly grated Parmigiano-Reggiano
- 2 tablespoons sherry vinegar
- 1 cup extra-virgin olive oil
- 2 teaspoons truffle oil (see Sources, page 290; optional)

FOR THE SAUTÉED MUSHROOMS

- 2 tablespoons olive oil
- 4 cups thinly sliced portobello mushroom caps
- 1/2 teaspoon kosher salt, or more to taste
  Freshly ground black pepper

- 2 cups thinly sliced small white button mushroom caps
- 1 cup fresh basil leaves, torn into small pieces
- 1 cup fresh flat-leaf parsley leaves
- 1/4 cup fresh tarragon leaves

If you have any leftover mushroom salad, toss all the mushrooms and herbs together, cover, and refrigerate. Serve cold as an accompaniment to any meat or game dish.

For the soft-cooked egg yolks, put 2 large eggs in a saucepan and cover with water. Bring to a boil, reduce the heat to a simmer, and cook for 2 minutes. Drain the eggs and cool them under cold running water. Crack each eggshell in half with a knife, carefully split the egg apart, and scoop out the yolk with a teaspoon.

1. **PREPARE THE PICKLED MUSHROOMS:** Put the mushrooms in a small bowl. Bring the vinegar to a boil in a small saucepan, and pour over the mushrooms. Cover, refrigerate, and let marinate for at least 6 hours, or overnight.

2. **PREPARE THE VINAIGRETTE:** In a small bowl, mash the garlic paste with the egg yolks and Parmesan. Whisk in the sherry vinegar. Whisking constantly, add the olive oil in a slow, steady stream. Whisk in the truffle oil, if using.

3. **PREPARE THE SAUTÉED MUSHROOMS:** Heat the oil in a large skillet over medium-high heat. Add the portobellos, sprinkle with the salt, and cook, stirring, for about 10 minutes, until the mushrooms have released their juices and the juices have cooked away. Season with additional salt, if necessary, and pepper to taste. Remove from the heat and set aside.

4. In a medium bowl, toss the sliced button mushrooms with 1/2 cup of the vinaigrette. Combine the herbs in a medium bowl and toss to mix well.

5. Drain the pickled mushrooms. Arrange the pickled mushrooms, sautéed mushrooms, and raw mushrooms in three rows on a large platter, separating each row with a sprinkling of the herbs. Serve.

Some of my happiest childhood memories recall days spent walking through fields and forests with my father and grandmother to forage for wild mushrooms. This salad, which makes a good first course for an autumn dinner, features three different types of mushrooms — white mushrooms, portobellos, and chanterelles — prepared in three different ways: raw, sautéed, and pickled. You can substitute other mushrooms, such as morels, porcini, or shiitake for the portobellos and chanterelles, but do use button mushrooms for the raw part of the salad.

APPLE ENDIVE SALAD WITH PISTACHIO OIL DRESSING

SERVES 4 TO 6

FOR THE PISTACHIO OIL

- 1 cup shelled pistachios (see Note)
- 1 cup olive oil
- 1 garlic clove, peeled
- 2 sprigs fresh thyme

- 5 thin slices prosciutto

FOR THE PISTACHIO OIL DRESSING

- 2 tablespoons freshly squeezed lime juice
- 1½ teaspoons sherry vinegar
- 1½ teaspoons honey

- 3–4 stalks celery
- 4 endives
- 4 Granny Smith apples
- 2 tablespoons freshly squeezed lemon juice

Be sure to use natural green pistachios, not the ones that have been dyed red.

Reserve the leftover pistachio oil for another salad dressing, or use it as a dip for raw figs, dates, apricots, or peaches, or even good crusty bread.

The leftover dressing can be covered and refrigerated for up to 2 days.

1. **PREPARE THE PISTACHIO OIL:** Combine the nuts, olive oil, garlic, and thyme in a small saucepan and bring just to a simmer over low heat. Reduce the heat to the lowest possible level (use a heat diffuser if you have one) and let the oil infuse for 2 hours; do not allow the oil to bubble at all. Remove the oil from the heat and let steep for 2 hours at room temperature.

2. Strain the oil into a bowl. Discard the garlic and thyme, and transfer the nuts to paper towels to drain, then crush them lightly.

3. Meanwhile, preheat the oven to 275°F. Line a baking sheet with parchment paper.

4. Arrange the prosciutto on the baking sheet in a single layer. Bake for 20 to 30 minutes, or until the prosciutto is very crisp. Let cool, then crumble into small pieces. Set aside.

5. **PREPARE THE DRESSING:** Whisk together ½ cup of the pistachio oil, the lime juice, vinegar, and honey in a small bowl.

6. Remove the tough strings from the celery stalks. Cut into 2-inch lengths, then cut into thin matchsticks. (You should have about 2 cups.) Cut the endives lengthwise in half, cut out the cores, and slice lengthwise into ½-inch-wide strips. Peel and core the apples, cut them into thin matchsticks, and toss with the lemon juice.

7. Combine the celery, endive, and apples in a salad bowl and toss with 2 to 4 tablespoons of the dressing. Sprinkle with the crushed pistachios and crumbled prosciutto and serve.

A great salad offers contrasts in flavors, textures, and colors — think of the ever-popular Caesar salad. This one combines salty prosciutto, tart-sweet Granny Smith apples, and bitter endive, tossed with a slightly sweet honey-pistachio dressing. It's a good salad to make in the winter when other salad greens are hard to come by.

RADICCHIO, BIBB, AND BLUE CHEESE SALAD WITH HAZELNUT VINAIGRETTE

SERVES 4 TO 6

FOR THE HAZELNUT VINAIGRETTE

¼ cup hazelnuts, toasted and skinned

1 garlic clove, thinly sliced

½ cup olive oil

¼ cup freshly squeezed lime juice

1 tablespoon red wine vinegar, or more to taste

1 teaspoon finely chopped fresh tarragon or a pinch of dried tarragon

¼ cup hazelnut oil

Kosher salt and freshly ground black pepper

FOR THE SALAD

½ cup 1-inch cubes sturdy white bread

1 head radicchio, leaves separated, washed, patted dry, and cut into thin slivers

8 hearts Bibb lettuce (outer leaves reserved for another use), washed, patted dry, and cut in half or into quarters, depending on size

2 tablespoons chopped toasted skinned hazelnuts

1 tablespoon Dried Garlic Chips (page 272; optional)

3 tablespoons crumbled Danish blue cheese

Freshly ground black pepper

Hazelnut oil is available in gourmet markets and many supermarkets. It is highly perishable and should be refrigerated after opening. If you can't find hazelnut oil, substitute ¼ cup extra-virgin olive oil; there will still be a good nut flavor from the garlicky hazelnut-infused oil.

The remaining vinaigrette can be covered and refrigerated for up to 2 days; use it to dress another salad of strong greens.

1. PREPARE THE VINAIGRETTE: Combine the hazelnuts, garlic, and oil in a small skillet and heat over medium-low heat for 2 to 3 minutes, or until the garlic just starts to color. Remove from the heat and let cool to room temperature.

2. Transfer the hazelnut-oil mixture to a blender, add the lime juice, vinegar, and tarragon, and blend until smooth. With the blender running, slowly pour in the hazelnut oil, blending until thoroughly mixed. Taste and add more vinegar, if needed, then season with salt and pepper.

3. PREPARE THE SALAD: Preheat the oven to 350°F.

4. Spread the bread cubes on a small baking sheet and toast in the oven for 5 to 7 minutes, until golden brown. Let cool.

5. Combine the radicchio, Bibb lettuce, hazelnuts, garlic chips (if using), and croutons in a large salad bowl. Add 2 to 4 tablespoons of the vinaigrette and toss to coat. Scatter the blue cheese over the top, season with pepper, and serve.

To toast and skin hazelnuts, preheat the oven to 350°F. Spread the hazelnuts on a rimmed baking sheet and toast in the oven for 15 minutes, or until fragrant and light golden brown. Remove from the oven, wrap the nuts in a kitchen towel, and rub them together to remove the skins; don't worry about removing every last bit of skin.

Radicchio and other slightly bitter lettuces are always a good match with the sharp flavor of blue cheese. You could substitute Roquefort or another good blue cheese for the Danish blue in this salad. Toasted hazelnuts add crunch to the crisp greens, and a hazelnut oil vinaigrette brings everything together. The optional garlic chips add another dimension to the salad, and they are easy to prepare (although you must allow time for them to dry overnight).

WATERMELON AND WATERCRESS SALAD AND SOUP
SERVES 4

This dish started as a salad only: sweet watermelon and spicy watercress. But I'd learned from my grandmother never to waste anything in the kitchen, and it bothered me to throw out the scraps from trimming the watermelon. I decided to puree those leftover melon bits, and this refreshing take on "soup and salad" is the result.

1½ pounds watermelon flesh, preferably seedless

3 tablespoons Swedish 1-2-3 Vinegar (page 262)

Juice of 1 lime

1–1¼ cups extra-virgin olive oil

1 shallot, finely chopped

Juice of 1 orange

Juice of 1 lemon

Juice of 1 lime

1 teaspoon fresh thyme leaves

Kosher salt and freshly ground black pepper

4 bunches watercress, coarse stems removed, leaves washed and patted dry

1 tablespoon sesame seeds, lightly toasted

½ cup cottage cheese

To toast sesame seeds, heat them in a small skillet over medium heat, shaking the pan frequently, for about 5 minutes, until they start to turn golden. Transfer to a plate (they can scorch if left in the hot pan) and let cool.

The leftover vinaigrette can be covered and refrigerated for at least 2 days.

1. PREPARE THE WATERMELON: Cut the watermelon flesh into rectangles 3 inches long, 2 inches wide, and ½ inch thick, discarding any seeds; you will need a total of 8 rectangles for the salad. Reserve all the scraps. Put the watermelon rectangles in a bowl, sprinkle with the vinegar and lime juice, and set aside to marinate for 45 minutes to 1 hour.

2. PREPARE THE VINAIGRETTE: Heat ½ cup of the oil in a small skillet over medium-high heat. Add the shallot and cook for 2 to 3 minutes, or until softened. Remove from the heat and let cool slightly.

3. Transfer the shallot, with the oil, to a blender. Add another ½ cup of the oil, the citrus juices, and thyme, and blend until smooth. Taste and add a little more olive oil, if necessary, then season with salt and pepper.

4. PREPARE THE SOUP: Drain the watermelon rectangles, reserving the marinade; set aside. Puree the watermelon scraps in a blender or food processor, and season to taste with the reserved marinade. Cover and refrigerate until cold.

5. Combine the watercress and sesame seeds in a bowl. Add 2 to 4 tablespoons of the vinaigrette and toss well.

6. To serve, make a thin stripe of cottage cheese down the center of each plate, using 2 tablespoons cottage cheese per serving. Arrange the watercress over the stripes. Place 2 watermelon rectangles on two opposite sides of each salad, standing them on a long side (lean them against the greens if necessary). Pour the soup into four small cups or bowls and serve alongside the salad.

GINGER POTATO SALAD

SERVES 4 TO 6

½ cup olive oil

1 tablespoon mustard seeds

8 medium red or white waxy potatoes

2 tablespoons Dijon mustard

2 tablespoons freshly squeezed lime juice

2 tablespoons balsamic vinegar

1 tablespoon grated fresh horseradish (see Pantry, page 281; see
   Note)

   Kosher salt and freshly ground black pepper

2 tablespoons finely chopped pickled ginger

If fresh horseradish is unavailable, substitute 1 tablespoon drained bot-

tled horseradish or omit the horseradish entirely, if you prefer.

Serve the salad soon after making it; refrigerating it will mute its flavors.

1. Combine the olive oil and mustard seeds in a small saucepan and bring just to a simmer over low heat. Reduce the heat to the lowest possible level (use a flame diffuser if you have one) and let infuse — the oil should barely bubble — for 1 hour. Remove from the heat and let cool.

2. Put the potatoes in a saucepan, add salted water to cover, and bring to a boil. Cook for 18 to 20 minutes, or until fork-tender. Drain and let cool until you are able to handle them.

3. Use a small, sharp knife to peel the potatoes, cutting away about ¼ inch of flesh with the skins. Slice the skins in half, and set aside. Cut the potatoes into ¼-inch-thick rounds and put in a salad bowl.

4. Put the mustard in a small bowl and gradually whisk in the cooled olive oil and mustard seeds. Whisk in the lime juice, balsamic vinegar, and grated horseradish (if using), and season with salt and pepper.

5. Add the pickled ginger and the reserved potato skins to the potatoes, then add the dressing and toss well. Serve.

In Sweden, everyone gets excited when new potatoes first appear in the market. We search out the tiniest, freshest potatoes and boil them quickly, let them cool a little, and cut away the peels, leaving at least 1/4 inch of the potato flesh still attached, then use the peels as well as the potato flesh in this salad. The skin of new potatoes has really great flavor; do try to find organic potatoes. ✣ The olive oil for the dressing is slowly cooked with mustard seeds to infuse their flavor and aroma, and the mustard seeds are added along with the oil to provide an interesting crunch. But the most unusual ingredient is the pickled ginger, which adds a sweet, spicy flavor.

CURRIED CAULIFLOWER, POTATO, AND SPROUT SALAD

SERVES 4 TO 6

FOR THE DRESSING

1 tablespoon Curry Paste (page 271) or store-bought
   Thai red curry paste

1 teaspoon curry powder

2 tablespoons sour cream

3 tablespoons extra-virgin olive oil

1 teaspoon Asian sesame oil

½ cup freshly squeezed lime juice

FOR THE SALAD

¾ pound large fingerling or medium Yukon Gold potatoes

1 head cauliflower, trimmed, cored, and cut into small florets

1 pint bean sprouts (or other sprouts), rinsed and patted dry

6 scallions, trimmed and finely chopped

2 tablespoons finely chopped store-bought mango chutney
   (optional)

Serve this salad as an accompaniment to Pan-Roasted Venison Chops (page 162), Rice-Smoked Duck Breasts (page 34), or Swedish Roast Chicken (page 136).

1. PREPARE THE DRESSING: Combine the Curry Paste and curry powder in a blender or food processor and process to blend. Add the sour cream and process to blend. With the machine running, gradually add the olive oil, sesame oil, and lime juice. Transfer to a bowl and set aside.

2. PREPARE THE SALAD: Put the potatoes in a medium saucepan and add cold salted water to cover. Bring to a boil and cook for 18 to 20 minutes, or until the potatoes are fork-tender. Drain and let cool slightly.

3. Meanwhile, bring another large pot of water to a boil. Add the cauliflower florets and cook for 5 to 6 minutes, or until crisp-tender. Drain and let cool slightly.

4. While the cauliflower is cooking, peel the potatoes. If using fingerling potatoes, cut into thin rounds; if using Yukon Gold potatoes, cut lengthwise in half or into quarters, then thinly slice crosswise.

5. Combine the potatoes, cauliflower, sprouts, scallions, and mango chutney (if using) in a salad bowl. Add the vinaigrette, tossing to coat, and serve.

Curry powder and other spices of Indian origin are very much a part of Scandinavian cooking, dating back to the eighteenth century, the heyday of the powerful Swedish East India Company. This tangy salad makes a great side dish for venison or other game, or for roast chicken.

ARUGULA WITH TOMATO–GOAT CHEESE TERRINE

SERVES 8

2 heads garlic, separated into cloves but not peeled

½ cup extra-virgin olive oil

6 medium yellow tomatoes

6 medium red tomatoes

¼ cup milk

1 ¼-ounce package powdered gelatin

2 cups (13½ ounces) fresh goat cheese

2 cups arugula leaves

1 cup fresh basil leaves

¼ cup freshly squeezed lime juice

1 tablespoon balsamic vinegar

1. Preheat the oven to 350°F.

2. Rub the garlic cloves with 1 tablespoon of the olive oil. Wrap them in foil and roast for about 35 minutes, until softened. Let cool, then peel the garlic cloves and slice them.

3. Meanwhile, bring a large pot of water to a boil. Fill a large bowl with ice and water. Core the tomatoes and cut an X in the bottom of each. Add 3 of the tomatoes at a time to the boiling water and blanch for about 15 seconds, until the skin at the X starts to loosen. Remove with tongs or a wire skimmer and immediately plunge into the ice water to cool briefly; drain. Peel the tomatoes and cut them into quarters. Put 12 red tomato quarters and 12 yellow tomato quarters in a small bowl for the salad. Add half the sliced garlic, cover, and refrigerate. Slice the pulp and seeds from the remaining tomato quarters, leaving only the flesh. Put ¼ cup of the seeds and pulp for the salad dressing in a separate small bowl; cover and refrigerate. Discard the remaining pulp. Transfer the tomato flesh to another bowl and add the remaining sliced garlic; set aside for the terrine.

4. Put the milk in a small saucepan, sprinkle the gelatin over it, and let stand for 5 minutes to soften the gelatin. Bring the milk to a simmer over low heat, whisking until the gelatin has dissolved. Transfer to a medium bowl, add the goat cheese, and whisk until well blended.

5. Line an 8½x4½-inch loaf pan with plastic wrap, leaving a 4-inch overhang on each long side. Lay 2 or 3 arugula leaves lengthwise down the center of the bottom of the pan. Add half the remaining arugula and half the basil to the tomatoes, tossing to mix. Spread one quarter of the goat-cheese mixture in the bottom of the loaf pan. Cover with one third of the tomato mixture. Spread with another layer of goat cheese and top with half the remaining tomatoes. Repeat one more time, and finish with a layer of goat cheese. Fold the plastic wrap over the top to cover the terrine. Refrigerate for at least 8 hours, or up to 12 hours.

6. Just before serving, in a medium bowl, whisk the remaining ¼ cup plus 3 tablespoons oil with the lime juice, balsamic vinegar, and the refrigerated tomato pulp. Add the refrigerated tomatoes and garlic. Stir gently to coat. Coarsely chop the remaining arugula and basil and add to the salad, stirring gently to mix.

7. To serve, peel back the plastic wrap from the top of the terrine, invert it onto a cutting board, and remove the plastic wrap. Cut into eight 1-inch slices. Serve the salad alongside the terrine.

Look for heirloom and other flavorful tomatoes at the farmers' market— and buy only those that are fully ripe and juicy. Use half each red and yellow tomatoes, or choose a mix of colors —or make the terrine with all red tomatoes.

Some of my favorite ingredients are combined in this dish: garlic, tomatoes, arugula, basil, and goat cheese. Make it in the summer, when tomatoes are at their peak and fresh basil is abundant, and serve with toasted bread. The terrine would also be good served with prosciutto, sliced tenderloin of beef, or even Gravlax-Cured Tuna (page 24).

ARUGULA SALAD WITH WALNUT PESTO

SERVES 4

FOR THE WALNUT PESTO

- 3 garlic cloves, unpeeled
- ¾ cup extra-virgin olive oil
- ½ cup walnuts
- 1 tablespoon freshly grated Parmigiano-Reggiano
- 6 large basil leaves
- ¼ cup freshly squeezed lime juice

  Kosher salt and freshly ground black pepper

FOR THE SALAD

- 1 cup Pickled Asparagus (page 182)
- 3 bunches arugula, tough stems removed, leaves washed and patted dry (about 6 cups)
- ½ cup crumbled fresh goat cheese
- 1 tablespoon aged balsamic vinegar
- ¼ cup finely chopped serrano ham or prosciutto

If you'd rather not turn on the oven for the pesto, you can roast the garlic in a toaster oven. Then toast the walnuts on the stovetop, in a dry skillet over medium-high heat, shaking the pan occasionally, for about 5 minutes.

The remaining pesto can be refrigerated, tightly covered, for up to a week. Use it for other salads, toss it with hot pasta, or drizzle it over roasted or grilled vegetables.

For the best flavor, choose an artisanal balsamic vinegar, one that has been aged for at least twelve years.

Serrano is a delicious mountain-cured Spanish ham. It's available in some gourmet and specialty markets. If you can't find it, prosciutto makes an excellent substitute.

1. **PREPARE THE PESTO:** Preheat the oven to 350°F.

2. Rub the garlic cloves with 1½ teaspoons of the olive oil. Wrap them in foil and roast for 30 minutes, or until they are soft enough to squeeze out of their skins. Meanwhile, spread the walnuts on a small baking sheet and toast them in the oven for about 10 minutes, stirring occasionally, until fragrant and lightly golden. Set aside to cool.

3. Squeeze the pulp from the garlic cloves into a blender or mini food processor. Add the walnuts, Parmesan, basil, and 1½ tablespoons of the olive oil and process to a paste. With the machine running, gradually add the remaining ½ cup plus 2 tablespoons olive oil, blending until thoroughly incorporated. Add the lime juice and season to taste with salt and pepper.

4. **PREPARE THE SALAD:** Put the asparagus and arugula in a bowl and toss with 3 tablespoons of the pesto. Transfer the salad to a platter and scatter the goat cheese over it. Drizzle the balsamic vinegar over the salad, scatter the ham or prosciutto over the top, and serve.

I like to pair arugula with something that can stand up to its bite, such as the pickled asparagus in this flavorful salad. Pickled Beets (page 181) are another good possibility. The salad is substantial enough to serve as a first course, but I also like to offer it as an accompaniment to Poached Lamb with Dried Mushrooms and Rosemary (page 154) or Herb-Roasted Rack of Lamb (page 156). ✣ Serve this in the spring, to celebrate the first asparagus and tender early arugula.

SCANDINAVIAN SEAFOOD SALAD
SERVES 6

6   fingerling potatoes or 2 Yukon Gold potatoes

2   cups (about 10 ounces) cooked and peeled small shrimp

1½ cups finely chopped smoked salmon (10 ounces)

1½ cups (about 10 ounces) crabmeat, picked through for shells and
      cartilage

4   hard-cooked eggs, finely chopped

2   shallots, finely chopped

2   anchovy fillets, finely chopped

1   tablespoon finely chopped fresh cilantro

1   tablespoon finely chopped fresh chives

½   cup freshly squeezed lime juice

3   tablespoons mayonnaise

2   tablespoons sour cream

    Kosher salt and freshly ground black pepper

2   small heads iceberg lettuce, cored, separated into leaves, washed,
      and patted dry

1. Preheat the oven to 400°F.

2. Roast the potatoes for 30 to 40 minutes, until fork-tender. Let cool until you can handle them, then peel and cut into ½-inch dice.

3. Combine the potatoes, shrimp, smoked salmon, crabmeat, eggs, shallots, anchovies, cilantro, and chives in a large bowl. In a small bowl, combine the lime juice, mayonnaise, and sour cream, stirring to blend well. Gently fold into the salad and season with salt and pepper to taste.

4. Arrange the lettuce leaves on a platter, and serve alongside the salad. Instruct your guests to roll up 2 tablespoons or so of salad in a lettuce leaf, like a spring roll, and eat.

Called *skagen* in Swedish, this salad is named for a Danish fishing village across the water from Sweden. It's a very traditional dish that appears on every smorgasbord table in the country. Here is our version, which includes smoked salmon, shrimp, and crabmeat. It makes a great lunch served with crusty French bread or whole-grain crispbread.

ROASTED LOBSTER SALAD

SERVES 4 TO 6

8 garlic cloves, unpeeled

3 tablespoons olive oil

4 1½-pound lobsters

¾ cup fromage blanc or mascarpone cheese

½ cup cooked and peeled fava beans (see Notes)

½ cup peas, cooked in boiling salted water just until tender

½ cup freshly squeezed lime juice

1 tablespoon finely chopped pickled ginger plus 1 tablespoon of the pickling liquid

6 fresh basil leaves

8 fresh mint leaves

Kosher salt and freshly ground black pepper

To prepare fava beans, remove them from their pods (you will need about 1¼ pounds favas in the pod to make ½ cup cooked and peeled). Cook in boiling water for about 3 minutes, or until soft. Cool under cold running water and drain well. To peel them, pinch the skins and slip out the beans.

If necessary, substitute cooked frozen baby lima beans for the fava beans.

Any leftover dressing makes a great dip for crudités.

1. Preheat the oven to 350°F.

2. Rub the garlic cloves with 1½ teaspoons of the olive oil and wrap them in foil. Roast for 25 to 30 minutes, or until they are soft enough to squeeze out of their skins. Remove from the oven and let cool. (Leave the oven on.)

3. Meanwhile, bring a large pot of salted water to a boil. Plunge the lobsters headfirst into the pot (do this in two batches if necessary) and cook for 3 minutes. Remove from the water and let cool.

4. Crack the lobster shells and remove the meat from the tails and claws. (Reserve the shells, if you like, to prepare Lobster Stock, page 265; you can freeze the shells until ready to make the stock.)

5. Put the remaining 2½ tablespoons oil in a roasting pan just large enough to hold all the lobster meat in a single layer. Put the pan in the oven for about 3 minutes, until the oil is hot. Add the lobster tails to the pan, turn several times to coat with the oil, and roast for 3 minutes.

6. Add the claw meat to the roasting pan, turn to coat with oil, and roast the lobster for 6 minutes longer, or until just cooked through. Let cool.

7. Meanwhile, squeeze the garlic pulp from the skins. Combine the garlic, fromage blanc or mascarpone, fava beans, peas, lime juice, and ginger pickling liquid in a food processor or blender and process until smooth. Transfer the dressing to a bowl and set aside.

8. Cut the lobster meat into bite-sized pieces and place in a large bowl. Slice the basil and mint leaves into a fine chiffonade (thin slivers) and toss with the lobster. Add just enough of the dressing to coat lightly, tossing gently. Add the pickled ginger, season to taste with salt and pepper, and serve.

When I use a special ingredient like lobster, I want it to be the main focus of the dish, so I avoid ingredients that would mask the flavor of the succulent meat. The delicate green dressing for this salad was inspired by a classic French pea soup. The dressing, made with sweet fresh peas and fava beans along with roasted garlic and just a little fragrant mint, both highlights the natural sweetness of the roasted lobster and serves as a beautiful foil to its coral-pink color. Serve with good crusty bread for an elegant lunch or supper.

SOUPS

MUSHROOM CONSOMMÉ
SERVES 4

4 cups Chicken Stock (page 263)

1 cup dry white wine

2 cups dried shiitake mushrooms

2 sheets kombu (see Pantry, page 281)

2 garlic cloves, smashed

1 shallot, finely chopped

2 sprigs fresh thyme

½ cup ruby port or Madeira

2 tablespoons Earl Grey tea leaves

Kosher salt and freshly ground black pepper

Truffle oil, for garnish (see Pantry, page 284; optional)

VARIATION

To make Mushroom Consommé with Oysters and Wild Mushrooms: Heat 1 table-spoon olive oil in a large skillet over high heat. Add 1 cup sliced wild (or cultivated) mushrooms, season with salt and freshly ground black pepper, and sauté for 5 to 8 minutes, just until the liquid the mushrooms release has evaporated and the mush-rooms are beginning to turn golden. Place 4 freshly shucked small oysters in each soup bowl, add the mushrooms, and pour the hot consommé over the oysters and mushrooms. Serve immediately.

1. Combine the stock, wine, dried mushrooms, kombu, garlic, shallot, and thyme in a large saucepan. Bring to a boil, reduce the heat to medium, and simmer for about 20 minutes, until reduced by half; during the last 5 minutes, add the port or Madeira and tea leaves. Remove from the heat and strain through a fine-mesh strainer into another saucepan.

2. Reheat the consommé over medium heat. Season with salt and pepper to taste. Divide the consommé among four bowls and add a few drops of truffle oil, if using, to each. Serve.

This is a quick consommé, without the usual complicated steps. In fact, it takes less than 30 minutes to prepare, yet I think it surpasses even the classic version made from meat or game. It combines flavors from the earth and sea, the essence of mushrooms and the briny taste of kelp, with the subtle sweetness of port. ✤ Serve this as a first course, on its own or with oysters and wild mushrooms (see the Variation), or, for a more substantial soup, add Mushroom Dumplings (page 199). Or take a thermos of the hot consommé along on a day of skiing or other winter outing, as a marvelous restorative broth. We also serve this with Steamed Sea Bass (page 124) and Warm Beef Carpaccio (page 36).

JUNIPER APPLE SOUP

SERVES 6 TO 8

1 tablespoon juniper berries

2 cardamom pods

2 allspice berries

1 2-inch cinnamon stick

2 sprigs fresh tarragon

2 tablespoons olive oil

2 apples, peeled, cored, and diced

1 shallot, finely chopped

1 3-inch piece of ginger, peeled and finely chopped

4 cups Chicken Stock (page 263)

2 cups heavy cream

Juice from 2 apples or 1 cup apple cider

¼ cup apple brandy

¼ cup cider vinegar

¼ cup ruby port or Madeira

Kosher salt and freshly ground black pepper

About ¼ cup Apple Saffron Jam (page 211), for garnish (optional)

Juniper berries, which are used a great deal in traditional Swedish cooking, especially in game dishes, make a perfect pairing with apples, another favorite ingredient. The berries have a wild, pungent flavor, full of piney, resinous notes. (They are the main flavoring in gin.) Here they flavor a creamy sweet-tart soup — just the thing on a cold winter's night.

1. Wrap the juniper berries, cardamom pods, allspice berries, cinnamon stick, and tarragon in a square of cheesecloth and tie with kitchen twine. Set aside.

2. Heat the oil in a large saucepan over medium-high heat. Add the apples, shallot, and ginger and sauté for 2 to 3 minutes, until the shallot starts to soften. Add the stock, cream, and apple juice or cider, stir, then add the spice bundle and bring to a brisk simmer. Reduce the heat slightly and simmer until the liquid is reduced by half, 30 to 40 minutes.

3. Remove the cheesecloth bundle and blend the soup with an immersion blender. Or transfer to a regular blender, in batches, and puree, then return the soup to the saucepan. Bring the soup to a boil, stir in the brandy, vinegar, and port or Madeira, and bring to a simmer. Season with salt and pepper to taste, and remove from the heat.

4. Divide the soup among four bowls, garnish each with a tablespoon of jam, if using, and serve.

Juniper and allspice berries are available in the spice section of many supermarkets, in gourmet markets, and by mail order (see Sources, page 289).

If you don't own a juicer, you can buy fresh apple juice at some health food stores or at juice bars; or simply substitute apple cider, as suggested above.

For a more substantial dish, add some duck confit to the soup (see Sources, page 289). Omit the jam, and place a few tablespoons shredded confit in each bowl before ladling in the hot soup.

Serve this soup as a first course before Slow-Cooked Squab (page 138), Pan-Roasted Venison Chops (page 162), or Spice-Rubbed Wild Boar Tenderloin (page 164).

CHILLED POTATO-CHIVE SOUP

SERVES 4

4 medium Yukon Gold potatoes, peeled and quartered

4 cups Chicken Stock (page 263)

2 garlic cloves, peeled

1 cup finely chopped fresh chives

1 tablespoon finely chopped fresh tarragon

3 tablespoons freshly squeezed lime juice

½ cup sour cream

Kosher salt and freshly ground white pepper

1. Put the potatoes in a medium pot, add the stock and garlic, and bring just to a boil. Reduce the heat slightly and simmer for 25 to 30 minutes, until the potatoes are very soft. Remove from the heat.

2. Puree the soup with an immersion blender, or transfer to a regular blender, in batches, and puree. Add the chives, tarragon, and lime juice and blend well, then add the sour cream. Season with salt and pepper to taste.

3. Transfer the soup to a bowl, cover, and refrigerate for 3 to 4 hours, or until thoroughly chilled, before serving.

On the hills of the west coast of Sweden, where I grew up, chives grow like weeds. For much of my youth, they were the only fresh herbs we had. This cold potato soup, generously flavored with chives, is my version of vichyssoise. The addition of lime juice is unusual, but it gives the soup a bright lift. You might serve the soup with a spoonful of Ginger Potato Salad (page 82) in the center of each bowl.

YELLOW SPLIT PEA SOUP

3 cups yellow split peas, picked over and rinsed

2 quarts cold water

2 quarts Chicken Stock (page 263)

2 medium onions, finely chopped

1 medium carrot, finely chopped

1 teaspoon dried thyme

1 bay leaf

1 cup diced cooked ham

Kosher salt and freshly ground black pepper

1. Put the split peas in a large heavy pot, add 6 cups of the cold water, and refrigerate for 6 to 8 hours, or overnight.

2. Add the stock, the remaining 2 cups water, the onions, carrot, thyme, and bay leaf to the split peas and bring to a simmer over medium heat. Reduce the heat to low, so that the soup barely simmers, and simmer gently for 3 hours, or until the peas are almost falling apart.

3. Stir in the ham and remove from the heat. Season to taste with salt and pepper and serve.

Like most soups, this tastes even better the day after it is made. It also freezes well (actually, I think the flavor improves if the soup is frozen), but if you plan to freeze it, don't add the ham before freezing. The soup can be frozen for up to 3 months. Then defrost and reheat it, stirring in the diced ham just before serving.

A great favorite from my childhood, this soup appeared on our table every Thursday night throughout the long winter, which lasted from mid-September to March. Called *ärtsoppa*, it was traditionally eaten on Thursday for the midday meal, or for dinner, throughout Scandinavia, and many households still maintain the tradition. This hearty, sustaining soup was probably served as far back as the Middle Ages, when dried peas were a staple winter food for most people of Europe. Again according to custom, the soup was usually followed by a dessert of Swedish Pancakes (page 236). Every Wednesday night, my grandmother would begin her preparations for the next night's dinner by soaking the peas and making the pancake batter. ✤ Serve the soup as a main course, with whole-grain bread and a platter of sliced smoked sausages (such as kielbasa) and other smoked meats, along with an assortment of mustards.

SALSIFY CAPPUCCINO

SERVES 6

   3 tablespoons unsalted butter
   2 shallots, finely chopped
   3 salsify, peeled and cut into ¹/₂-inch pieces
 ¹/₂ pound fingerling or Yukon Gold potatoes, peeled and cut into
       ¹/₂-inch pieces
   1 parsnip, peeled and finely chopped
   4 cups Chicken Stock (page 263)
   2 cups Fish Stock (page 264)
 ¹/₂ cup dry white wine
   2 bay leaves
   2 sprigs fresh thyme
   2 tablespoons sour cream
      Kosher salt and freshly ground white pepper

If salsify is unavailable, you can make the soup using an additional 2 or 3 parsnips instead.

You can purchase fresh or frozen fish stock at most seafood markets, if you don't have the time to make it yourself. Or you could simply use 2 additional cups of chicken broth instead of the fish stock, although the soup will not have the same depth of flavor. Do not be tempted to substitute bottled clam juice for the fish stock—its taste is wrong for this soup.

VARIATION

For an elegant variation, add a few thin strips of rare tuna to each bowl of soup. Or, for a more earthy touch, garnish it with Caramelized Chestnuts (page 161).

Salsify, a root vegetable resembling a long, slender parsnip, is sometimes called oyster plant because its flavor is said to be somewhat reminiscent of oysters. Widely used in Scandinavian and northern European cooking, it is becoming more available in produce markets here. The most common variety of salsify has pale gray skin, but there is also a type with dark brown skin, which is sometimes called scamorza; you can use either type for this creamy winter soup. ✢ I call this a cappuccino because right before serving, I froth the soup in a blender. The color of the soup also reminds me of the creamy froth on a good cappuccino.

1. Melt 1 tablespoon of the butter in a large saucepan over medium heat. Add the shallots and sauté for 1 to 2 minutes, or until just softened. Add the salsify, potatoes, parsnip, both kinds of stock, white wine, bay leaves, and thyme, and bring just to a boil. Reduce the heat and simmer for 20 to 25 minutes, until all the vegetables are tender.

2. Remove from the heat and remove the bay leaves and thyme sprigs. Add the sour cream and the remaining 2 tablespoons butter to the soup and puree with an immersion blender. Or transfer to a regular blender, in batches, and puree, then return to the pan and reheat gently over low heat. Season with salt and white pepper.

3. Divide the soup among four bowls and serve.

CREAMY CURRY SOUP
SERVES 6 TO 8

2 tablespoons unsalted butter

1 apple, peeled, cored, and finely diced

2 shallots, finely chopped

1 4-inch piece ginger, peeled and finely chopped

1 stalk fresh lemongrass, tough outer leaves removed, tender inner
   stalk lightly smashed and chopped

1 garlic clove, finely chopped

1 tablespoon Curry Paste (page 271) or store-bought
   Thai red curry paste

2 quarts Chicken Stock (page 263)

2 cups canned unsweetened coconut milk

1 cup heavy cream

6 tablespoons fresh lime juice

3 star anise

3 sprigs fresh thyme

1 2-inch sprig fresh rosemary

   Kosher salt and freshly ground black pepper

I like to serve this soup with a spoonful of Israeli couscous in the center of

each bowl.

1. Melt the butter in a large pot over medium-high heat. Add the apple, shallots, ginger, lemongrass, and garlic, and sauté for 5 minutes, or until the apple is soft. Add the Curry Paste and cook, stirring, for 2 minutes, or until fragrant. Add the stock, coconut milk, cream, lime juice, star anise, thyme, and rosemary, and bring to a boil. Reduce the heat to low and simmer gently for 30 minutes.

2. Strain the soup into another pot, pressing down on the solids to extract as much liquid as possible. Reheat the soup gently over low heat. Season to taste with salt and pepper and serve.

Curry and other Indian spices have been important seasonings in Scandinavia for hundreds of years. More recently, Southeast Asian food has become popular, and this curried soup is somewhat reminiscent of the famous Thai soup *tom yum gai* — although it is not as spicy. I like to serve this as a first course before a fish dish such as Glazed Salmon with Wasabi Sabayon (page 110) or Dill-Crusted Arctic Char with Pinot Noir Sauce (page 113).

CORN SOUP WITH SMOKED SALMON
SERVES 4

1/2 pound fingerling or small Yukon Gold potatoes

6 ears corn, shucked

2 tablespoons grapeseed oil or canola oil

Bones from 2 salmon, chopped into pieces with a cleaver (optional)

2 shallots, finely chopped

1 garlic clove, finely chopped

4 cups Chicken Stock (page 263)

1 cup sour cream

Kosher salt and freshly ground black pepper

6 ounces Tandoori-Smoked Salmon (page 26) or regular smoked salmon (in one chunk), cut into 1/2-inch cubes

1 tablespoon finely chopped fresh tarragon

1 tablespoon finely chopped fresh cilantro

Most fish markets will sell you the salmon bones at little cost.

1. Preheat the oven to 400°F.

2. Pierce the potatoes in a few places with a fork. Put the corn and the potatoes on a baking sheet and roast, turning occasionally, for 25 to 30 minutes, until the potatoes are fork-tender. Let cool.

3. Cut the kernels off the corncobs and set aside. Break each corncob into 2 or 3 pieces and set aside.

4. Heat the oil in a large pot over medium-high heat. Add the salmon bones (if using), shallots, and garlic, and sauté for about 3 minutes, until the shallots start to soften. Add the corncobs and stock, bring to a simmer, and simmer for 30 minutes.

5. Meanwhile, peel the potatoes and cut into chunks; set aside.

6. Strain the stock into a large bowl and add the corn kernels and potatoes. Transfer to a blender, in batches if necessary, and puree. Add the sour cream and blend well.

7. Pour the soup into a large saucepan and reheat gently over medium heat; do not let boil. Remove from the heat and season with salt and pepper.

8. Ladle the soup into bowls. Garnish with the smoked salmon, sprinkle with the tarragon and cilantro, and serve immediately.

This is a sturdy but elegant soup, thick with pureed corn kernels and garnished with Tandoori-Smoked Salmon (or regular smoked salmon), cilantro, and tarragon. The stock is flavored with salmon bones, but it can certainly be made without them. The corncobs are also used, contributing even more flavor. ✣ The soup is also good served at room temperature.

SUMMER SOUP OF YELLOW TOMATOES WITH SALMON "RAVIOLI"

SERVES 4

2 tablespoons olive oil

1 medium red onion, finely chopped

4 garlic cloves, finely chopped

2 jalapeño peppers, seeded and finely chopped

1 cup freshly squeezed orange juice

½ cup dry white wine

6 tablespoons freshly squeezed lime juice

2 tablespoons finely chopped fresh mint

2 tablespoons finely chopped fresh basil

1 cup frozen mango puree, thawed, or 1 ripe mango, peeled, pitted, and pureed (in a food processor or blender)

7 pounds yellow tomatoes, cut in half

Kosher salt and freshly ground black pepper

FOR THE SALMON "RAVIOLI" (OPTIONAL)

¼ pound sushi-quality salmon fillet, Gravlax (page 18), or smoked salmon, cut horizontally into 4 slices ½–⅓ inch thick

2 teaspoons sour cream

4 teaspoons salmon caviar

Frozen mango puree is available in some supermarkets and in Latin and other ethnic markets; or substitute fresh mango puree, as suggested above.

If you are using raw salmon for the "ravioli," be sure to buy the best and freshest salmon you can find.

Serve this soup as a first course before Poached Lamb with Dried Mushrooms and Rosemary (page 154) or Herb-Roasted Rack of Lamb (page 156). Or serve it, without the optional "ravioli," together with Steamed Crab Rolls (page 48) or Roasted Lobster Salad (page 88).

1. Heat the oil in a medium saucepan over medium-high heat. Add the onion, garlic, and jalapeños, and sauté for 5 minutes, or until the onion has softened. Add the orange juice, white wine, lime juice, mint, and basil, and bring just to a boil, then reduce the heat to low and simmer gently for 10 minutes.

2. Whisk the mango puree into the orange juice mixture and bring to a boil, then remove from the heat. Strain the broth into a bowl, cover, and refrigerate for at least 2 hours, until cold.

3. Puree the tomatoes in batches in a food processor. Strain the tomatoes through a sieve set over a large bowl, pressing on the solids with the back of a wooden spoon to extract as much liquid as possible. (You should have 2½ to 3 cups tomato juice.)

4. Gradually whisk the orange-mango broth into the tomato juice, tasting as you go, until you reach a nice balance of flavors (you may not need all the broth — it shouldn't overpower the tomato). Season with salt and pepper, cover, and refrigerate until thoroughly chilled.

5. WHILE THE SOUP CHILLS, PREPARE THE "RAVIOLI" (OPTIONAL): Pound each salmon slice between two sheets of plastic wrap until it is about ¼ inch thick. Cut each slice in half. Put ½ teaspoon of the sour cream in the center of each of 4 slices of the salmon and top with 1 teaspoon salmon caviar each. Cover with the remaining slices of salmon and press together gently to seal. Transfer to a plate, cover, and refrigerate until ready to serve.

6. To serve, divide the soup among four shallow soup bowls. Place a "ravioli" in each bowl, and serve.

This chilled soup, tart, sweet, and spiced with chiles, is perfect for a warm summer's night, when tomatoes are at their peak. The salmon "ravioli" are thin slices of salmon (fresh, cured, or smoked, as you prefer) enclosing a filling of sour cream and salmon caviar. You could serve the soup on its own, but the "ravioli" make an elegant and unusual garnish.

LOBSTER TOMATO SOUP
SERVES 4

I like to make this rich, spicy soup in the late summer or early fall when ripe tomatoes are still abundant. Serve it with crusty bread and a salad of greens for an elegant light meal.

2 tablespoons unsalted butter

2 shallots, finely chopped

2 jalapeño peppers, seeded and finely chopped

1 3-inch piece ginger, peeled and finely chopped

2 tablespoons chopped fresh dill, plus ½ cup chopped dill stems

1 garlic clove, finely chopped

½ cup brandy

4 cups Lobster Stock (page 265)

1 tablespoon white wine vinegar

1 tablespoon sugar

4 medium tomatoes, peeled, quartered, and seeded

½ cup freshly squeezed lime juice

   Kosher salt and freshly ground black pepper

2 cups chopped cooked lobster meat (from two 1½-pound lobsters; see Note), at room temperature

   Chive blossom, for garnish (optional)

1. Melt the butter in a large saucepan over medium-high heat. Add the shallots, jalapeños, ginger, dill stems, and garlic, and sauté for 2 to 3 minutes, or until the shallots have softened. Add the brandy and lobster stock and bring to a simmer. Reduce the heat to low and simmer gently for 20 minutes.

2. Strain the broth into a clean saucepan. Add the vinegar, sugar, tomatoes, lime juice, and salt and pepper to taste, and bring to a simmer over medium-high heat. Simmer for 3 minutes to blend the flavors, and remove from the heat.

3. Divide the lobster among four soup bowls and ladle the soup over it. Garnish with the chopped dill and chive blossoms, if desired, and serve.

To cook lobsters, bring a large pot of water to a boil and throw in a couple of handfuls of salt; the water should be almost as salty as seawater. Plunge the lobsters headfirst into the water, cover the pot, and cook for 12 to 15 minutes after the water returns to a boil, depending on size. Remove the lobsters with tongs and let sit until cool enough to handle. Crack the tails and claws, and remove the meat.

You can substitute small cooked and peeled shrimp for the lobster.

MY GRANDMOTHER'S CHICKEN SOUP

SERVES 4 TO 6

1 tablespoon grapeseed oil or canola oil

1 tablespoon unsalted butter

1 tablespoon garam masala (see Pantry, page 281)

2–3 pounds chicken wings and backs

2 medium onions, coarsely chopped

3 large carrots, chopped

1 garlic clove, peeled

3 quarts water

1 bay leaf

1 teaspoon dried thyme

1 teaspoon kosher salt

1 medium Granny Smith apple, peeled, cored, and chopped

2 cups sliced white button mushrooms

2 cups cooked long-grain white rice (²/₃ cup raw rice)

½ cup chopped fresh chives

1. Preheat the oven to 350°F.

2. Put the oil and butter in a large roasting pan and place it in the oven for about 2 minutes, until the butter has melted. Add the chicken backs and wings and roast for 20 to 25 minutes, or until lightly browned.

3. Add the onions and half of the carrots to the roasting pan, stir well, and roast for another 10 minutes.

4. Transfer the bones and cooked vegetables to a stockpot. Add about 1 cup of the water to the roasting pan and stir to release the browned bits on the bottom of the pan. Pour the liquid into the stockpot, then add the remaining water, bay leaf, thyme, and salt, and bring to a simmer over medium-high heat. Skim off the foam from the top of the stock, reduce the heat to low, and simmer gently for 1 hour, skimming off the foam from time to time.

5. Strain the broth into a clean pot. Add the remaining carrots and the apple, bring to a simmer, and simmer for 10 minutes. Add the mushrooms and rice and simmer for 5 minutes.

6. Ladle the soup into bowls, garnish with the chives, and serve.

In Scandinavia, as in most places, soup cuisine has its origins in kitchen economy. Every Sunday night, my grandmother prepared a wonderful meal of roast chicken (see page 136), redolent of curry and other spices. If there was any chicken left over, she would use that for a second meal, and then the carcass and any remaining scraps of meat would be turned into a hearty curry-flavored soup. This is my version of her recipe. ✤ At home we always accompanied the soup with a spoonful of Corn Mashed Potatoes (page 189) in the center of each serving, or with the rice as suggested here, and my grandmother's rustic homemade bread.

FISH

AND

SHELLFISH

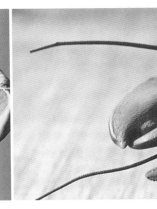

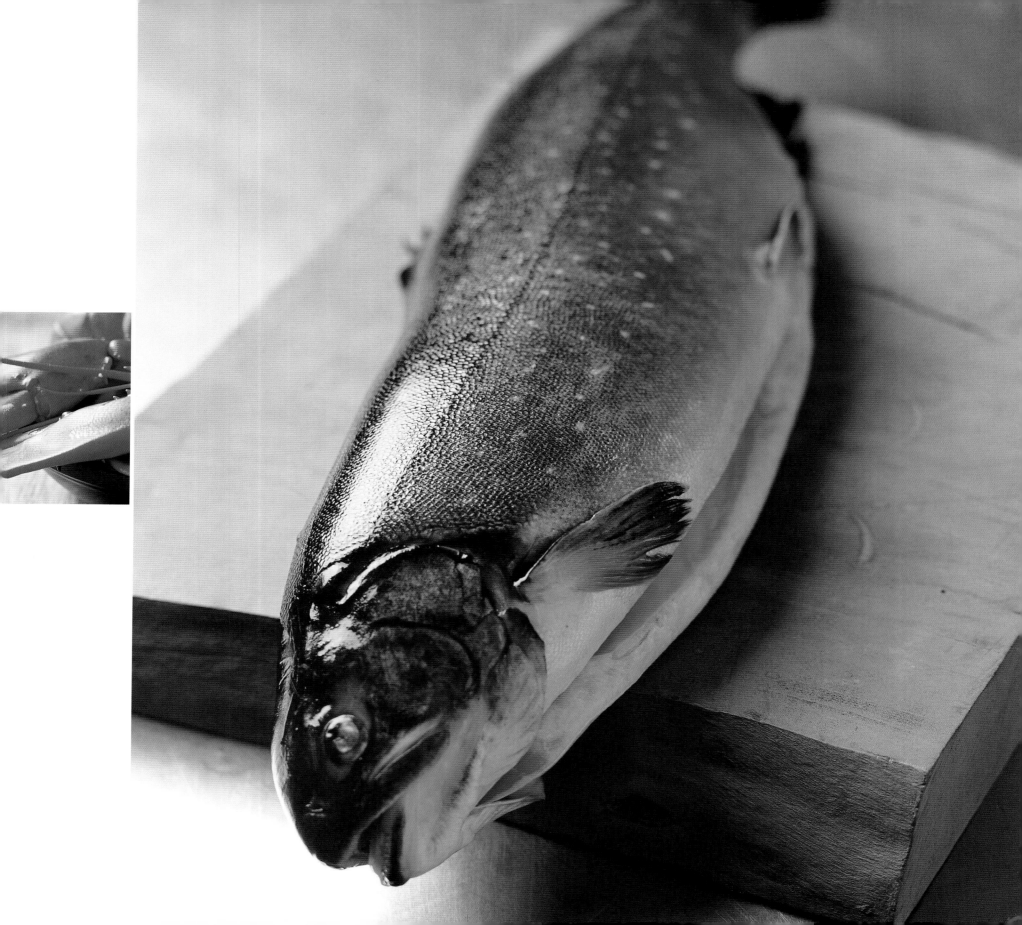

CRISPY SEARED SALMON BUNDLES WITH ORANGE-FENNEL BROTH

SERVES 4

For this festive dish, salmon fillets are topped with thinly sliced potatoes, rolled up in spring roll wrappers to make neat cylinders, and seared until crisp. These packets are served in a fragrant broth, which envelops the fish with sweet-tart, anise-tinged flavors. ✢ Though fennel is a familiar ingredient in Scandinavia and I have always loved its licorice flavor, I had never thought to combine it with the sweetness of citrus until I came to New York City, where my cooking became more adventuresome. ✢ Despite the long list of ingredients, this recipe is easy to make. The broth can be prepared up to a day ahead, and once the potatoes are cooked, it takes only 15 minutes or so to assemble the cylinders of salmon and quickly pan-sear them.

I like to garnish this dish with Pickled Asparagus and Onion Marmalade (page 182). Place a spoonful of the marmalade next to the sliced salmon cylinders.

The broth makes a wonderful light soup on its own, served hot or cold. Simmer it for 1 hour and strain as directed, but don't reduce it further.

2 tablespoons olive oil

2 fennel bulbs, trimmed, cored, and cut into small dice

2 shallots, finely chopped

2 garlic cloves, finely chopped

1 3-inch piece ginger, peeled and thinly sliced

1 stalk fresh lemongrass, tough outer leaves removed, tender inner
 stalk lightly smashed and finely chopped

2 tablespoons honey

 Grated zest of 2 oranges

 Grated zest of 2 limes

4 cups Fish Stock (page 264)

1²/₃ cups freshly squeezed orange juice

¹/₂ cup dry white wine

6 tablespoons freshly squeezed lime juice

2 kaffir lime leaves (see Pantry, page 281)

4 sprigs fresh mint

2 sprigs fresh basil

2 star anise

1 bird's-eye chile or other small dried chile

4 small Yukon Gold potatoes

4 square spring roll wrappers

2 tablespoons unsalted butter, melted

4 6-ounce salmon fillets, skin removed

 Kosher salt and freshly ground black pepper

3 tablespoons chopped fresh dill

2 tablespoons olive oil

 Fennel fronds, for garnish (optional)

1. PREPARE THE BROTH: Heat the oil in a large saucepan over medium-high heat. Add the fennel, shallots, garlic, ginger, and lemongrass, and sauté for about 3 minutes, until the shallots are translucent. Add the honey and cook, stirring, for 2 minutes.

2. Add the orange and lime zests, stock, orange juice, wine, lime juice, kaffir lime leaves, mint sprigs, basil sprigs, star anise, and chile pepper, and bring just to a boil. Reduce the heat and simmer gently for 1 hour.

3. Meanwhile, put the potatoes in a medium saucepan, add salted water to cover, and bring to a boil. Reduce the heat slightly and boil gently until the potatoes are fork-tender, 18 to 20 minutes. Drain and let cool, then cut into thin slices.

4. Strain the broth into a clean saucepan. Bring to a simmer and simmer until reduced to 2 cups. Remove from the heat and cover to keep warm. (The broth can be made up to 1 day ahead, covered, and refrigerated.)

5. Lay the spring roll wrappers on a work surface and brush with the melted butter. Season the salmon with salt and pepper. Place one salmon fillet on the lower part of each spring roll wrapper, about 2 inches from the bottom, and cover the salmon with the potato slices, overlapping them as necessary. Sprinkle the dill over the potatoes. Fold the bottom of each wrapper over the salmon and potatoes, then roll up into a cylinder, leaving the sides open.

6. In a skillet large enough to hold the salmon cylinders without crowding (or use two skillets and divide the oil between them), heat the olive oil over medium-high heat until almost smoking hot. Place the salmon cylinders seam side down in the pan and sauté for 3 minutes, or until the wrappers are crisp and golden brown on the bottom. Turn and cook for 3 minutes on the other side, for medium-rare salmon. (Cook for an additional minute on each side if you like your salmon more well done.)

7. Meanwhile, reheat the broth gently over low heat.

8. To serve, cut each salmon bundle into 2 or more pieces and stand on end in a large soup plate. Ladle the broth around the salmon, garnish with a fennel frond, if desired, and serve immediately.

GLAZED SALMON WITH WASABI SABAYON

SERVES 4

FOR THE WASABI SABAYON

- 4 large egg yolks
- ½ cup dry white wine
- ¼ cup freshly squeezed lime juice
- 2 tablespoons white wine vinegar
- 2 teaspoons wasabi powder (see Pantry, page 285)
  Kosher salt

FOR THE SALMON

- 1 tablespoon olive oil
- 4 6-ounce salmon fillets, with skin
- ¼ cup freshly squeezed lime juice
- 2 tablespoons ketjap manis (see Pantry, page 281)
- 1 teaspoon wasabi powder

Because the ketjap manis is quite salty, there is no need to season the salmon with salt.

I like to serve this with Potato Pancakes (page 186). Place each salmon fillet on a potato pancake, and garnish with the sabayon.

1. **PREPARE THE SABAYON:** In the top of a double boiler or a medium heatproof bowl, whisk the egg yolks, wine, lime juice, and vinegar until well blended. Set over gently simmering water and cook, whisking constantly, until the sabayon is thick and fluffy, about 10 minutes.

2. Whisk in the wasabi powder and season with salt to taste. Turn off the heat and keep the sabayon warm over the hot water until ready to serve.

3. **PREPARE THE SALMON:** Heat the oil in a large cast-iron or other heavy skillet over medium-high heat until very hot. Add the salmon skin side down, reduce the heat to medium, and cook for 5 minutes, or until the skin is crisp but the salmon is still quite rare. Remove from the heat, cover the pan, and let stand for 3 minutes to finish cooking.

4. Whisk the lime juice, ketjap manis, and wasabi together in a small bowl. Transfer the salmon to a plate and cover loosely with foil to keep warm. Add the ketjap manis mixture to the skillet, set over medium heat, and cook, stirring, until reduced to a syrupy glaze.

5. Brush the salmon on both sides with the glaze, and place skin side up on serving plates. Garnish each fillet with a dollop of sabayon, and pass the remaining sabayon at the table.

Taking my cue from traditional Swedish sweet-salty flavor combinations, I use Asian ingredients to achieve the same effect in this dish, painting pan-seared salmon fillets with a glaze of ketjap manis (a sweet-salty, syrupy soy-based Indonesian sauce) and lime juice. Since the salmon is seared only on the skin side, the skin becomes very crisp but the fish remains medium-rare, moist, and succulent. Wasabi, the pungent spice sometimes called Japanese horseradish, adds its heat to both the glaze and the accompanying sabayon.

BRAISED SALMON WITH CANNELLINI BEANS

SERVES 4

FOR THE CANNELLINI BEANS

- 2 cups cannellini beans, soaked in cold water to cover for at least 4 hours, or overnight, and drained
- 2 slices bacon, finely chopped
- 1 teaspoon fresh thyme leaves
- 1 tablespoon finely chopped fresh tarragon
- 2 garlic cloves, finely chopped
- 1/2 teaspoon kosher salt, or more to taste
  Freshly ground black pepper

FOR THE SALMON

- 4 6-ounce salmon fillets, with skin
  Kosher salt and freshly ground black pepper
- 2 tablespoons olive oil
- 6 shiitake mushrooms, stems removed, caps very thinly sliced
- 1/2 cup white port or dry sherry
- 1 tablespoon soy sauce
- 1 tablespoon finely chopped fresh tarragon
- 2 tablespoons unsalted butter, cut into pieces
- 1 teaspoon truffle oil (see Sources, page 290; optional)

You might also serve the salmon with Mustard Greens with Bacon (page 174).

1. **PREPARE THE BEANS:** Combine the beans, bacon, thyme, tarragon, and garlic in a large heavy saucepan, add water to cover generously, and bring to a boil. Boil for 2 minutes, then reduce the heat and simmer gently, partially covered, for 1 1/2 to 2 hours, or until the beans are tender; add more water if necessary as the beans cook. Shortly before the beans are cooked, season with the salt and pepper to taste. Remove from the heat and cover to keep warm.

2. **PREPARE THE SALMON:** Pat the salmon fillets dry with paper towels. Season with salt and pepper to taste. Heat the oil in a large skillet over medium-high heat until almost smoking hot. Add the salmon fillets skin side down and cook for 3 minutes, or until the skin is crisp. Turn the salmon over, lower the heat slightly, and add the mushrooms, port or sherry, soy sauce, and tarragon. Cook for 2 minutes, then scatter the pieces of butter around the salmon and cook for 1 to 2 minutes longer, just until the salmon is medium-rare. Remove from the heat, add the truffle oil, if using, to the braising liquid, and baste the salmon fillets.

3. To serve, using a slotted spoon, transfer the beans to four serving plates. Place the salmon fillets on the beans, spoon the mushrooms and some of the braising liquid around them, and serve.

In Sweden, we prepare salmon in every possible way, from curing and smoking it to poaching, roasting, and sautéing it. In this recipe, salmon is cooked in two stages, first seared until the skin is crisp, then gently braised in a simple broth flavored with shiitake mushrooms, port, and soy sauce. It's served on a bed of cannellini beans, with the fragrant braising liquid spooned around.

DILL-CRUSTED ARCTIC CHAR WITH PINOT NOIR SAUCE

SERVES 4

FOR THE PINOT NOIR SAUCE

- 3 cups Pinot Noir or other dry red wine
- 2 garlic cloves, smashed but not peeled
- 1 shallot, finely chopped
- 1 3-inch sprig fresh rosemary
  Kosher salt and freshly ground black pepper

FOR THE CHAR

- 4 fingerling potatoes or 2 small Yukon Gold potatoes, peeled
- 1 tablespoon Dijon mustard
- 2 large egg yolks
- 1 cup chopped fresh dill
  Kosher salt and freshly ground black pepper
- 1 cup panko (see Pantry, page 283) or other coarse dry bread crumbs
- 4 6-ounce Arctic char fillets, with skin
- 2 tablespoons unsalted butter
- 1 tablespoon olive oil

- 2–3 tablespoons unsalted butter

Serve with Cauliflower, Potato, and Artichoke Ragout (page 170).

This recipe also works well using trout, mackerel, or salmon in place of the char.

The combination of dill, fish, and potato is the essence of comfort food to every Swede, and that homey trio inspired this more sophisticated variation on the theme. I spread a topping of dilled mashed potatoes over char fillets, coat the topping with coarse bread crumbs, and sauté the fish over high heat until the potato crust is very crisp but the inside is still moist and tender. A simple rosemary-scented red wine sauce finishes the dish.

1. **PREPARE THE SAUCE:** Combine the wine, garlic, shallot, and rosemary in a medium saucepan and bring to a simmer over medium heat. Reduce the heat to low and simmer gently until the liquid is reduced to $1/2$ cup, 45 minutes to 1 hour. Strain the sauce into a bowl, pressing down on the solids to extract as much liquid as possible. Season with salt and pepper, pour into a small saucepan, and set aside.

2. Meanwhile, put the potatoes in a medium saucepan, add salted water to cover, and bring to a boil. Reduce the heat slightly and boil gently for 18 to 20 minutes, or until the potatoes are fork-tender; drain. Transfer the potatoes to a medium bowl and mash with a fork. Let cool.

3. Mix the mustard with the egg yolks in a small bowl. Add to the potatoes, mixing well. Stir in the dill and season with salt and pepper to taste.

4. **PREPARE THE CHAR:** Spread the panko on a plate. Lay the fish fillets skin side down on a work surface and spread a layer of the potato mixture onto each fillet. Dip the potato-coated sides of each fillet in the panko.

5. In a heavy skillet large enough to hold the fish fillets in one layer without crowding, melt 1 tablespoon of the butter with the oil over medium-high heat. When the bubbles have subsided, slide in the fish fillets, potato side down, and cook for 3 to 4 minutes, or until the crust is golden brown. Turn the fillets over, raise the heat to high, and cook for another 2 to 3 minutes, or until the skin is golden and crisp and the fish is just cooked through. Remove the pan from the heat, add the remaining 1 tablespoon butter to the pan, and let it melt, then baste the fillets with the oil and butter mixture.

6. Meanwhile, reheat the sauce over low heat. Whisk in the butter bit by bit. Remove from the heat.

7. To serve, spoon about 2 tablespoons of the sauce to make a large oval pool on each plate and top with a char fillet, crust side up. Pass the remaining sauce at the table.

HORSERADISH-CRUSTED ARCTIC CHAR WITH CURRIED MUSSELS
SERVES 4

FOR THE CURRIED MUSSELS

- 2 tablespoons olive oil
- 1 carrot, finely chopped
- 1 shallot, finely chopped
- 3 garlic cloves, finely chopped
- 1 tablespoon Curry Paste (page 271) or store-bought Thai yellow curry paste
- 3 ripe tomatoes, peeled, seeded, and coarsely chopped, or 1½ cups chopped canned tomatoes
- 2 cups fresh carrot juice
- 6 tablespoons freshly squeezed lime juice
- 1 tablespoon crème fraîche
- 2 pounds mussels, scrubbed and debearded

FOR THE CHAR

- 1 large horseradish root (about 12 inches long; see Pantry, page 281), peeled
- 4 6-ounce Arctic char fillets, with skin
- 1 tablespoon unsalted butter, melted
  Kosher salt and freshly ground black pepper

If you don't have a vegetable juicer, you can find fresh carrot juice at
health food stores or juice bars.

You can substitute cod, salmon, or sea bass fillets for the char.

1. Preheat the oven to 400°F. Grease a baking sheet with olive oil.

2. PREPARE THE BROTH: Heat the oil in a large pot over medium heat. Add the carrot, shallot, garlic, curry paste, and tomatoes, and cook, stirring, for 2 minutes, or until the vegetables just begin to soften. Add the carrot juice, lime juice, and crème fraîche, and bring to a simmer. Cook, stirring, for 2 minutes. Turn off the heat until you are ready to cook the mussels. (The broth can be prepared up to 6 hours ahead, covered, and refrigerated.)

3. PREPARE THE CHAR: Grate the horseradish on the fine holes of a box grater; it should be the consistency of wet sawdust. Or grate it using a food processor: first grate it using the grating blade, then switch to the metal cutting blade and process until fine.

4. Lay the fillets skin side down on the prepared baking sheet and brush with the melted butter. Season with salt and pepper to taste. Pat about ½ cup of the grated horseradish evenly onto each fillet.

5. Roast the fish for 7 to 9 minutes, or until the crust is golden brown and the fish is just cooked through.

6. Meanwhile, bring the broth to a boil over medium-high heat. Add the mussels, cover the pot, and steam, shaking the pot every few minutes to move the mussels around, for 5 to 7 minutes, until they open. Discard any mussels that don't open.

7. To serve, place the fillets in large soup plates and ladle the mussels and broth around them.

When you first make this dish, you may think it calls for much too much horseradish—your kitchen will be filled with its bracing, sinus-clearing aroma. But the cooking process smooths everything out, leaving just enough heat in the crust to complement the sweetness of the carrot juice in the spicy mussel broth. ✣ You can prepare the broth hours ahead of time. The horseradish crust takes only minutes to prepare, and both the salmon and the mussels cook in about 10 minutes. Be sure to serve with crusty bread for mopping up the last drops of the flavorful broth.

Most of the mussels sold today are farm-raised, and they are usually already quite clean. Scrub them briefly if necessary, and just before cooking, pull off the wiry beards.

The Curried Mussels make an excellent dish on their own, served with crusty bread. To serve 4, double the amount of mussels, but use the same amount for broth.

ROASTED RED SNAPPER WITH DILL SAUCE
SERVES 4

One of the most popular fish in America, red snapper isn't found in European waters, but it's become one of my favorites. And it pairs especially well with a dill sauce, as classic a Swedish touch as you will ever find — though I added a splash of nontraditional mustard oil to give the sauce a bit of a kick. ✦ Cooking fish on the bone keeps it moist and flavorful. Although the idea of roasting a whole fish might seem intimidating, it's actually simple — and it's easy to remove the bones from snapper once it's cooked.

To fillet a whole cooked fish, slit the skin down the back of the fish. Slide a sharp knife under the top fillet to separate it from the backbone, then cut the fillet into serving pieces and, using a wide metal spatula, transfer to a platter. Cut through the backbone at the head and tail, and lift out and discard it. Cut the bottom fillet into serving pieces and transfer to the platter.

1   4-pound red snapper, cleaned and scaled

2   lemons, thinly sliced

2   sprigs fresh dill

2   bay leaves

3   tablespoons olive oil

1   tablespoon mustard oil (see Pantry, page 282), grapeseed oil, or canola oil

1   head garlic, cut horizontally in half

2   shallots, finely chopped

6   fingerling potatoes, halved, or 3 medium Yukon Gold potatoes, quartered

1   stalk fresh lemongrass, tough outer leaves removed, tender inner stalk lightly smashed

2   tablespoons unsalted butter

FOR THE DILL SAUCE

1   tablespoon olive oil

1   garlic clove, finely chopped

1   shallot, finely chopped

1   tablespoon mustard seeds (see Pantry, page 282)

1   tablespoon white wine vinegar

2   teaspoons mustard oil or 1 tablespoon whole-grain mustard

1   cup Chicken Stock (page 263)

½   cup heavy cream

1   tablespoon unsalted butter

2   teaspoons sugar

½   cup chopped fresh dill

    Pinch of kosher salt, or to taste

You could also make this dish using sea bass.

Serve the fish with Celery Root and Pear Puree (page 169).

1.   Preheat the oven to 400°F.

2.   PREPARE THE SNAPPER: Score 4 diagonal slashes in each side of the snapper. Pat dry with paper towels. Stuff the lemon slices, dill, and bay leaves into the cavity of the fish. In an ovenproof skillet large enough to hold the snapper, heat the oils over medium-high heat until almost smoking (if you don't have a very large skillet, use a heavy roasting pan, set over two burners if necessary). Add the snapper, reduce the heat to medium, and add the garlic, shallots, potatoes, and lemongrass. Cook for 3 to 5 minutes, pressing down on the fish with a heavy metal spatula, until the skin is very crisp. Turn the fish and crisp the skin on the other side, pressing down on the fish with the spatula again.

3.   Transfer the pan to the oven and roast for about 18 minutes, turning the fish once about halfway through the cooking time, until it is just opaque throughout. Just before the fish is done, add the butter to the pan and let it melt. Remove the fish from the oven and spoon the pan juices over it.

4.   MEANWHILE, PREPARE THE SAUCE: Heat the oil in a medium saucepan over medium heat. Add the garlic, shallot, and mustard seeds, and sauté for 1 minute, or until the mustard seeds start to pop. Add the vinegar, mustard oil or mustard, stock, and cream, bring to a simmer, and simmer gently for 10 minutes, or until the liquid is slightly reduced and thickened.

5.   Strain the sauce and pour it into a small saucepan. Stir in the butter, sugar, dill, and salt. Just before serving, reheat the sauce over low heat.

6.   To serve, transfer the fish to a serving platter and present it at the table. Cut the fish into serving portions (see Note on facing page). Spoon 1 to 2 tablespoons of the dill sauce onto each plate, top with a portion of fish, and spoon another tablespoon of sauce onto the fish.

PROSCIUTTO-WRAPPED HALIBUT WITH DARK BEER SAUCE

SERVES 4

FOR THE DARK BEER SAUCE

- 1 tablespoon olive oil
- 1 shallot, finely chopped
- 1 garlic clove, finely chopped
- 1 teaspoon honey
- 2 cups Chicken Stock (page 263)
- ½ cinnamon stick
- 3 cardamom pods
- ½ cup dark beer
- 1 tablespoon unsalted butter
- 1 tablespoon sour cream

FOR THE HALIBUT

- 1½ tablespoons finely chopped fresh basil
- 1½ tablespoons finely chopped fresh cilantro
- 4 6-ounce halibut fillets, skin removed
- 4 thin slices prosciutto
- 2 tablespoons grapeseed oil or canola oil

Instead of halibut, you could use other firm-fleshed white fish, such as monkfish, Chilean sea bass, or another bass.

1. **PREPARE THE SAUCE:** Heat the oil in a medium saucepan over medium heat. Add the shallot and garlic and sauté for 2 minutes, or until softened. Add the honey and cook for about 5 minutes, or until the shallots and garlic are golden brown and caramelized.

2. Add the stock, cinnamon, and cardamom pods, and bring to a boil. Reduce the heat and simmer gently until the liquid is reduced to ½ cup, about 20 minutes.

3. Strain the broth, pressing against the solids to release as much liquid as possible, and pour into a small saucepan. Add the beer and simmer for 3 minutes to blend the flavors. Remove from the heat.

4. **PREPARE THE HALIBUT:** Sprinkle the chopped basil and cilantro over both sides of the fish fillets. Wrap a slice of prosciutto around each fillet.

5. Heat the oil in a large skillet or sauté pan over medium-high heat until almost smoking hot. Add the fillets and cook, turning once, for 4 minutes on each side, or until the prosciutto is crisp and the fish is just cooked through.

6. Meanwhile, just before serving, reheat the sauce over low heat. Whisk in the butter and sour cream and heat through; do not allow to boil. Remove from the heat.

7. To serve, transfer the halibut fillets to four plates. Pour the sauce around the fish, and serve.

With its firm, meaty white flesh, halibut can stand up to all kinds of hearty preparations. In this recipe, I treat the fish as I might treat a mild-flavored meat, serving it in a spicy beer sauce. The sauce is very Scandinavian, typical of the northern beer-drinking countries. ✣ This is a good cold-weather dish, especially when served with Spicy Sauerkraut (page 184).

COCONUT-POACHED COD

1   14-ounce can unsweetened coconut milk

¼   cup olive oil

2   cups crushed canned tomatoes

6   tablespoons freshly squeezed lime juice

1   stalk fresh lemongrass, tough outer leaves removed, tender inner
    stalk lightly smashed and cut into 3-inch lengths

2   tablespoons finely chopped fresh cilantro

4   6-ounce cod fillets
    Kosher salt and freshly ground black pepper

For a more elaborate dish, serve this with Tomato-Crab Risotto (page 130).

Place a mound of risotto in the center of each soup plate, top with a cod

fillet, and spoon the sauce over and around the fish.

You can also prepare this with Chilean sea bass or another bass instead

of the cod.

1. Combine the coconut milk, oil, tomatoes, lime juice, lemongrass, and cilantro in a deep skillet large enough to hold the cod in one layer, and bring to a simmer over medium heat. Reduce the heat to medium-low and simmer gently, stirring occasionally, for 15 minutes to allow the flavors to blend.

2. Season the cod with salt and pepper to taste and slide the fish into the pan. Bring to a simmer, then reduce the heat to low and simmer for 5 minutes. Remove from the heat and let stand for 5 minutes to finish the cooking. Remove the lemongrass pieces just before serving.

3. With a slotted spatula, transfer the fillets to large soup plates. Spoon a generous amount of sauce around each one, and serve.

In my early twenties, I spent some time traveling in the Caribbean, cooking on cruise ships. The colors, the tropical scents, and the balmy air were heavenly to someone accustomed to a northern European climate, and the foods I discovered — the spectacular seafood, the different curries, the starchy vegetables such as yuca and taro root, and coconut — were exciting. ✤ Years later, those Caribbean discoveries gave me the idea of poaching fish in well-seasoned coconut milk, a technique that works extremely well. The rich broth made with coconut milk and tomatoes becomes a superb sauce for the fish, and the result is a special dish that is very simple to prepare.

MISO-CURED MONKFISH IN CARROT-GINGER BROTH
SERVES 4

FOR THE MONKFISH

- 4 8-ounce monkfish steaks (on the bone)
- ¼ cup white miso (see Pantry, page 282)
- 3 tablespoons freshly squeezed lime juice
- 1 tablespoon olive oil

FOR THE CARROT-GINGER BROTH

- Grated zest of 1 lime
- 6 tablespoons freshly squeezed lime juice
- 1 3-inch piece ginger, chopped
- 1 shallot, chopped
- ¼ cup water
- 1½ teaspoons rice wine vinegar
- 2 cups fresh carrot juice
- 1 teaspoon Pastrami Spices (page 268)

- 1 tablespoon olive oil
- 1 tablespoon unsalted butter

If you don't have a vegetable juicer, you can find fresh carrot juice at health food stores or juice bars.

For a finishing touch, top each portion of fish with 1 to 2 tablespoons Corn Flake, Pine Nut, and Bacon Crumbs (page 273).

The Carrot-Ginger Broth is delicious served on its own as a light, spicy soup.

1. MARINATE THE MONKFISH: Place each monkfish steak between two sheets of plastic wrap and pound gently with a meat mallet to break the connective fibers and flatten slightly.

2. Whisk the miso, lime juice, and olive oil together in a small bowl. Lay the monkfish in a shallow baking dish and pour the miso mixture over it, turning the fish several times to coat. Cover and marinate in the refrigerator for at least 12 hours or up to 24 hours.

3. SHORTLY BEFORE SERVING, PREPARE THE BROTH: Combine the lime zest, lime juice, ginger, shallot, water, and rice wine vinegar in a medium saucepan, bring to a simmer, and simmer for 4 minutes, or until reduced by half.

4. Strain the broth into another medium saucepan. Add the carrot juice and spices and bring to a simmer. Turn off the heat and cover to keep warm.

5. SAUTÉ THE MONKFISH: Lift the monkfish fillets out of the marinade and pat dry with paper towels. Heat the 1 tablespoon olive oil in a large skillet over medium-high heat until it is almost smoking hot. Add the monkfish and cook, turning once, for 3 to 5 minutes on each side, until lightly browned and cooked to the desired doneness.

6. Meanwhile, reheat the broth. Whisk in the butter and remove from the heat.

7. To serve, transfer the monkfish to shallow soup plates. Spoon the broth around, and serve immediately.

I discovered miso, the Japanese fermented soybean paste, the way many people do, in miso soup, and I fell in love with its rich taste. Miso's saltiness gave me the idea of using it as a curing agent to flavor and tenderize fish, much as I would use a traditional Swedish salt cure. I serve the miso-cured fish in a carrot-ginger broth—its sweet, hot flavors are a great complement to the salty richness of the monkfish. ✣ For best results, the monkfish should marinate for at least 1 day before you cook it. If you're impatient, though, you can reduce the curing time to just a few hours and still have excellent results.

CURRIED CHILEAN SEA BASS WITH CHILLED TOMATO SOUP

SERVES 4

FOR THE TOMATO SOUP

12 pounds ripe tomatoes (see Note)

1 tablespoon olive oil

1/2 cup chopped shallots

2 garlic cloves, chopped

1 stalk fresh lemongrass, tough outer leaves removed, tender inner stalk lightly smashed and coarsely chopped

1 1/2 teaspoons chopped ginger

5 ripe plum tomatoes, halved, seeded, and coarsely chopped

3 tablespoons honey

2 cups Chicken Stock (page 263)

1 cup dry white wine

Finely chopped zest of 1 lime

3/4 cup freshly squeezed lime juice

2 sprigs fresh mint

4 sprigs fresh cilantro

Kosher salt and freshly ground black pepper

FOR THE BASS

2 tablespoons store-bought mango chutney

1 teaspoon Curry Paste or store-bought Thai green curry paste

4 6-ounce Chilean sea bass fillets, skin removed

1 tablespoon unsalted butter

2 tablespoons olive oil

2 tablespoons citrus-flavored vodka

Fresh cilantro leaves, for garnish

If ripe tomatoes are not available, you can prepare the soup with high-quality canned tomato juice. Substitute 2 quarts juice for the 12 pounds tomatoes and proceed as directed.

You can substitute halibut, skate, or turbot for the sea bass.

For finely chopped citrus zest, remove the zest with a zester (or a Microplane rasp-type grater), then finely chop. If you don't have a zester, remove the zest with a vegetable peeler (avoid the bitter white pith) and cut into thin strips, then chop.

I like to serve the fish topped with a few plantain chips (page 43) to add a crunchy element. Or you could add flavor and crunch with Corn Flake, Pine Nut, and Bacon Crumbs (page 273).

Seasoned with a puree of curry paste (homemade or store-bought) and store-bought mango chutney, this cod is intensely flavorful. Curry seems to be one of those flavors with worldwide appeal, and curry spices have been used in Swedish cuisine for hundreds of years. ✣ The spiciness of the fish is complemented by the clear, sharp flavors of a chilled soup, which is the essence of sun-ripened tomatoes. On its own, the rosy soup makes a terrific first course on a hot summer night. It's not difficult to make, but you do need to allow time for it to chill.

1. **PREPARE THE SOUP:** Core the tomatoes and cut them into quarters. Puree them in a food processor, in batches if necessary. Strain the tomatoes through a sieve set over a large bowl, pressing on the solids with the back of a wooden spoon to extract as much liquid as possible; you should have at least 8 cups juice.

2. Heat the oil in a large pot over medium-low heat. Add the shallots, garlic, lemongrass, ginger, and plum tomatoes, and cook, stirring, for about 10 minutes, until the tomatoes have softened. Add the honey and continue cooking until the vegetables begin to caramelize.

3. Add 8 cups tomato juice, the stock, wine, lime zest, lime juice, mint, and cilantro, and bring to a simmer. Reduce the heat to low and simmer for 1 hour.

4. Strain the soup into a bowl. Season to taste with salt and pepper. Let cool, then cover and refrigerate for at least 3 hours, or until very cold.

5. **PREPARE THE BASS:** Puree the mango chutney with the curry paste or powder in a blender. Spread the mixture over both sides of each fillet.

6. Melt the butter with the olive oil in a large skillet over medium-high heat. When the bubbles have subsided, add the fish and cook, turning once, for about 4 minutes per side, until golden brown.

7. Meanwhile, stir the vodka into the chilled soup. Taste and add more salt or pepper if necessary.

8. To serve, ladle the soup into four large soup bowls and place a fillet in each bowl. Garnish with cilantro leaves.

VARIATION

For another version of the dish with an intriguing contrast of hot and icy-cold, turn the soup into a granita: Prepare the soup as directed and chill it, then add the vodka and pour it into a shallow metal pan. Freeze for 30 minutes, or until ice crystals have started forming around the edges of the pan. Stir the crystals into the center of the mixture and continue to freeze until solid, stirring the granita every 20 minutes or so. Shortly before serving, scrape up the granita with the edge of a metal spoon to make ice shavings; return the granita to the freezer. Cook the fish as directed, place a portion of granita in each bowl, and top with the fish. Serve immediately.

STEAMED SEA BASS WITH MUSHROOM CONSOMMÉ

SERVES 4

FOR THE TORTELLINI (OPTIONAL)

About 2 tablespoons olive oil

1 shallot, finely chopped

1 garlic clove, finely chopped

1 large portobello mushroom cap (about 4 inches in diameter), finely chopped

½ teaspoon kosher salt

1 cup fresh or thawed frozen corn kernels

½ teaspoon fresh thyme leaves

Freshly ground black pepper

2 tablespoons mascarpone cheese or fresh goat cheese

1 teaspoon truffle oil (see Sources, page 290; optional)

1 cup finely chopped arugula

16 wonton wrappers

1 large egg white, whisked with 1 teaspoon water for egg wash

FOR THE BASS

4 cups water

1 cup dry white wine

Reserved solids from Mushroom Consommé (below)

1 head garlic, cut horizontally in half

2 3-inch pieces ginger, peeled and coarsely chopped

1 bunch fresh cilantro

4 dried shiitake mushrooms

6 fresh thyme sprigs

8 fresh basil leaves

4 6-ounce black sea bass fillets

½ teaspoon kosher salt

Freshly ground black pepper

1 lime, halved

Mushroom Consommé (page 92)

Wonton wrappers, or wonton skins, are available in the freezer or refrigerated section of Asian markets and some supermarkets or by mail order (see Sources, page 289). Most packages contain 80 or more wrappers, but they freeze well; wrap the leftovers well and freeze for another use.

The Corn and Mushroom Tortellini also make a delicious appetizer on their own, tossed with a few tablespoons of butter.

If you prefer to steam the tortellini, place them on a steamer rack over boiling water, without touching one another (or they will stick together), and steam for 5 to 10 minutes, until the wrappers are al dente. Or, if you have a large steamer or a stackable Chinese bamboo steamer, you can simply steam the dumplings along with the fish.

You can substitute halibut or cod fillets for the sea bass.

1. **PREPARE THE OPTIONAL TORTELLINI:** Heat 1 tablespoon of the olive oil in a large skillet over medium heat. Add the shallot, garlic, portobello, and salt, and cook, stirring, for about 10 minutes, until the juices released by the mushrooms have cooked away. Add the corn kernels and cook for about 3 minutes, or until tender. Remove from the heat and stir in the thyme and pepper to taste. Transfer to a bowl and let cool.

2. Stir the mascarpone and the truffle oil (if using) into the cooled mushroom filling, then stir in the arugula.

3. Lay out 8 of the wonton wrappers on a work surface. Place about 1 teaspoon of mushroom filling in the center of each wrapper. Using your index finger or a pastry brush, brush the edges of each wrapper with the egg wash, then fold it over to form a triangle and press the edges together to seal. Transfer to a small baking sheet. Repeat with the remain-

ing wrappers and filling. Cover with wax paper and refrigerate until ready to cook.

4. PREPARE THE BASS: Pour the water and white wine into the bottom of a steamer. Add the reserved solids from the consommé, 1 of the garlic halves, half the ginger, half the cilantro, 2 of the shiitake mushrooms, 3 of the thyme sprigs, and 4 of the basil leaves. Bring to a boil and simmer for 5 minutes to infuse the steaming liquid with flavor.

5. Line the steamer rack with the remaining cilantro, thyme, and basil. Season the fish fillets with the salt and pepper to taste and place on the steamer rack. Scatter the remaining garlic, ginger, and shiitakes around them. Squeeze the juice of the lime over the fish, then add the lime halves to the steamer rack. Set the steamer rack over the boiling liquid, cover, and steam for 10 to 15 minutes, until the fish is opaque throughout.

6. MEANWHILE, COOK THE TORTELLINI, IF USING: Bring a large pot of salted water to a boil. Add 1 tablespoon olive oil and the tortellini and cook for about 3 minutes, or until they float to the surface. Using a slotted spoon or a wire skimmer, transfer the tortellini to a shallow bowl. Gently toss with a little olive oil to keep them from sticking together.

7. Just before serving, heat the consommé over low heat.

8. Transfer the fillets to shallow soup plates. Ladle the consommé around the fish, arrange 4 tortellini (if using) in each plate, and serve.

We don't have bass in Sweden, but I've come to love cooking with it. I use black sea bass for this recipe. The pure white fillets are steamed over a garlicky mushroom-infused broth, then served in my easy but intensely flavorful Mushroom Consommé. (Be sure to save the solids from the consommé when you make it, to use in the broth.) ✣ At Aquavit, we float Corn and Mushroom Tortellini in the consommé, which adds a hint of sweetness to the earthy flavors, but these are entirely optional—the dish is more than satisfying without them.

SEARED TUNA AND SCALLOPS WITH SOY BEURRE BLANC

SERVES 4

FOR THE TUNA

6 dried shiitake mushrooms

1 pound sushi-quality tuna, cut into 4 loins (see Note)

1 tablespoon olive oil

¼ cup white miso (see Pantry, page 282)

2 tablespoons water

FOR THE SOY BEURRE BLANC

1½ cups Chicken Stock (page 263)

2 tablespoons soy sauce

1 shallot, finely chopped

½ teaspoon fresh thyme leaves

1 tablespoon heavy cream

2 tablespoons unsalted butter

Freshly ground black pepper

1 tablespoon olive oil

1 large portobello mushroom cap, cut into 12 slices

FOR THE SCALLOPS

12 large sea scallops

Kosher salt and freshly ground black pepper

1 tablespoon olive oil

1 tablespoon unsalted butter

Ask the fishmonger to cut a thick chunk of tuna into 4 "loins" — you want long rectangles, about 1½ inches thick, rather than the thinner steaks sold in most markets.

1. **PREPARE THE TUNA:** Break the dried mushrooms into smaller pieces, put them in a food processor, and process until ground to a powder. Spread on a large plate and set aside.

2. Pat the tuna dry with paper towels. Heat the olive oil in a large skillet over medium-high heat until it is almost smoking hot. Sear the tuna loins for about 20 seconds on each of the four sides; the tuna should remain very rare. Transfer to a plate.

3. Whisk the miso and water together in a small bowl. Brush the tuna on all sides with the miso, then roll it in the dried mushroom powder. Cover and set aside for 30 minutes. Preheat the oven to 450°F.

4. **PREPARE THE BEURRE BLANC:** Combine the stock, soy sauce, shallot, and thyme in a small saucepan and bring to a boil over high heat. Boil until reduced to ½ cup, about 15 minutes. Strain the liquid and return it to the pan. Cover and keep warm. Just before serving, add the cream, butter, and pepper, and use a whisk or an immersion blender to whip the sauce until it is frothy.

5. Meanwhile, heat the 1 tablespoon olive oil in a medium skillet over medium-high heat. Add the sliced portobello and sauté for about 5 minutes, or until tender and any juices have evaporated. Remove from the heat, cover, and set aside in a warm place.

6. **PREPARE THE SCALLOPS:** Pat the scallops dry with paper towels. Season with salt and pepper. Heat the olive oil in a large ovenproof skillet over medium-high heat until almost smoking. Add the scallops and sear for about 30 seconds on each side. Add the butter to the pan and place in the oven for about 1½ minutes, until the butter turns brown. Remove the skillet from the oven, turn the scallops over, and let stand for about 5 minutes to finish the cooking.

7. To serve, slice each tuna loin across the grain into 4 pieces. Arrange 4 tuna slices, 3 scallops, and 3 portobello slices in a row down the center of each plate, starting and ending with a tuna slice. Pass the beurre blanc separately at the table.

Although I was raised in a seafood-loving culture, fish served rare was unfamiliar to me before I came to the United States — in Sweden, as in the rest of Europe, fish has traditionally been cooked until well done. But certain fish, such as tuna, are at their best served rare. ✣ This multicultural dish blends French techniques with Asian and American flavors. The rare tuna has the flavor and texture of sushi, but to give it a more Western appeal, I sear it briefly over high heat before brushing it with miso. Then I add soy sauce to beurre blanc, the classic French sauce. ✣ This recipe plays with similar textures rather than contrasting ones. The buttery texture of the scallops echoes that of the moist tuna, and the seafood in turn complements the rich, silky beurre blanc. But if you'd like to add a crispy, crunchy contrast, garnish the dish with a few Root Vegetable Chips (page 43).

TUNA CONFIT WITH AVOCADO SOUP

SERVES 4

FOR THE TUNA CONFIT

- 4 6-ounce tuna steaks
- 2 garlic cloves, smashed
- 2 sprigs fresh thyme
- 2–3 cups olive oil, plus more if necessary

FOR THE AVOCADO SOUP

- ¼ pound fingerling or baby Yukon Gold potatoes
- 1 tablespoon olive oil
- 3 ounces chorizo sausage, finely chopped
- 2 garlic cloves, finely chopped
- 1 shallot, finely chopped
- 1 jalapeño pepper, seeded and finely chopped
- 1 cup heavy cream
- 1 cup Chicken Stock (page 263)
- 1 cup dry white wine
- 2 ripe Hass avocados
- 1½ tablespoons freshly squeezed lime juice
- ¼ cup white miso (see Pantry, page 282)
- 1 tablespoon finely chopped fresh cilantro, for garnish

You can substitute skinless salmon fillets for the tuna.

Chorizo is a spicy Spanish smoked pork sausage. It's available in Latin markets and specialty markets, as well as some supermarkets.

The soup can also be served on its own, in small portions, as an appetizer, with some good crusty bread.

1. **PREPARE THE TUNA:** Place the tuna in one layer in a small baking dish that will hold it snugly. Add the garlic, thyme, and olive oil. The oil should completely cover the fish; add additional oil if necessary. Refrigerate for at least 3 hours, or overnight.

2. **PREPARE THE SOUP:** Preheat the oven to 400°F.

3. Place the potatoes on a small baking sheet, pierce them in a few places with a fork, and roast for 20 to 30 minutes, until fork-tender. Remove the potatoes from the oven and let cool slightly.

4. **MEANWHILE, PREPARE THE SOUP BASE:** Heat the oil in a deep heavy pot over medium heat. Add the chorizo, garlic, shallot, and jalapeño, and sauté for 3 minutes, or until the garlic and shallot have softened. Add the cream, stock, and white wine, and bring to a simmer, then reduce the heat to medium-low and simmer gently for 10 minutes, or until slightly reduced. Turn off the heat and cover to keep warm.

5. Peel the roasted potatoes and put them in a bowl. Halve and pit the avocados and scoop the flesh into the bowl of potatoes. Mash the avocados and potatoes together with a fork. Return the soup to a simmer and stir in the avocado mixture. Remove from the heat and whisk in the lime juice. Cover to keep warm.

6. Remove the tuna fillets from the oil (set the oil aside) and pat dry.

Brush on all sides with the miso. Heat 2 tablespoons of the oil from the tuna in a large skillet over medium-high heat until almost smoking hot. Add the tuna and sear for 1 to 1$^{1}/_{2}$ minutes on each side, or until golden brown and crisp. Remove from the heat.

7. Meanwhile, reheat the soup over low heat, stirring occasionally.

8. To serve, ladle the soup into shallow soup plates. Cut each tuna steak in half on the diagonal, and lay the tuna in the soup. Garnish with the cilantro, and serve.

Traditionally, the French term *confit* refers to duck or goose (or sometimes pork) that has been salted and slowly cooked in its own fat, then stored in the cooking fat as a way to preserve it. In this takeoff on that classic dish, the tuna is instead marinated in olive oil for several hours, or overnight, to flavor it and keep it moist. It's then sautéed briefly in a little of the marinating oil and served in a rich, spicy avocado soup.

TOMATO-CRAB RISOTTO

SERVES 4

¼ cup heavy cream

2 cups tomato juice

1 cup Chicken Stock (page 263)

1 cup canned unsweetened coconut milk

2 tablespoons olive oil

1 shallot, finely chopped

1 garlic clove, finely chopped

5 oil-packed sun-dried tomatoes, finely chopped

1 tablespoon finely chopped fresh tarragon

1 cup Arborio or Carnaroli rice

¼ cup dry white wine

2 tablespoons unsalted butter

3 large egg yolks, lightly beaten

1 tablespoon soy sauce

1 tablespoon freshly grated Parmigiano-Reggiano

1 cup jumbo lump crabmeat (about 6 ounces), picked over for shells and cartilage

1. Whip the cream in a medium bowl until it holds soft peaks. Cover and refrigerate.

2. Combine the tomato juice, stock, and coconut milk in a medium saucepan and bring to a simmer over medium-high heat. Reduce the heat to very low to keep the liquid at the barest simmer.

3. Heat the olive oil in a large heavy saucepan over medium-high heat. Add the shallot, garlic, sun-dried tomatoes, and tarragon, and sauté for 2 minutes, or until the shallot has softened. Add the rice and cook, stirring, until all the grains are coated with oil. Add the wine and cook, stirring, until it has evaporated.

4. Add about ½ cup of the stock mixture, reduce the heat, and cook, stirring, until almost all of it has been absorbed. The liquid should bubble gently as you stir; adjust the heat as necessary. Continue cooking, stirring, and adding the stock mixture, ½ cup at a time, once each previous addition has been absorbed, until the rice is al dente and the risotto is creamy, 18 to 20 minutes from the time you first added the liquid (if you run out of liquid, add hot water as necessary). Remove from the heat.

5. Fold the egg yolks, soy sauce, and Parmesan into the whipped cream, then fold the cream into the risotto. Fold in the crabmeat, and serve immediately.

Both rich and delicately flavored, this risotto makes an elegant lunch or light supper dish, or you could serve it as an appetizer. The risotto is cooked in a mixture of tomato juice, stock, and coconut milk instead of just stock, a combination that accentuates the sweetness of the crabmeat.

GRILLED LOBSTER WITH GRAPEFRUIT SALSA
SERVES 4

This is a luxurious dish for a summer dinner party. The lobster is grilled, and a sprinkling of ground tea adds an unexpected accent. Threading the lobster tails on skewers prevents them from curling up as they cook, and for a casual presentation, you could serve them on the skewers. Citrus and shellfish are a natural combination, and the refreshing grapefruit salsa is a light and flavorful alternative to the traditional melted butter.

2 pink grapefruit

¼ cup olive oil

1 shallot, finely chopped

1 garlic clove, finely chopped

1 teaspoon finely chopped pickled ginger

1 roasted red bell pepper (see page 73), finely chopped

2 tablespoons finely chopped fresh cilantro

2 tablespoons finely chopped fresh mint

Grated zest of 1½ limes

3 tablespoons freshly squeezed lime juice

1 tablespoon honey

1 tablespoon sherry vinegar

Pinch of cayenne pepper

Kosher salt and freshly ground black pepper

FOR THE LOBSTER

4 1½-pound lobsters

2 tablespoons olive oil

1 tablespoon mint tea, ground to a powder

Sherry vinegar, which comes from Spain, is available in gourmet shops and some supermarkets. If you can't find it, substitute white wine vinegar.

Use a spice grinder (or a clean coffee grinder) to grind the tea leaves to a powder.

The lobsters can also be broiled instead of grilled.

1. **PREPARE THE SALSA:** Slice off both ends of the grapefruit right down to the flesh. Stand each grapefruit on a cutting board and, using a serrated knife or sharp paring knife, cut away the peel and white pith from top to bottom in strips, following the curve of the grapefruit. Working over a bowl to catch the juices, slice between the membranes of the fruit with a sharp paring knife to release the segments. Transfer the grapefruit segments to another bowl, and set the fruit and the juice aside.

2. In a large skillet or sauté pan, heat 2 tablespoons of the oil over medium-high heat. Add the shallot, garlic, pickled ginger, roasted red pepper, cilantro, mint, and lime zest, and sauté for 3 minutes, or until the shallot has softened. Remove from the heat and add the grapefruit juice, lime juice, honey, and vinegar. Let cool.

3. Transfer the grapefruit-juice mixture to a small bowl and add the grapefruit segments, cayenne, the remaining 2 tablespoons oil, and salt and pepper to taste. Cover and refrigerate.

4. **PREPARE THE LOBSTERS:** Prepare a hot fire in a grill. Meanwhile, bring a large pot of water to a boil. Plunge the lobsters headfirst into the pot and cook for just 2 minutes. Remove from the water and let cool slightly.

5. Pull off the lobster tails, crack the shells or cut them open, and remove each tail in one piece. Run a metal or wooden skewer lengthwise through each tail to keep it flat, and set aside. Pull off the claws and crack them open so that the meat will be easy to pull out (do not remove the meat). Brush the lobster tails and claws with the olive oil and sprinkle with the mint tea.

6. Grill the lobster tails and claws, turning once, for about 5 minutes, or until the meat is cooked through.

7. Place 1 lobster tail and 2 claws on each plate. Top each with several tablespoons of salsa and pass the rest of the salsa at the table.

BIRDS, MEAT, AND GAME

SWEDISH ROAST CHICKEN WITH SPICED APPLE RICE
SERVES 4

This recipe comes from my grandmother, who roasted a chicken for dinner every Sunday night. The chicken is seasoned with cinnamon, cardamom, star anise, and cloves, spices that have been an important part of Swedish cuisine since the eighteenth century, when the Swedish East India Company first brought them to Sweden from Asia. ✧ The spices are used to season the apple-vegetable stuffing as well as the bird. Although some recipes call for roasting chicken at high temperatures, I prefer to cook it at 350°F so that the spices have time to penetrate the flesh inside and out with their flavors. After the chicken is cooked, the stuffing mixture of apples, sweet potato, and onion is added to hot rice, along with a spoonful of yogurt to cool and soften the spicy flavors, and served alongside.

- 1 medium sweet potato, peeled and cut into ½-inch cubes
- 1 large onion, cut into ½-inch cubes
- 2 Granny Smith apples, peeled, cored, and cut into ½-inch cubes
- 2 shallots, coarsely chopped
- 1 garlic clove, chopped
- 1 teaspoon fresh thyme leaves
- 1 tablespoon finely chopped fresh mint
- 2 tablespoons water
- 1 tablespoon olive oil
- ½ teaspoon ground cinnamon
- 2 cardamom pods or ¼ teaspoon ground cardamom
- 2 star anise
- 2 whole cloves or ⅛ teaspoon ground cloves
- 2 black peppercorns
- 4 white peppercorns (or 4 additional black peppercorns)
- 1 teaspoon kosher salt
- 1 3½-pound chicken, preferably free-range

FOR THE SPICED APPLE RICE

- 1 cup long-grain white rice
- 1 cup water
- 1 teaspoon kosher salt, or to taste
- 1½ tablespoons yogurt
- Freshly ground black pepper

1. PREPARE THE CHICKEN: Preheat the oven to 350°F.

2. Blanch the sweet potato in boiling water for 2 minutes. Drain, rinse under cold water, and drain again. In a medium bowl, combine the sweet potato, onion, apples, shallots, garlic, thyme, and mint. Combine the water and olive oil and add to the vegetable mixture, tossing to coat.

3. Using a mortar and pestle, lightly crush the cinnamon, cardamom, star anise, cloves, black peppercorns, and white peppercorns with the salt. (Or combine the spices on a cutting board and crush with the bottom of a heavy pot.) Add half the spice mixture to the vegetables, and reserve the rest.

4. Rinse the chicken inside and out and pat dry with paper towels. Remove all the excess fat. Lightly stuff the bird's cavity with about half the vegetable mixture and tie its legs together with kitchen string. Place the chicken on a rack in a roasting pan and rub it all over with the reserved spice mixture. Scatter the remaining vegetable mixture around the chicken.

5. Roast for about 1½ hours, or until an instant-read thermometer inserted into the thigh reaches 160°F. After the first hour, or when the vegetables in the pan are tender, remove them from the pan and set aside in a bowl. Check the pan occasionally as the chicken roasts, adding a bit of water if it becomes completely dry.

6. When the chicken is cooked, transfer it to a cutting board. Remove the vegetables from the cavity and add to the vegetables in the bowl. Cover the chicken loosely with foil and let rest while you cook the rice.

7. Add a few tablespoons hot water to the roasting pan, stirring well to deglaze the pan. Pour the liquid into a measuring cup and skim off as much of the fat as possible. Add enough additional water to make 1 cup.

8. PREPARE THE RICE: Combine the rice, water, deglazing liquid, and salt in a medium saucepan. Bring to a boil over high heat, reduce the heat to low, cover, and cook for about 18 minutes, until the rice is tender and all the liquid is absorbed. Remove from the heat, fold in the yogurt and reserved vegetables, and season with salt if necessary and pepper.

9. Carve the chicken and serve with the rice.

SLOW-COOKED SQUAB

SERVES 4

4   squabs (see Note)
2   cups Curry Oil (page 270) or 2 cups grapeseed oil or canola oil plus
     2 tablespoons curry powder
     Kosher salt and freshly ground black pepper

Cutting up the squab is quite easy, but if you prefer, you can buy what are called boneless squabs. They are actually semi-boneless—the breasts are boned, but the legs are not. Boneless squabs are available at some specialty butchers and by mail order (see Sources, page 289).

You can also make this recipe with pheasant; substitute four 6- to 7-ounce boneless pheasant breasts for the squab and cook them in exactly the same way.

Serve the squab with Asparagus-Potato "Risotto" (page 194).

Although squab is usually served fairly rare, I sometimes like to cook it until the meat is almost falling-apart tender. The idea for this dish came from a meal I had in Chinatown, where poultry of all types is slow-cooked. Marinating and then cooking the squab in curry-infused oil flavors the meat and keeps it succulent.

1.   Cut the legs off each squab at the thigh joint. Using a sharp thin-bladed knife, slice each half-breast from the bones. (Discard the carcasses, or reserve for poultry stock.) Put the squab breasts and legs in a baking dish just large enough to hold them in one layer. If using the Curry Oil, pour the oil over them; it should just cover them. Or, toast the curry powder in a small dry skillet over medium heat, stirring, for about 30 seconds, until fragrant. Stir in the grapeseed or canola oil and pour over the squab. Cover and marinate in the refrigerator for at least 8 hours, or overnight.

2.   Preheat the oven to 325°F.

3.   Transfer the squab breasts to a plate and return to the refrigerator. Put the legs in a baking pan that will hold them and the breasts snugly, and pour the oil over them. Bake for 1 hour.

4.   Add the squab breasts to the baking pan and bake for 45 minutes to 1 hour longer, until the meat of the legs and the breasts is very tender; remove the breasts first if they are done before the legs. Transfer the squab to a platter; cover the legs to keep them warm.

5.   Heat a large skillet over medium-low heat until hot. Add the squab breasts, skin side down, and cook for 3 to 5 minutes, until the skin is crispy. Season all the squab with salt and pepper, arrange on serving plates, and serve.

COFFEE-ROASTED DUCK BREASTS
SERVES 4

FOR THE MARINADE

- 2 cups hot coffee
- 4 cardamom pods, crushed
- 1 2-inch cinnamon stick

- 4 6-ounce boneless skin-on duck breasts, trimmed of excess fat
- 1 teaspoon cardamom pods
- 2 2-inch cinnamon sticks, broken into pieces
- 2 cups coffee beans
- ½ cup ruby port or Madeira

Serve the duck with Pear and Fingerling Potato Ragout (page 191).

We drink a lot of coffee in Scandinavia, but I got the idea for this recipe while traveling in my birth country, Ethiopia. There, being invited to someone's house for coffee involves an hour-long ritual. First, the host slowly roasts green (raw) coffee beans in a frying pan on the stove. As the coffee beans gradually turn brown, the house fills with their fragrance. It occurred to me that I could cook duck breasts in a frying pan along with coffee beans, using their wonderful taste to flavor the meat. ✣ For even more flavor, I first marinate the duck breasts in coffee spiced with cardamom and cinnamon. Be sure to allow time for marinating the duck — at least 6 hours (or overnight).

1. PREPARE THE MARINADE: Combine the coffee, crushed cardamom pods, and cinnamon stick in a bowl. Let cool.

2. Prick the skin of the duck breasts all over with a sharp kitchen fork. With a small sharp knife, score the skin of each breast a few times. Place the breasts skin side up in a baking dish. Pour the coffee mixture over them, cover, and marinate in the refrigerator for at least 6 hours, or overnight.

3. Remove the duck breasts from the marinade and pat them dry with paper towels; discard the marinade. Heat a large skillet over medium-low heat. Add the duck breasts, skin side down, the cardamom pods, and the cinnamon sticks, and cook for 3 minutes. Scatter the coffee beans around the duck breasts and cook, gradually increasing the heat as the duck breasts render their fat, for about 5 minutes longer, or until the skin is crisp and brown.

4. Transfer the duck breasts to a plate and discard the coffee beans and spices. Return the duck, skin side up, to the skillet, add the port or Madeira, and bring to a simmer over medium-low heat. Braise the duck breasts for 5 minutes. Remove from the heat and let stand for 5 minutes to finish the cooking.

5. To serve, cut the duck breasts into ½-inch-thick slices and fan them out on four plates. Drizzle the pan juices over the duck and serve immediately.

CRISPY DUCK WITH GLÖGG SAUCE

SERVES 4

FOR THE MARINADE

2 cups freshly squeezed orange juice

¹/₂ cup red wine vinegar

2 tablespoons honey

1 2-inch cinnamon stick

6 cardamom pods

4 6-ounce boneless skin-on duck breasts,
    trimmed of excess fat

FOR THE GLÖGG SAUCE

2 star anise

1 cinnamon stick

2 whole cloves

³/₄ cup ruby port or Madeira

¹/₄ cup dry red wine

Grated zest of 2 limes

Grated zest of 2 oranges

1 bay leaf

4 white peppercorns

1 tablespoon olive oil

1 shallot, finely chopped

¹/₂ teaspoon fresh thyme leaves

2 tablespoons unsalted butter

Serve the duck with Mango Risotto (page 196)

or Lime Risotto (page 195).

After marinating duck breasts in a sweet-spicy orange juice–vinegar mixture, I let them air-dry in the refrigerator for several hours (overnight is even better) so the skin will cook to a wonderful crispness. The sauce, which has some of the same flavors as the duck marinade, is based on the Swedish drink glögg, a hot spiced wine with citrus zest, cinnamon, cloves, and other fragrant spices.

1. **MARINATE THE DUCK:** Combine the orange juice, vinegar, honey, cinnamon stick, and cardamom pods in a small saucepan and bring to a boil. Remove from the heat and let cool for 5 minutes.

2. Prick the skin of the duck breasts all over with a sharp kitchen fork. Lay the breasts skin side up in a baking dish and pour the warm marinade over them. Cover and refrigerate for at least 8 hours, or, preferably, overnight.

3. **MEANWHILE, PREPARE THE SAUCE BASE:** Toast the star anise, cinnamon stick, and cloves in a small dry skillet over medium-low heat for 2 to 3 minutes, until fragrant. Transfer the spices to a small bowl and add the port or Madeira, wine, lime and orange zests, bay leaf, and peppercorns. Cover and let sit at room temperature for 6 to 8 hours, or overnight.

4. **PREPARE THE DUCK:** Lift the duck breasts out of the marinade (set the marinade aside) and pat dry with paper towels. Lay the breasts skin side up on a plate and refrigerate, uncovered, for 2 to 6 hours, to air-dry. Pour 1 cup of the marinade into a small bowl, cover, and refrigerate; discard the remaining marinade.

5. Heat the olive oil in a large saucepan over medium-high heat. Add the shallot and thyme and sauté for 2 minutes, or until the shallot has softened. Add the reserved marinade and the sauce base, bring to a simmer, and simmer for about 20 minutes, until the liquid has reduced by almost half. Remove from the heat and set aside.

6. Heat a large heavy skillet over medium heat until hot. Add the duck, skin side down, and cook for 6 minutes, or until the skin is crisp and brown. Turn the breasts over and cook for 4 to 6 minutes longer, or until the meat is browned. Turn off the heat and let the duck breasts sit for another 4 minutes to finish cooking.

7. Meanwhile, reheat the sauce over medium-low heat. Whisk in the butter and remove from the heat.

8. To serve, arrange the duck on serving plates and spoon some sauce over each duck breast. Pass the remaining sauce at the table.

SWEDISH MEATBALLS
SERVES 4 TO 6

FOR THE MEATBALLS
- ½ cup fine dry bread crumbs
- ¼ cup heavy cream
- 2 tablespoons olive oil
- 1 medium red onion, finely chopped
- ½ pound ground chuck or sirloin
- ½ pound ground veal
- ½ pound ground pork
- 2 tablespoons honey
- 1 large egg
  - Kosher salt and freshly ground black pepper
- 3 tablespoons unsalted butter

FOR THE SAUCE
- 1 cup Chicken Stock (page 263)
- ½ cup heavy cream
- ¼ cup lingonberry preserves (below)
- 2 tablespoons juice from Quick Pickled Cucumbers (below)
  - Kosher salt and freshly ground black pepper

FOR SERVING
- Garlic Mashed Potatoes (page 188)
- Lingonberry preserves (see Sources, page 289)
- Quick Pickled Cucumbers (page 181)

1. **PREPARE THE MEATBALLS:** Combine the bread crumbs and heavy cream in a small bowl, stirring with a fork until all the crumbs are moistened. Set aside.

2. Heat the oil in a small skillet over medium heat. Add the onion and sauté for about 5 minutes, until softened. Remove from the heat.

3. In a large bowl, combine the ground beef, veal, pork, onion, honey, and egg, and mix well with your hands. Season with salt and pepper to taste. Add the bread crumb–cream mixture and mix well. With wet hands (to keep the mixture from sticking), shape the mixture into meatballs the size of a golf ball, placing them on a plate lightly moistened with water. You should have about 24 meatballs.

4. Melt the butter in a large skillet over medium-high heat. Add the meatballs, in batches if necessary, and cook, turning frequently, for about 7 minutes, until browned on all sides and cooked through. Transfer the meatballs to a plate, and discard all but 1 tablespoon of fat from the skillet.

5. **PREPARE THE SAUCE:** Return the skillet to the heat, whisk in the stock, cream, preserves, and pickle juice, and bring to a simmer. Season to taste with salt and pepper. Add the meatballs to the sauce, reduce the heat to medium, and simmer for about 5 minutes, until the sauce thickens slightly and the meatballs are heated through. Serve hot with the mashed potatoes, preserves, and pickled cucumbers.

Many supermarkets and meat markets sell a meat loaf mix of ground beef, pork, and veal. However, if the mixture isn't available or you can't buy ground pork or ground veal separately, you can grind the meat yourself in small batches in a food processor.

Although lingonberry preserves are the traditional accompaniment to these meatballs, some sweet-tart Fresh Cranberry Relish (page 210) would be a good stand-in.

These meatballs are served at least once a week in many Swedish homes, and they always appear on a traditional smorgasbord table. What makes them unique are the accompaniments, which are as important as the meatballs themselves — cream sauce, mashed potatoes, and the traditional condiments, lingonberry preserves and pickled cucumber. The meatballs are always made with a combination of beef, veal, and pork, for flavor and moistness.

RYDBERG (PAN-SEARED BEEF AND POTATOES IN RED WINE SAUCE)

SERVES 4

FOR THE RED WINE SAUCE

- 2 cups Chicken Stock (page 263)
- 2 cups dry red wine
- 2 shallots, finely chopped
- 2 sprigs fresh thyme

- 3 tablespoons grapeseed oil or canola oil
- 1 large onion, cut into ½-inch dice
  Kosher salt and freshly ground black pepper
- 3 Idaho or other baking potatoes, peeled, cut into
  ¼-inch cubes, and soaked in cold water to
  cover until needed
  Splash of white wine vinegar
- 4 large eggs
- 1½ pounds beef tenderloin, cut into ¾-inch cubes
  and patted dry
- 2 tablespoons unsalted butter

At Aquavit, we use veal stock to make the sauce, but we've substituted the more common chicken version in this recipe. However, many gourmet markets sell good-quality fresh or frozen veal stock, which you could use instead for a richer flavor.

Served at inns and grand hotels, Rydberg is virtually the only fancy dish in the traditional Swedish repertoire. Made with seared beef tenderloin and sautéed cubed potatoes, and served with a red wine sauce and raw egg yolks in a presentation somewhat similar to that of steak tartare, it's definitely not poor man's food. ✣ The egg yolks are typically served in half-shells on top of the meat, and each diner mixes the yolk into the hot beef, potatoes, and wine sauce, to add an element of creamy richness. I prefer to serve Rydberg with poached eggs.

1. **PREPARE THE SAUCE:** Combine the stock, wine, shallots, and thyme in a medium saucepan and bring to a boil over medium-high heat. Reduce the heat slightly and simmer for 30 to 40 minutes, until reduced to $1^1/_2$ cups. Strain the sauce. Transfer half the sauce to a small saucepan, and set the remaining $^3/_4$ cup sauce aside.

2. Heat 1 tablespoon of the oil in a large cast-iron skillet over medium-high heat. Add the onion, season with salt and pepper, and cook, stirring frequently, until golden brown, about 10 minutes. Transfer to a bowl and wipe the skillet clean.

3. Drain the potatoes and pat them dry. Heat 1 tablespoon of the oil in the skillet over medium-high heat. Add the potatoes, season with salt and pepper, and sauté until browned on the outside and soft inside, 15 to 20 minutes.

4. Meanwhile, bring a large deep skillet of water just to a simmer. Add the vinegar. One at a time, break each egg into a cup and carefully slip it into the water. Poach the eggs for 3 to 4 minutes, until the whites are set but the yolks are still runny. Using a slotted spoon, transfer the eggs to a bowl of cold water. Set the skillet of hot water aside.

5. Heat $1^1/_2$ teaspoons of the remaining oil in a large skillet over high heat until almost smoking. Season the beef with salt and pepper. Toss half the beef cubes into the pan and cook, tossing frequently, for 3 to 4 minutes, until the beef is seared on all sides and cooked just to rare. Transfer to a plate and repeat with the remaining $1^1/_2$ teaspoons oil and the remaining meat. Add the reserved $^3/_4$ cup red wine sauce to the pan, stirring to deglaze, and simmer until reduced to $^1/_4$ cup. Keep warm.

6. Just before serving, reheat the red wine sauce in the saucepan until hot. Whisk in the butter, remove from the heat, and cover to keep warm.

7. Bring the skillet of water back to a simmer, carefully add the poached eggs, and heat through, about 1 minute. Meanwhile, return all the beef to the skillet of the reduced sauce and toss to coat.

8. Arrange the meat in a line down the center of a long platter. Spread the onion in a line down the center of the meat, then use the back of a spoon to make four hollows in the onion and meat to hold the eggs. Surround the meat with the potatoes and drizzle some of the sauce around them. Using a slotted spoon, remove the poached eggs from the hot water, draining them thoroughly, and place in the hollows in the onions and meat. Serve, passing the remaining sauce at the table.

SJÖMAN'S BEEF IN SPICY BROTH
SERVES 6

FOR THE BEEF

- 2 cups pale beer (lager)
- 2 tablespoons soy sauce
- 1 tablespoon sake
- 1 tablespoon white miso (see Pantry, page 282)
- ½ cup grapeseed oil or canola oil
- 2 bird's-eye or other small dried chiles, broken into pieces
- 6 tablespoons freshly squeezed lime juice
- 2 pounds flank steak

FOR THE SPICY BROTH

- 1 tablespoon olive oil
- 2 shallots, finely chopped
- 1 3-inch piece ginger, peeled and finely chopped
- 1 stalk fresh lemongrass, tough outer leaves removed, tender inner stalk lightly smashed and chopped
- 4 black peppercorns
- 3 cups Chicken Stock (page 263)
- ½ cup sake
- 6 tablespoons freshly squeezed lime juice
- 1 tablespoon soy sauce
- 1 tablespoon fish sauce
- 1 tablespoon white miso
- 1 bird's-eye or other small dried chile
- ½ cup pale beer (lager)

- 2 scallions, trimmed and thinly sliced, for garnish

Sake is a Japanese rice wine used both in cooking and for drinking; look for it in well-stocked liquor stores.

Fish sauce — nam pla is the Thai name, nuoc nam the Vietnamese — is available in Asian markets and many supermarkets.

1. MARINATE THE STEAK: Combine the beer, soy sauce, sake, miso, oil, chiles, and lime juice in a shallow baking dish large enough to hold the meat snugly. Add the steak, turning to coat. Cover and refrigerate for at least 4 hours, or overnight, turning the steak occasionally in the marinade.

2. Prepare a medium-hot fire in a charcoal or gas grill.

3. MEANWHILE, PREPARE THE BROTH: Heat the olive oil in a large saucepan over medium-high heat. Add the shallots, ginger, lemongrass, and peppercorns, and cook, stirring, for 2 to 3 minutes, until the shallots have softened. Add the stock, sake, lime juice, soy sauce, fish sauce, miso, and chile, reduce the heat to low, and simmer for 20 minutes. Add the beer, remove from the heat, and remove the chile pepper. Set aside, covered to keep warm.

4. Remove the steak from the marinade and pat dry with paper towels. Grill, turning once, until cooked to rare (4 to 5 minutes per side for a 1-inch-thick steak, 8 to 10 minutes per side for a 2-inch-thick steak) or medium-rare (6 to 8 minutes per side for a 1-inch-thick steak, 10 to 12 minutes per side for a 2-inch-thick steak); do not overcook, or the meat will be tough. Transfer to a platter and let rest for 5 minutes.

5. Meanwhile, reheat the broth over low heat. Remove from the heat.

6. Slice the steak against the grain into ¼-inch-thick slices. Divide the steak among four shallow soup plates and ladle the broth over it. Garnish with the scallions, and serve.

At Aquavit, we use veal stock to make the sauce, but we've substituted the more common chicken version in this recipe. However, many gourmet markets sell good-quality fresh or frozen veal stock, which you could use instead for a richer flavor.

Sjöman's beef, made with flank steak marinated in beer, is one of the many rustic meat dishes popular in Sweden. The word *sjöman* means "seaman" and refers here to the type of hearty meal a sailor craves when he's finally back on land after a long voyage. I've added chiles and other Asian seasonings to the marinade and the broth to spice them up a bit.

CARAMELIZED RIB-EYE STEAKS
SERVES 4

1 cup Thai red chile dipping sauce or sweet chile sauce (see Pantry, page 284)

½ cup soy sauce

6 tablespoons freshly squeezed lime juice

3 garlic cloves, finely chopped

2 tablespoons Dijon mustard

1 teaspoon wasabi powder (see Pantry, page 285)

2 tablespoons olive oil

4 6-ounce boneless rib-eye steaks

1.   Preheat the oven to 450°F.

2.   Whisk together the chile sauce, soy sauce, lime juice, garlic, mustard, and wasabi in a small bowl. Set aside.

3.   Heat 1 tablespoon of the oil in a large skillet over high heat until very hot. Add 2 of the steaks and sear for 2 minutes on each side, or until lightly browned. Transfer to a baking dish large enough to hold all the steaks. Heat the remaining 1 tablespoon oil, sear the remaining steaks, and add to the baking dish.

4.   Pour the soy sauce mixture over the steaks and roast for about 7 minutes, until medium-rare. Let rest for 5 minutes before serving.

Rib-eye is my favorite cut of steak because of the satisfying beefy flavor of the perfectly marbled meat. For this dish, the steaks are first seared in a hot skillet, then basted with a sweet-salty, spicy sauce that caramelizes slightly as the meat finishes cooking in the oven. ✛ Serve with Asparagus-Potato "Risotto" (page 194).

PEPPER-CRUSTED BEEF TENDERLOIN STEAKS WITH CABBAGE TZATZIKI

SERVES 4

FOR THE BEEF

- 2 tablespoons white peppercorns
- 2 tablespoons black peppercorns
- 2 tablespoons pink peppercorns
- 2 tablespoons Asian sesame oil
- 4 anchovy fillets
- 3 garlic cloves
- 1 tablespoon olive oil
- 1½ pounds center-cut beef tenderloin, cut into 4 steaks

FOR THE CABBAGE TZATZIKI

- 1 cup yogurt (see Note)
- 3 garlic cloves
- Juice of 1 lime
- 2 tablespoons chopped fresh dill
- 1 tablespoon chopped fresh flat-leaf parsley
- 3 cups thinly sliced napa cabbage
- Kosher salt

Pink peppercorns, spicy and slightly sweet, aren't actually peppercorns at all but the berries of a rose plant. They are available at gourmet markets and by mail order (see Sources, page 289). If necessary, you can substitute additional black and white peppercorns, but the rosy pink peppercorns add both flavor and color to the mix. Blanching the peppercorns removes some of their sharp bite.

You can substitute boneless rib-eye steaks for the beef tenderloin.

Thick yogurt is best for the tzatziki; sheep's milk yogurt is especially good. If your yogurt seems very liquid, let it drain in a cheesecloth-lined strainer set over a bowl for 8 to 12 hours in the refrigerator before making the tzatziki.

1. PREPARE THE BEEF: Put the peppercorns in a small saucepan, add water to cover, and bring to a boil; drain. Add cold water to cover, bring to a boil, and drain again; repeat 2 more times. Spread the peppercorns on paper towels and let dry thoroughly.

2. Preheat the oven to 425°F.

3. Put the peppercorns in a mini processor or blender and process until coarsely crushed. Add the sesame oil, anchovies, and garlic, and blend to a coarse paste. Transfer to a small bowl.

4. Heat the olive oil in a large cast-iron or other heavy ovenproof skillet over high heat until almost smoking hot. Add the tenderloin steaks and sear for 1 minute on each side. Transfer the skillet to the oven and roast the steaks for 6 minutes, or until cooked to medium-rare.

5. Transfer the steaks to a warm platter and rub the peppercorn mixture all over them. Let rest for 10 minutes.

6. MEANWHILE, PREPARE THE TZATZIKI: Combine the yogurt, garlic, lime juice, dill, and parsley in a food processor or blender and process until smooth. Put the cabbage in a bowl, add the yogurt mixture, and toss to coat. Season with salt to taste.

7. To serve, slice the steaks and arrange on four plates, with a spoonful of the tzatziki alongside. Pass the remaining tzatziki at the table.

Serve this with Chorizo Mashed Potatoes or any of the other mashed potato dishes on pages 188–190.

This is my version of steak au poivre, incorporating intriguing flavors from other cuisines into a French dish. Rather than using just one kind of pepper, I combine white, black, and pink peppercorns as well as anchovies and Asian sesame oil to make the crust for the beef. And instead of the classic pan sauce, I serve Cabbage Tzatziki, with crisp napa cabbage standing in for the usual cucumbers. The cool, creamy yogurt salad provides the perfect foil for the heat of the peppercorns.

SALT-CURED BRISKET IN MUSTARD BROTH

SERVES 8 TO 10

FOR THE BRINE

- 4 quarts water
- 3 cups kosher salt
- 6 white peppercorns

- 1 5-pound beef brisket, trimmed of excess fat
- 2 carrots, peeled and cut into 1-inch pieces
- 2 medium onions, peeled and cut into 1-inch pieces
- 1 parsnip, peeled and cut into 1-inch pieces
- 1 celery root, peeled and cut into 1-inch pieces
- 2 sprigs fresh rosemary
- 2 bay leaves

FOR THE MUSTARD BROTH

- 1 tablespoon mustard oil (see Pantry, page 282) or grapeseed oil or canola oil
- 2 Granny Smith apples, peeled, cored, and finely chopped
- 4 shallots, finely chopped
- 2 garlic cloves, finely chopped
- 1 tablespoon light brown sugar
- 1 cup dry white wine
- 4 sprigs fresh thyme
- 2 sprigs fresh rosemary
- 2 tablespoons Dijon mustard
- 1 tablespoon unsalted butter

- 1 3-inch piece horseradish (see Pantry, page 281), peeled and grated

Substitute bottled horseradish for the fresh if necessary.

1. **PREPARE THE BRINE:** Bring the water and salt to a boil in a large pot, stirring occasionally to dissolve the salt. Remove from the heat and add the peppercorns. Let cool to room temperature.

2. Cut the brisket crosswise in half. Place in a deep baking dish or bowl and pour the brine over the meat; it should cover it completely. Cover and refrigerate for 12 hours to cure.

3. **COOK THE BRISKET:** Remove the meat from the brine (discard the brine), place it in a large pot, and cover with cold water. Bring to a boil, then drain and rinse out the pot (blanching the beef removes excess salt). Return the beef to the pot and add the carrots, onions, parsnip, celery root, rosemary, bay leaves, and enough cold water to cover. Bring to a boil and skim any scum and fat from the surface. Reduce the heat and simmer gently for $3^{1}/_{2}$ to 4 hours, or until the meat is fork-tender. Remove from the heat and let the meat cool in the stock.

4. Transfer the brisket to a platter and cover with plastic wrap. Place a flat platter or a cutting board on top of the meat and put a heavy weight, such as a cast-iron skillet with a 28-ounce can in it, on top. Refrigerate for 12 hours.

5. Meanwhile, strain the stock and let stand briefly, then skim off as much fat as possible. Reserve 4 cups of the stock for the brisket, cover, and refrigerate. (Refrigerate or freeze the rest for another use.)

6. **PREPARE THE MUSTARD BROTH:** Heat the oil in a medium saucepan over medium-high heat. Add the apples, shallots, and garlic, and sauté for about 3 minutes, or until just softened. Add the brown sugar, the reserved 4 cups stock, the wine, thyme, and rosemary, and bring to a simmer. Reduce the heat and simmer gently for 30 minutes.

7. Strain the stock into another saucepan, and whisk in the mustard and butter. Keep warm over low heat.

8. To serve, cut the meat into $^{1}/_{2}$-inch-thick slices. Pour a little of the

broth into a large skillet and heat over medium heat. Add the slices of brisket, in batches if necessary, and heat through. Arrange several slices of brisket in each shallow soup plate and ladle the broth around it. Pass the grated horseradish in a small bowl at the table.

In many households in Sweden, a dish like this is a weekly standard. While the recipe looks long, it is not difficult — but it does take time. Slow cooking is essential for tough but flavorful cuts of meat like brisket, to make sure the meat becomes very tender. First the brisket is cured in a salt brine for 12 hours, then it is simmered and allowed to cool in the broth. Finally, it is weighted and refrigerated for another 12 hours before being reheated and served.

For more on celery root, see page 169. Use a sharp paring knife to peel it.

For a complete meal, serve with Roasted Caramelized Root Vegetables (page 168) and, instead of the grated horseradish, Horseradish Applesauce (page 213). Arrange a bed of the root vegetables in each bowl, place the meat on top, and add the broth. Pass the applesauce at the table.

Freeze the flavorful leftover brisket cooking liquid in small plastic containers to use in any recipe that calls for beef stock.

STEAMED VEAL TENDERLOIN WITH CREAMED BABY BOK CHOY

SERVES 4 TO 6

FOR THE STEAMING LIQUID

4–6 medium portobello mushrooms (1 per serving), trimmed and
     cleaned
  4 heads garlic
  4 shallots, coarsely chopped
  8 sprigs fresh thyme

FOR THE CREAMED BOK CHOY

4–6 baby bok choy (about 1 pound total) or 1 small mature bok choy
     (1–1¼ pounds), rinsed well
  2 oranges
  1 14-ounce can unsweetened coconut milk
  1 cup Chicken Stock (page 263)

FOR THE VEAL

  8 fresh thyme sprigs
  1 veal tenderloin (1½ to 2 pounds)
     Kosher salt and freshly ground black pepper

The idea of steaming a veal tenderloin roast may seem unusual, but I love to use this technique for meat. Like other forms of "enclosed cooking," it intensifies the flavor and gives moist, succulent results. ✣ You will probably have to order veal tenderloin from a good butcher. It is a luxury cut, tender and full of delicate flavor. (If you're lucky enough to have any veal left over, it's absolutely delicious cold.) ✣ I like to serve the veal with creamy bok choy. I hadn't encountered boy choy until I began cooking outside Scandinavia, but its crispness reminds me of cabbage, and it can be cooked in similar ways. Rather than stir-frying it in garlic and oil, I blanch it briefly, Asian style, then serve it in a creamy, orange-flavored coconut milk sauce that also acts as a second sauce for the veal.

1. **PREPARE THE STEAMING LIQUID:** Remove the mushroom stems from the caps; set the caps aside. Coarsely chop the stems and put them in the bottom of a steamer pot. Cut off the top third of each garlic head and place all the garlic in the bottom of the steamer. Add the shallots, the 8 thyme sprigs, and just enough water to come up to the top of the garlic. Bring to a boil, reduce the heat to low, cover, and simmer for 20 minutes.

2. Meanwhile, bring a large saucepan of salted water to a boil. If using baby bok choy, trim the root ends, leaving the boy choy whole, and slice them lengthwise in half. If using 1 large bok choy, remove any tough outer stalks, and cut the bok choy crosswise into 1-inch pieces. Blanch in the boiling water for 1 minute; drain and set aside.

3. **PREPARE THE SAUCE FOR THE BOK CHOY:** Grate the zest from 1 of the oranges, then halve the orange and squeeze the juice. Set the zest and juice aside. Slice off both ends of the remaining orange, right down to the flesh. Stand it on a cutting board and, using a serrated or other sharp knife, cut away the peel and white pith from top to bottom in strips, following the curve of the orange. Use a sharp paring knife to slice between the membranes to release the orange segments; set aside.

4. Combine the coconut milk, stock, orange juice, and zest in a medium saucepan, bring to a simmer, and simmer for 30 minutes, or until reduced by half.

5. **MEANWHILE, STEAM THE VEAL:** Arrange the 8 thyme sprigs on the steamer rack. Season the veal with salt and pepper and place it on top. Arrange the mushroom caps, gill side up, around or next to the veal and sprinkle with salt and pepper. Set the steamer rack over the simmering liquid, bring the liquid to a boil, and cover the steamer. Steam for 15 minutes, then turn off the heat and let stand, covered, for 5 minutes.

6. Transfer the veal and mushrooms (be careful not to spill the juices in the mushroom caps) to a platter and cover with foil to keep warm. Strain the steaming liquid, pressing down on the solids to extract as much liquid as possible; reserve the garlic.

7. Pour the steaming liquid into a medium saucepan, bring to a boil over medium-high heat, and reduce to 1 cup. Meanwhile, squeeze the garlic pulp out of the skins.

8. Just before serving, stir the bok choy into the coconut milk mixture. Fold in the orange segments and heat through. Whisk the garlic into the reduced steaming liquid and season to taste with salt and pepper.

9. To serve, cut the veal into 4 to 6 thick slices. Carefully transfer the mushroom caps to serving plates and set a slice of veal on top of each one. Arrange the bok choy next to the veal, and pass the garlic sauce on the side.

POACHED LAMB WITH DRIED MUSHROOMS AND ROSEMARY
SERVES 4

FOR THE SAUCE

- 2 cups Chicken Stock (page 263)
- ½ cup truffle juice (see Sources, page 290; optional)
- 2 garlic cloves, smashed
- 2 sprigs fresh rosemary
- Grated zest of 2 lemons
- Kosher salt and freshly ground black pepper

FOR THE LAMB

- 1 cup Chicken Stock (page 263)
- 1 cup olive oil
- 10 dried shiitake mushrooms
- 2 garlic cloves, peeled
- 2 sprigs fresh rosemary
- ½ cup truffle juice (optional)
- 2 lamb loins (12–14 ounces each)
- Kosher salt and freshly ground black pepper

- 1 tablespoon unsalted butter
- 1 teaspoon truffle oil, or more to taste (see Pantry, page 284; optional)

Serve the lamb with Caramelized Sunchokes (page 179).

At Aquavit, we use veal stock for both the poaching liquid and the sauce, but we've substituted the more common chicken version in this recipe. However, many gourmet markets sell good-quality fresh or frozen veal stock, which you could use instead for a richer flavor.

You will probably have to special-order the lamb loins from the butcher. They are expensive, but they are very tender and flavorful, a great delicacy to serve on special occasions.

1. **PREPARE THE SAUCE:** Combine the stock, truffle juice (if using), garlic, rosemary, and lemon zest in a medium saucepan, bring to a simmer, and simmer until the liquid is reduced by half, about 30 minutes. Strain the stock into a clean saucepan. Season to taste with salt and pepper and set aside.

2. **PREPARE THE LAMB:** Bring the stock to a boil in a Dutch oven or other large pot. Add the oil, 4 of the shiitake mushrooms, the garlic, rosemary, and truffle juice (if using), and bring just to a simmer. Season the lamb with salt and pepper and add to the pot. Reduce the heat to the lowest possible setting, so that the liquid just barely simmers, cover, and poach for 12 minutes, turning the meat once.

3. Meanwhile, break the remaining 6 shiitake mushrooms into small pieces. Put them in a spice grinder (or a clean coffee grinder) and grind to a fine powder.

4. Just before serving, reheat the reduced stock. Whisk in the butter, then whisk in the truffle oil, if using.

5. Remove the lamb loins from the poaching liquid and pat dry on paper towels. Roll the loins in the mushroom powder.

6. To serve, cut the loins into 1-inch-thick slices, arrange on serving plates, and spoon some of the sauce over them. Pass the remaining sauce at the table.

Poaching lamb is one of the best ways not only to impart flavor but also to keep the meat meltingly tender and moist. Using olive oil as part of the poaching liquid ensures that the lamb will be especially succulent. The truffle juice contributes intense flavor and extra depth to the poaching liquid and the sauce, but it is optional.

SLOW-COOKED LEG OF LAMB WITH MUSTARD SAUCE

SERVES 4 TO 6

FOR THE LAMB

- ¼ cup olive oil
- 1 cup Dijon mustard
- ½ cup pitted brined-cured black olives, coarsely chopped
- 6 garlic cloves, finely chopped
- 1 teaspoon fresh thyme leaves
- 1 tablespoon kosher salt
- 1 5- to 6-pound leg of lamb (ask your butcher to remove the hip bone)

FOR THE MUSTARD SAUCE

- ½ cup water
- ½ cup dry red wine
- ½ cup Chicken Stock (page 263)
- 1½ teaspoons mustard seeds
- 2 cloves
- 3 sprigs fresh thyme
- 1 tablespoon unsalted butter
- 1 tablespoon grainy mustard

At Aquavit, we use veal stock to make the sauce, but we've substituted the more common chicken version in this recipe. However, many gourmet markets sell good-quality fresh or frozen veal stock, which you could use instead for a richer flavor.

Serve the lamb with the Goat Cheese and Artichoke Tart (page 56).

1. PREPARE THE LAMB: Preheat the oven to 275°F.

2. Mix the oil and mustard in a small bowl. Stir in the olives, garlic, thyme, and salt. Rub the mustard mixture all over the lamb. Place the lamb in a roasting pan and roast for 6 hours, or until the meat almost falls off the bone.

3. Increase the oven temperature to 425°F and roast for another 20 minutes, or until a crisp crust forms. Transfer the lamb to a cutting board, cover loosely with foil, and let rest for 20 minutes.

4. PREPARE THE SAUCE: Add the water to the roasting pan to deglaze, scraping up the browned bits in the bottom of the pan. Transfer ½ cup of the pan juices to a small saucepan, add the red wine, stock, mustard seeds, cloves, and thyme, and bring to a simmer over medium heat. Simmer for about 10 minutes, or until reduced by half.

5. Strain the sauce into another saucepan, and keep warm over low heat. Just before serving, whisk in the butter and mustard.

6. To serve, carve the lamb and transfer to serving plates. Spoon some of the sauce over the meat, and pass the remaining sauce at the table.

This is one of my favorite ways of cooking leg of lamb. Slow-cooking meat gives you more control over the flavors than pan-searing or roasting—you can baste it repeatedly, or slowly build up a delicious crust. And the result is meat so moist and tender that it almost falls off the bone, with a richness of flavor that quick-cooking simply cannot achieve.

HERB-ROASTED RACK OF LAMB
SERVES 4

FOR THE LAMB

1 large egg yolk
1 tablespoon Dijon mustard
1 tablespoon plus 1 teaspoon olive oil
1 tablespoon freshly grated Parmigiano-Reggiano
3 tablespoons fine dry bread crumbs
1 teaspoon fresh thyme leaves
1 teaspoon finely chopped fresh rosemary
2 racks of lamb (1½–2 pounds each)
Kosher salt and freshly ground black pepper

FOR THE SAUCE

1 cup ruby port or Madeira
1 cup Chicken Stock (page 263)
3 tablespoons balsamic vinegar
1 teaspoon fresh thyme leaves
Grated zest of 1 lemon
1½ tablespoons freshly squeezed lemon juice
1 tablespoon unsalted butter
Kosher salt and freshly ground black pepper

You could also serve this as part of a special buffet. Cut the racks into individual ribs, arrange them on a platter, and drizzle with a little of the sauce; serve the remaining sauce alongside the meat.

Serve the lamb with Orzo with Mushrooms (page 193).

1. PREPARE THE LAMB: Preheat the oven to 450°F.

2. Combine the egg yolk, mustard, 1 teaspoon of the olive oil, the Parmesan, bread crumbs, thyme, and rosemary in a small bowl and mix well.

3. Heat the remaining 1 tablespoon oil in a large skillet over medium-high heat until almost smoking hot. Add the racks of lamb and sear for about 3 minutes on each side, or until lightly browned. Transfer to a platter and let cool.

4. Season the lamb with salt and pepper. Spread the herb mixture over the meaty part of the lamb. Place the lamb, fat side up, on a rack in a roasting pan. Roast for 15 to 20 minutes, or until the internal temperature registers 125°F on an instant-read thermometer, for medium-rare. Remove from the oven and let rest for 10 minutes.

5. MEANWHILE, PREPARE THE SAUCE: Combine the port or Madeira, stock, vinegar, thyme, and lemon zest in a medium saucepan, bring to a simmer, and simmer for 20 minutes, or until reduced to 1 cup. Remove from the heat and cover to keep warm.

6. Just before serving, reheat the sauce if necessary, and whisk in the lemon juice and butter. Season with salt and pepper to taste.

7. To serve, cut the racks into individual chops and arrange 3 or 4 chops on each plate. Pass the sauce at the table.

Rack of lamb is a superb dinner party dish, easy to prepare but always elegant. The meat is nicely marbled, giving it a great flavor, and meat cooked on the bone is juicy. It always surprises me that lamb isn't more popular in America, especially because it's so good here. ✤ The lamb is coated with a mixture or herbs, mustard, and bread crumbs, which roasts into a crisp crust. A lemony wine sauce balances the richness of the meat.

PRUNE-STUFFED PORK ROAST
SERVES 6

We used to eat this dish all the time at home, with red cabbage and roasted potatoes. Prunes, both in the meat itself and in the sauce, complement the flavors of the roast pork. At Aquavit, we like to accompany this with lingonberry preserves; you could also serve it with Fresh Cranberry Relish (page 210).

FOR THE PORK

- 1 3-pound pork loin roast
- 2 teaspoons finely chopped fresh marjoram
- 2 3-inch pieces ginger, peeled and finely chopped
- 5 garlic cloves, peeled and halved
- 5 pitted prunes, quartered
- 1 tablespoon caraway seeds
- 2 teaspoons kosher salt
  Freshly ground black pepper
- 1 tablespoon olive oil

FOR THE SAUCE

- 1¼ cups dry white wine, Chicken Stock (page 263), or water
- 1 tablespoon olive oil
- 2 shallots, finely chopped
- 1 3-inch piece ginger, peeled and finely chopped
- 5 pitted prunes, quartered
- 2 cups Chicken Stock
- ½ cup balsamic vinegar
- 1 tablespoon unsalted butter
  Kosher salt and freshly ground black pepper

At Aquavit, we use veal stock to make the sauce, but we've substituted the more common chicken version in this recipe. However, many gourmet markets sell good-quality fresh or frozen veal stock, which you could use instead for a richer flavor.

Serve with Braised Red Cabbage (page 175) and Curry Potatoes (page 192).

1. PREPARE THE PORK: Preheat the oven to 425°F.

2. Use a sharp knife to cut away most of the excess fat from the pork roast, leaving a thin layer of fat on top. (Reserve ¼ cup of the scraps for Braised Red Cabbage, if you are serving it with the pork.)

3. Mix the marjoram and ginger together in a small bowl. Use a sharp knife to poke 10 holes about 1½ inches deep all over the pork roast, then use a sharpening steel or the handle of a wooden spoon to make the holes a bit wider. Stuff 1 or 2 prune quarters, half a garlic clove, and a large pinch of the marjoram mixture into each hole.

4. Combine the remaining marjoram mixture with the caraway seeds, the salt, and pepper to taste. Rub the roast all over with the olive oil, then rub the seasoning mixture over the roast.

5. Put the roast in a roasting pan and roast for 20 minutes. Reduce the heat to 350°F and roast for 40 minutes to 1 hour longer, until the center of the roast reaches 150° to 155°F on an instant-read thermometer. Transfer the roast to a cutting board, cover loosely with foil, and let rest while you make the sauce.

6. PREPARE THE SAUCE: Set the roasting pan over medium-high heat and deglaze the pan with the wine or other liquid, scraping up the browned bits in the bottom of the pan with a wooden spoon. Remove from the heat and set aside.

7. Heat the oil in a small saucepan over medium heat. Add the shallots and ginger and sauté for about 2 minutes, until the shallots start to soften. Add the prunes, stock, vinegar, and the deglazing liquid, bring to a simmer, and simmer gently for 10 minutes, until slightly reduced. Whisk in the butter, season with salt and pepper to taste, and remove from the heat.

8. To serve, cut the roast into thick slices and arrange them on a platter. Spoon some of the sauce over the meat, and pass the remaining sauce at the table.

HONEY-GLAZED PORK RIBS
SERVES 4 TO 6

1 28-ounce can crushed tomatoes

1 cup soy sauce

½ cup honey

¼ cup Thai red chile dipping sauce or sweet chile sauce (see Pantry, page 284)

2 garlic cloves, crushed

2 fresh thyme sprigs

2 sprigs fresh basil

16 country-style pork ribs

Country-style ribs are actually chops cut from the blade, or shoulder, end of the pork loin, sold split or butterflied.

1. Combine the crushed tomatoes, soy sauce, honey, chile sauce, garlic, thyme, and basil in a bowl, mixing well. Put the pork ribs in a large baking dish and pour the marinade over them, turning to coat. Cover and refrigerate overnight.

2. About 30 minutes before you plan to bake them, remove the ribs from the refrigerator. Preheat the oven to 325°F.

3. Bake the ribs for 4 to 6 hours, turning them occasionally, until the meat is falling off the bones; add water to the baking dish if necessary to prevent scorching.

4. Transfer the ribs to a platter and serve.

I created this casual, homey dish in honor of this country's rib-eating enthusiasts. Country-style pork ribs are among the most succulent and delicious part of the pig, and they take well to long, slow cooking. The ribs are marinated overnight in a sweet, spicy sauce, then baked slowly for hours until the meat is meltingly tender. If there is any sauce left over, freeze it to use as a sauce for pasta. ✤ Corn Mashed Potatoes (page 189) is a natural accompaniment to these ribs.

MARJORAM-STUFFED VENISON ROLLS WITH CARAMELIZED CHESTNUTS

SERVES 4

FOR THE CARAMELIZED CHESTNUTS

- 1 pound whole chestnuts
- 1 orange
- 1 lemon
- 1 lime
- ½ cup Chicken Stock (page 263)
- 1 cup freshly squeezed orange juice
- ½ cup ruby port or Madeira
- 1 tablespoon sugar

FOR THE VENISON ROLLS

- 2 1-pound venison tenderloins
- 1 tablespoon olive oil
- Kosher salt and freshly ground black pepper
- 4 sprigs fresh marjoram, leaves only
- 2 tablespoons clarified butter (see Pantry, page 279)

1. PREPARE THE CHESTNUTS: Preheat the oven to 450°F.

2. Use a sharp paring knife to score an X in the flat side of each chestnut. Spread the chestnuts on a baking sheet and roast for 15 to 20 minutes, or until the shells start to peel away at the X. Remove from the oven and let cool slightly, then peel away the shells, using a paring knife if necessary. Remove the inner skins and set aside.

3. Meanwhile, grate the zest from the orange, lemon, and lime; set aside. Slice off the top and bottom of the orange, lemon, and lime right down to the flesh. Stand each one on a cutting board, and, using a serrated or other sharp knife, cut away the peel and white pith from top to bottom in strips, following the curve of the fruit. Working over a bowl to catch the juices, slice between the membranes with a small sharp knife to release the segments. Transfer the citrus segments to another bowl and set aside.

4. Combine the stock, reserved citrus juices, orange juice, port or Madeira, sugar, and citrus zest in a medium saucepan and bring to a boil over medium-high heat. Reduce the heat and simmer for about 25 minutes, until the liquid is reduced by slightly more than half. Remove from the heat and cover to keep warm.

5. Meanwhile, preheat the oven to 400°F.

6. BUTTERFLY THE VENISON TENDERLOINS: One at a time, place each tenderloin on a cutting board. Using a sharp knife, start at one long side, keep the blade horizontal to the cutting board, and cut the meat horizontally almost but not quite in half, so you can open it up like a book. Brush the inside of each tenderloin with olive oil and season with salt and pepper. Sprinkle half the marjoram over each tenderloin, fold over the tenderloins, and secure with toothpicks. Sprinkle with salt and pepper.

7. Heat the clarified butter in a large skillet over high heat until very hot. Add the tenderloins and sear for about 1 minute on each side, until lightly browned. Transfer the tenderloins to a baking sheet and roast for 5 minutes, or until the internal temperature registers 125°F on an instant-read thermometer, for medium-rare. Transfer the tenderloins to a cutting board, cover loosely with foil, and let rest for 10 minutes.

8. While the venison is resting, reheat the citrus juice mixture. Stir in the chestnuts, then carefully fold in the citrus segments. Remove from the heat.

9. To serve, slice the tenderloins and arrange on serving plates. Spoon the caramelized chestnuts alongside the venison, and serve immediately.

You can get venison tenderloins at specialty butcher shops or by mail order (see Sources, page 289). ✤ Serve this dish in the fall, when both fresh chestnuts and game are in season, and accompany with Spicy Sauerkraut (page 184).

PAN-ROASTED VENISON CHOPS WITH FRUIT AND BERRY CHUTNEY
SERVES 4

¼ cup plus 1 tablespoon olive oil

2 tablespoons aquavit or gin

2 sprigs fresh thyme

1 garlic clove, smashed

2 allspice berries, slightly crushed

2 juniper berries, slightly crushed

4 venison rib chops

Kosher salt and freshly ground black pepper

Fruit and Berry Chutney (page 215)

Juniper berries and allspice berries are available in the spice section of many supermarkets, in gourmet markets, and by mail order (see Sources, page 289).

Venison chops are available at good butcher shops (you may have to order them in advance) or by mail order (see Sources, page 289).

1. Combine ¼ cup of the oil, aquavit or gin, thyme, garlic, allspice, and juniper berries in a small bowl. Put the venison chops in a large baking dish, add the marinade, turning to coat, and cover the dish. (Or put them in a zipper-lock plastic bag, add the marinade, and seal the bag.) Refrigerate for 8 to 24 hours, turning the chops (or the bag) several times.

2. Preheat the oven to 375°F. Remove the venison from the refrigerator and let stand at room temperature for 15 minutes.

3. Heat a large cast-iron or other heavy ovenproof skillet (use two skillets if necessary) over high heat until hot, then add the remaining 1 tablespoon oil and heat until hot. Remove the venison chops from the marinade, dry them on paper towels, and season with salt and pepper on both sides. Add to the skillet and sear for about 2 minutes on each side, until lightly browned.

4. Transfer the skillet to the oven and roast for 4 to 5 minutes for rare (120°F on an instant-read thermometer), 7 to 8 minutes for medium-rare (125°F); do not overcook. Transfer the chops to a platter, cover loosely with foil, and let rest for 5 minutes.

5. To serve, spoon some chutney into the center of each plate and place the chops on top. Pass the remaining chutney at the table.

When Swedes want to treat guests to something special, they are most likely to serve game, especially in the fall, during hunting season. The lean meat is more tasty and strongly flavored than ordinary beef, pork, or lamb. I prefer to serve game with traditional Swedish condiments, such as Fruit and Berry Chutney, rather than old-fashioned heavy cream sauces. ✤ Aromatic juniper berries are a traditional seasoning for venison, and for this dish, the meat is marinated in a combination of herbs, juniper and allspice berries, and aquavit or gin (which is flavored with juniper berries). The sweet-tart chutney offers a nice contrast to the rich flavor of the meat.

SPICE-RUBBED WILD BOAR TENDERLOIN

2 tablespoons Pastrami Spices (page 268)

1 tablespoon kosher salt

2 1-pound wild boar tenderloins, trimmed

1 tablespoon grapeseed oil or canola oil

2 tablespoons grainy mustard

1 tablespoon honey

1 tablespoon fresh thyme leaves

½ teaspoon crushed black peppercorns

Wild boar tenderloin is available at some specialty butchers (you may have to order it in advance) and by mail order (see Sources, page 289).

Serve with Horseradish Applesauce (page 213) and Sweet Potato Tårta (page 180).

1. Preheat the oven to 400°F.

2. Mix the spices and salt in a small bowl, and rub the mixture all over the tenderloins. Heat the oil in a large skillet over high heat until very hot. Add the tenderloins and sear, turning occasionally, for 4 to 5 minutes, until browned on all sides.

3. Transfer the tenderloins to a baking pan and roast for 15 minutes, or until the internal temperature registers 150°–155°F on an instant-read thermometer. Remove from the oven and let rest for 10 minutes.

4. Meanwhile, combine the mustard, honey, thyme, and peppercorns in a small bowl, mixing well.

5. Brush the mustard mixture over the tenderloins. Slice them into ½-inch-thick medallions, arrange on a platter, and serve.

The taste of wild boar is unique, something like the best pork with a rich, gamy quality, and wild boar tenderloin is both tender and flavorful. This festive dish may seem exotic, but it's easy to prepare — the spice-rubbed meat is seared briefly and then finished in the oven. You could substitute pork tenderloins for the boar, but they will have a milder flavor.

SIDES

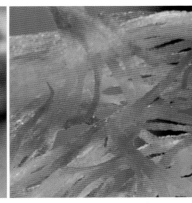

ROASTED CARAMELIZED ROOT VEGETABLES

SERVES 4 TO 6

1 cup heavy cream

½ cup maple syrup

1 teaspoon finely chopped fresh thyme

3 carrots, peeled and cut into 2-inch pieces

2 parsnips, peeled and cut into 2-inch pieces

1 small celery root (about 1 pound), peeled and cut into 2-inch pieces

2 small rutabagas (2½–3 pounds), peeled and cut into 2-inch pieces

2 tablespoons unsalted butter

1 tablespoon olive oil

1 pound mustard greens, washed and shredded, tough stems removed

½ cup Chicken Stock (page 263)

2 teaspoons mustard oil (see Pantry, page 282)

Freshly grated nutmeg

Kosher salt and freshly ground black pepper

1. Preheat the oven to 400°F.

2. Combine the cream, maple syrup, and thyme in a roasting pan large enough to hold all the root vegetables in a single layer. Add the vegetables, tossing to coat, and dot with the butter. Roast for 45 minutes to 1 hour, stirring occasionally, until the vegetables are tender and slightly caramelized.

3. Meanwhile, heat the olive oil in a large saucepan over medium-high heat. Add the mustard greens and cook, stirring, until they have wilted. Add the stock, cover the pan, reduce the heat to low, and cook for 30 minutes, or until the greens are very tender. Remove from the heat, stir in the mustard oil, and cover to keep warm.

4. Transfer the root vegetables to a large bowl and toss with the mustard greens. Season with a few gratings of nutmeg and salt and pepper to taste, and serve.

For more on celery root, see page 169. Use a sharp paring knife to peel it.

You can substitute turnips for the rutabagas.

This recipe doubles easily if you are serving a crowd.

Root vegetables are at the heart of Swedish cooking, part of the national cuisine. The long, cool growing season gives the vegetables heightened sweetness, so they are particularly tasty. Roasting root vegetables caramelizes their natural sugars, which are bolstered by the maple syrup, and the mustard oil and greens add a bit of spice.

CELERY ROOT AND PEAR PUREE

SERVES 4 TO 6

1 tablespoon unsalted butter

1 tablespoon olive oil

1 large celery root (about 1 pound), peeled and diced

1 ripe Bosc pear, peeled, cored, and diced

1 medium onion, chopped

1–2 cups Chicken Stock (page 263)

2 tablespoons sour cream

Kosher salt and freshly ground black pepper

1. Melt the butter with the olive oil in a large skillet over medium heat. Add the celery root, pear, and onion, and sauté for 3 to 4 minutes, until the vegetables start to soften and turn golden.

2. Add just enough stock to the pan to cover the vegetables. Bring to a boil over high heat, reduce the heat slightly, and boil gently for 15 to 20 minutes, or until the celery root is tender and the broth has cooked away.

3. Transfer to a food processor and puree until smooth. Add the sour cream and process to blend. Season to taste with salt and pepper, and serve.

Use a sharp paring knife to peel celery root.

Celery root, also called celeriac, is a knobby root vegetable that has a great crunchy texture when eaten raw. Simmered in chicken stock, it can be transformed into a creamy puree. ✤ The idea of balancing the earthy flavor of the celery root with the sweetness of pears comes from my chef and friend Vinny Chirioco; sour cream adds just a hint of tanginess. You could serve this, instead of mashed potatoes, with Swedish Meatballs (page 142) or with almost any meat, poultry, or fish main course.

CAULIFLOWER, POTATO, AND ARTICHOKE RAGOUT

½ head cauliflower, trimmed and separated into florets

4 medium Yukon Gold potatoes, peeled and quartered

3 cups Chicken Stock (page 263)

2 tablespoons clarified butter (see Pantry, page 279)

1 large Idaho or other baking potato, peeled and cut into ½-inch dice

3 artichoke hearts (see Note), cut into ½-inch dice

¼ cup heavy cream

2 tablespoons unsalted butter

Kosher salt and freshly ground black pepper

To prepare artichoke hearts, fill a large bowl with water and squeeze the juice of 1 lemon into it; set the lemon halves aside. Bend back and snap off the outer green leaves from each artichoke until you get to the inner cone of tender yellowish green leaves; slice off the cone of leaves. Trim off the stem of each artichoke and scrape out the fuzzy choke (a grapefruit spoon works well for this). Rub the cut surfaces of the artichokes occasionally with the lemon halves as you work, and drop the artichoke hearts into the lemon water to prevent discoloration. When ready to cook the artichokes, drain them thoroughly and pat dry before dicing.

Serve with Dill-Crusted Arctic Char (page 113) or any simple fish, chicken, or meat main course.

1. In a large saucepan, combine the cauliflower, Yukon Gold potatoes, and stock, and bring to a boil. Reduce the heat slightly and simmer until the vegetables are soft, 15 to 20 minutes.

2. Meanwhile, heat the clarified butter in a large skillet over high heat. Add the Idaho potato and sauté for about 10 minutes, until golden brown and tender. With a slotted spoon, transfer the potatoes to a plate; set aside in a warm spot. Add the artichokes to the skillet, sprinkle with salt, and sauté for about 5 minutes, until golden brown. Add to the plate with the potatoes.

3. Drain the cauliflower and Yukon Gold potatoes and put them through a food mill or potato ricer into a large bowl. Stir in the cream and butter and season with salt and pepper to taste. Stir in the sautéed potatoes and artichoke hearts, and serve immediately.

This ragout started as a simple puree of Yukon Gold potatoes and cauliflower enriched with cream and butter, terrific on its own. But I wanted some texture to play off against the smoothness, so I added crispy chunks of sautéed Idaho potato and artichoke hearts. The recipe calls for two types of potatoes because each has its own flavor and texture.

MUSHROOM RAGOUT WITH SALSIFY

4 large salsify (about ½ pound), peeled and cut into 1-inch pieces

1 tablespoon unsalted butter

1 tablespoon olive oil

2 shallots, finely chopped

2 garlic cloves, finely chopped

3 cups sliced porcini mushrooms or portobello mushroom caps (about ¾ pound), or use a combination of mushrooms

Kosher salt and freshly ground black pepper

1 cup heavy cream

½ cup sour cream

2 tablespoons ruby port or Madeira

1 tablespoon finely chopped fresh marjoram or 1 teaspoon dried marjoram

1. Cook the salsify in a large saucepan of boiling salted water for about 8 minutes, until barely crisp-tender. Drain.

2. Melt the butter with the olive oil in a deep skillet over medium heat. Add the shallots and garlic and sauté for 2 minutes, or until just softened. Add the mushrooms and salsify, season with salt and pepper to taste, and sauté for 5 minutes, or until the mushrooms have given up their liquid and it has mostly cooked away. Add the cream, sour cream, port or Madeira, and the dried marjoram, if using, whisking until smooth (reserve the fresh, if using). Bring to a simmer and simmer for about 10 minutes, until most of the liquid has cooked away.

3. Stir in the fresh marjoram, if using, season with salt and pepper to taste, and serve.

Mushrooms and the root vegetable salsify combine in an easy vegetable stew perfect for a fall or winter evening. The ragout can hold its own against other big flavors; serve it with roast beef or pork or another hearty main course.

Salsify, also known as oyster plant, is a root vegetable resembling a long, slender parsnip. The most common variety has pale gray skin, but there is also a type with dark brown skin, which is sometimes called scamorza. If salsify is unavailable, you can substitute ½ pound parsnips, peeled, halved lengthwise, and cut into 1-inch pieces.

You could also make this recipe using ¾ pound celery root, peeled and cut into 1-inch chunks, instead of the salsify, or ½ pound cauliflower, cut into 1-inch florets; celery root will take somewhat longer to cook, and cauliflower may take slightly less time.

SALSIFY "TAGLIATELLE" WITH SMOKED SALMON
SERVES 4

For this whimsical dish, thin strips of salsify act as a vegetable "pasta" and are tossed with a rich, creamy sauce and smoked salmon. This goes very well with simple grilled fish, and on its own it serves as a light lunch or an appetizer.

6 salsify (about 3/4 pound) (see Notes, page 171)
2 tablespoons olive oil
2 shallots, finely chopped
4 garlic cloves, finely chopped
2 cups heavy cream
1 cup Chicken Stock (page 263)
2 large egg yolks, lightly beaten
2 tablespoons freshly grated Parmigiano-Reggiano
4 ounces thinly sliced smoked salmon, cut into thin strips about 1 1/2
   inches long
   Kosher salt and freshly ground black pepper
6 fresh basil leaves, finely shredded

1.   Bring a large pot of salted water to a boil. Meanwhile, peel the salsify with a vegetable peeler and rinse it, then use the peeler to cut the salsify lengthwise into thin ribbons. Lay the ribbons on a cutting board and cut each one lengthwise into strips about $1/3$ inch wide. Add the salsify to the boiling water and cook for 3 minutes, or until just tender; drain.

2.   Heat the olive oil in a large skillet over medium-high heat. Add the shallots and garlic and sauté for about 2 minutes, until softened. Add the cream and stock and bring to a simmer, then reduce the heat slightly and simmer for about 10 minutes, until reduced by almost half. Add the salsify and cook, tossing gently to coat it with the sauce, for about 1 minute.

3.   Remove the pan from the heat and stir in the egg yolks, then the Parmesan. Add the smoked salmon, tossing gently, and season to taste with salt and pepper. Add the basil, toss to mix, and serve immediately.

MUSTARD GREENS WITH BACON
SERVES 4 TO 6

6 slices bacon

3 tablespoons olive oil

1 tablespoon unsalted butter

4 garlic cloves, halved

½ cup heavy cream

¼ cup ketjap manis (see Pantry, page 281)

1 tablespoon grainy mustard

4 cups very thinly sliced mustard greens (about 6 ounces)

4 cups very thinly sliced bok choy (about 1½ pounds)

Mustard greens can sometimes be sandy; be sure to rinse them well under cold running water.

For a more sophisticated presentation, for individual servings, pack the greens into a ⅓-cup measure, then unmold onto the plate next to the main course you are serving.

For a somewhat richer dish, substitute ½ cup diced or finely chopped duck confit (see Sources, page 289) for the bacon.

1. Cook the bacon in a large skillet until crisp. Drain on paper towels, then crumble into small pieces. Set aside.

2. Combine the olive oil and butter in a small saucepan, add the garlic, and bring just to a simmer over low heat. Reduce the heat and simmer gently for 10 minutes, or until the garlic is pale golden brown; be careful not to let it burn. Lift the garlic out of the oil with a slotted spoon and set aside. Set the oil aside.

3. In another small saucepan, bring the cream and katjap manis to a boil. Remove from the heat and stir in the mustard and bacon.

4. Heat 2 tablespoons of the reserved garlic oil in a large skillet over high heat. Add the mustard greens and bok choy and cook, stirring frequently, until the greens start to wilt. Stir in the cream mixture and cook for about 20 minutes, until the greens are tender and the sauce has thickened.

5. Stir the reserved garlic into the greens and serve.

I love Asian flavors, and ketjap manis, a sweet-salty Indonesian sauce, mixes with a little heavy cream to transform an ordinary pot of braised greens. Also, to the traditional combination of mustard greens and bacon I've added bok choy, another typical Asian ingredient. ✷ This is a great fall or winter dish.

WATER CHESTNUTS AND CUCUMBERS

1 English (hothouse) cucumber

2 tablespoons grapeseed oil or canola oil

1 cup julienned fresh or canned water chestnuts

1 teaspoon garam masala (see Pantry, page 281)

1 tablespoon ketjap manis (see Pantry, page 281)

When shopping for fresh water chestnuts, choose carefully. Look for firm, shiny ones with no shriveling or soft spots. Larger ones will be easier to peel. Scrub them gently to remove all traces of mud, then peel them with a sharp paring knife; be sure to cut away any brown spots. Store unpeeled water chestnuts in a plastic bag in the refrigerator; once peeled, they can be kept for at least a day if covered with cold water.

If using canned water chestnuts, rinse them thoroughly under cold running water.

1. Peel the cucumber, cut it lengthwise in half, and scoop out the seeds. Cut it into 3-inch pieces and cut the pieces lengthwise in half. Set aside.

2. Heat 1 tablespoon of the oil in a wok or a large skillet over high heat. Add the water chestnuts and sauté for about 3 minutes if using fresh chestnuts, $1\frac{1}{2}$ minutes if using canned. Transfer to a medium bowl and set aside in a warm spot.

3. Add the remaining 1 tablespoon oil to the pan and heat until hot. Add the cucumbers and sauté for about $1\frac{1}{2}$ minutes, until hot. Add them to the water chestnuts, then add the garam masala and ketjap manis, toss well, and serve.

Although you can now often find fresh water chestnuts at Asian markets, they are one of the few vegetables that are good canned. I had never cooked with them in Sweden, but now I love them; they have a crisp texture, but the flavor reminds me somewhat of potatoes. You could also make this with jicama instead of the water chestnuts, as it has a similar slightly sweet taste and crisp texture. ✦ Most people don't think of cooking cucumbers, but the French often sauté them in butter for a delicious side dish. Here they are cooked briefly, then added to the water chestnuts, and the vegetables are tossed with spicy Asian seasonings. This is a good choice when you want to add a crunchy element to your plate; I like to serve it as a topping for Miso-Cured Monkfish in Carrot-Ginger Broth (page 120) or Steamed Sea Bass with Mushroom Consommé (page 124).

CARAMELIZED SUNCHOKES
SERVES 4

About 2 cups coarse salt
1 pound sunchokes (Jerusalem artichokes)
2 heads garlic
2 tablespoons unsalted butter
3 tablespoons water
2 tablespoons rice vinegar
2 tablespoons honey
1 tablespoon sugar
4 large sorrel leaves, finely slivered
Kosher salt and freshly ground black pepper

Sorrel is an herb with a distinctive citrusy taste. Wild sorrel is in season from early summer to the fall; cultivated sorrel is at its best in the spring and summer. Look for sorrel in specialty produce markets; if it is unavailable, you could substitute tender arugula leaves, although the flavor will be different.

Serve with any lamb or game dish.

1.   Preheat the oven to 400°F.

2.   Make a bed of coarse salt on a baking sheet and place the sunchokes and garlic on it. Roast for 20 minutes, or until the garlic is just tender. Remove the garlic and set aside to cool. Roast the sunchokes for another 10 minutes, or until tender. Remove from the oven and let cool slightly.

3.   Peel the sunchokes; the peels should slip off easily, but don't worry if you don't get every last bit. Separate the garlic cloves and peel them.

4.   Melt the butter in a large skillet over medium-high heat. Add the sunchokes and sauté for about 5 minutes, until browned on all sides. Add the water, rice vinegar, honey, and sugar, and cook, tossing the chokes in the mixture, until the pan juices thicken and the sunchokes are lightly caramelized. Stir in the sorrel and garlic, season with salt and pepper to taste, and serve.

Sunchokes, also known as Jerusalem artichokes, are small, lumpy, brown-skinned tubers with crisp white flesh and a sweet, nutty flavor. Native to North America, they are used a lot in Swedish cooking, and they make a good substitute for potatoes in many recipes. I roast them on a bed of salt to keep them moist and sweet, then caramelize them in a buttery glaze of rice wine and vinegar. The garlic roasted along with the sunchokes adds another layer of savory sweetness.

SWEET POTATO TÅRTA

SERVES 4 TO 6

1 tablespoon unsalted butter, at room temperature

Grated zest of 1 orange

1 cup freshly squeezed orange juice

1 cup heavy cream

2 tablespoons honey

2 2-inch cinnamon sticks

2 sprigs fresh tarragon

2 large sweet potatoes

Kosher salt and freshly ground black pepper

Serve with Spice-Rubbed Wild Boar Tenderloin (page 164) or any simple roasted meat or poultry main course.

1. Preheat the oven to 350°F. Grease a 9½-inch deep-dish pie plate or round 2-quart baking dish with the butter.

2. Combine the orange zest, orange juice, cream, honey, cinnamon, and tarragon in a medium saucepan and bring just to a boil. Reduce the heat and simmer for 30 minutes, until reduced and thickened. Remove from the heat and discard the cinnamon sticks.

3. Peel the sweet potatoes and cut them into very thin slices. Layer the potatoes in the pie plate or baking dish, pouring some of the cream mixture over each layer and seasoning each layer with salt and pepper. Pour any remaining liquid over the last layer of potatoes.

4. Bake for 1 to 1½ hours, until the sweet potatoes are tender and the liquid has been absorbed. Cut into wedges and serve.

Thinly sliced and baked in a mixture of cream and orange juice, sweet potatoes make a sweet-spicy gratin. Like a tart, this colorful dish holds together nicely, though it has no crust. ✤ The thinner you slice the potatoes, the better; use a mandoline or other vegetable slicer if you have one.

QUICK PICKLED CUCUMBERS

SERVES 4 TO 6 (MAKES ABOUT 1½ CUPS)

1 English (hothouse) cucumber
1 tablespoon kosher salt
1½ cups water
½ cup white wine vinegar
1 cup sugar
1 bay leaf
2 allspice berries

1. Slice the cucumber as thin as possible (use a mandoline or other vegetable slicer if you have one). Put the slices in a colander, toss them with the salt, and let stand for about 30 minutes.

2. Meanwhile, combine the water, vinegar, sugar, bay leaf, and allspice in a medium saucepan and bring to a boil. Remove from the heat and let cool.

3. Rinse the salt off the cucumbers, and squeeze out as much moisture as possible. Put the cucumbers in a medium bowl and add the pickling solution; they should be completely covered by the brine. Cover and refrigerate for 3 to 6 hours before serving.

The pickled cucumbers will keep in the refrigerator for up to 5 days.

After lingonberry preserves, these pickled cucumbers are the most popular condiment in Scandinavia. They are a traditional accompaniment to Swedish Meatballs (page 142), simple salmon dishes, and roasts and other meats. They are even served with frankfurters sold at street kiosks, much like the sauerkraut that often tops the hot dogs sold here.

PICKLED BEETS

SERVES 4 TO 6 (MAKES ABOUT 2 CUPS)

4 medium beets, trimmed and scrubbed
2 bay leaves
2 allspice berries
1 3-inch piece horseradish (see Pantry, page 281), peeled and cut into chunks
2 quarts water
2 cups Swedish 1-2-3 Vinegar (page 262)

1. Put the beets in a medium pot, add the bay leaves, allspice, horseradish, and water, and bring to a boil. Boil for 30 to 45 minutes, or until the beets are tender. Drain and let cool slightly.

2. While the beets are still warm, peel them and cut into quarters. Put in a quart jar or other container with a lid and pour the vinegar over them. Cover and refrigerate for at least 2 days before serving.

These will keep in the refrigerator for about 1 month.

Serve with Pickled Herring Sushi-Style (page 22) or Kippers on Crispbread (page 68), or with Swedish Meatballs (page 142), Rydberg (page 144), or Salt-Cured Brisket in Mustard Broth (page 150).

Pickled beets are another traditional Swedish condiment that appears on dinner and smorgasbord tables all over the country. They are the classic accompaniment to any sort of herring and to many beef dishes.

PICKLED ASPARAGUS AND ONION MARMALADE
SERVES 6 TO 8 (MAKES ABOUT 3 CUPS)

A rich onion marmalade accented with orange makes a terrific condiment for any number of hearty dishes. With the addition of pickled asparagus, it becomes much more complex, with sweet and piquant flavors and contrasting textures: crisp (from the asparagus) and soft (from the long-simmered onions). ✳ Serve this savory-sweet marmalade with Crispy Seared Salmon Bundles with Orange-Fennel Broth (page 108) or any poultry dish, or use it in sandwiches.

³/₄ cup water

¹/₂ cup sugar

¹/₄ cup distilled white vinegar

5 thick spears white asparagus (about ¹/₂ pound), tough ends snapped off and peeled

5 medium spears green asparagus (about ¹/₃ pound), tough ends snapped off and peeled

FOR THE ONION MARMALADE

2 tablespoons unsalted butter

3 large red onions, thinly sliced

5 shallots, thinly sliced

2 garlic cloves, sliced

2 cups ruby port or Madeira

1 cup Chicken Stock (page 263)

2 tablespoons honey

2 star anise

1 bay leaf

Grated zest of 2 oranges

Although the thickness of the spears has little to do with the quality of green asparagus, with white asparagus, the thicker stalks are usually sweeter and better. Because they are thicker, they need to be marinated for a longer time than the green in this recipe. Also, green asparagus starts to lose color while standing in the pickling liquid.

This keeps well in the refrigerator, tightly covered, for at least 5 days.

1. PREPARE THE ASPARAGUS: Combine the water, sugar, and vinegar in a small saucepan and bring to a boil, stirring to dissolve the sugar. Remove from the heat and let cool completely.

2. Meanwhile, bring a large saucepan of salted water to a boil. Add the white asparagus and cook for 5 to 7 minutes, or until just tender. Lift out of the water and cool in an ice-water bath. Add the green asparagus to the boiling water and cook for 3 to 5 minutes, or until just tender. Drain, and add to the ice bath to cool. Drain the asparagus. Cut the white asparagus into 1-inch pieces, and put in a medium bowl. Cut the green asparagus into 1-inch pieces, put into a small bowl, cover, and refrigerate.

3. Pour the cooled pickling solution over the white asparagus. Cover and refrigerate for 6 to 8 hours, or overnight.

4. PREPARE THE ONION MARMALADE: Melt the butter in a large skillet over medium heat. Add the onions, reduce the heat to medium-low, and cook, stirring, for 10 to 15 minutes, until the onions start to turn golden brown.

5. Add the shallots and garlic to the onions and cook, stirring, for 3 minutes, or until they have just softened. Add the port or Madeira, stock, honey, star anise, bay leaf, and orange zest, and bring to a simmer, then reduce the heat and simmer gently, stirring occasionally, for about 1 hour, until the onions are very soft and the liquid has cooked away. Remove from the heat and let cool. (The marmalade can be made up to 1 day ahead, covered, and refrigerated.)

6. About 1 hour before serving, add the green asparagus to the white asparagus, stirring to mix well.

7. To serve, drain the asparagus and fold into the onion marmalade.

SPICY SAUERKRAUT

SERVES 4 TO 6 (MAKES 2½ TO 3 CUPS)

1   tablespoon olive oil

1   medium onion, halved and thinly sliced

1   Granny Smith apple, peeled, cored, and diced

1   3-inch piece ginger, peeled and finely diced

2   cups sauerkraut, rinsed, squeezed dry, and coarsely chopped

½   cup kimchi, homemade (page 185) or store-bought, finely chopped

Look for plastic bags of sauerkraut in the refrigerated section of the supermarket, or buy freshly made sauerkraut from a delicatessen. Avoid canned sauerkraut, which has a metallic taste.

If you don't have time to make kimchi for this recipe, you can find jarred kimchi in Asian markets, usually in the refrigerated section.

The sauerkraut will keep for several weeks in the refrigerator.

1.   Heat the olive oil in a medium skillet over medium heat. Add the onion and sauté for about 3 minutes, until wilted. Add the apple and ginger and sauté for 3 minutes longer, or until the apple is softened. Transfer to a medium bowl.

2.   Add the sauerkraut to the onions and apples and mix well, then fold in the kimchi. Serve at room temperature or chilled.

Although sauerkraut is usually associated with Germany, it plays a major role in Scandinavian cooking. Koreans make a hot, spicy version of sauerkraut, and I bring these influences together in a variation on the classic Scandinavian condiment.

QUICK KIMCHI

SERVES 6 TO 8 (MAKES 4 TO 5 CUPS)

6 anchovy fillets

2 whole pickled herring fillets, coarsely chopped, or one 6-ounce jar pickled herring (home-style or in wine sauce, not in sour cream), drained and coarsely chopped

12 garlic cloves, peeled

2 jalapeño peppers, cut lengthwise in half and seeded

3 fresh bird's-eye chiles or 1–2 serrano chiles, seeded and finely chopped

2 tablespoons peanut oil

2 daikon radishes (about 1½ pounds)

Whole pickled herring fillets can be found in some specialty markets and delis. If you can't find them, jars of pickled herring pieces are available in most supermarkets; look for them in the refrigerated section.

The kimchi will keep in the refrigerator for at least 1 week.

1. Combine the anchovies, herring, garlic, jalapeños, chiles, and oil in a food processor or blender and process to a puree.

2. Peel the daikon. Cut them in half, then cut each half lengthwise in half. Put in a small baking dish and pour the anchovy mixture over the daikon, turning to coat thoroughly. Cover and refrigerate for 8 to 12 hours, or overnight.

3. Remove the daikon from the marinade and cut it into ¼-inch-thick julienne strips. Serve, or cover and refrigerate until ready to serve.

There are dozens of versions of the hot, spicy, pungent Korean condiment called kimchi, made with everything from cabbage to turnips to radishes to cucumbers, which are first pickled and then allowed to ferment for several days or more. My quicker version uses the Asian daikon radish, but it can also be made with napa cabbage, bok choy, or even asparagus. Traditional kimchi always includes fish sauce, or dried salted shrimp, or another preserved fishy ingredient; I use a Scandinavian equivalent: pickled herring. The strong pickled and fermented flavors of this condiment reflect the way that today's Swedish cooks are using accompaniments.

POTATO PANCAKES

SERVES 4

1½ pounds Idaho or other baking potatoes

1 Spanish onion, finely chopped

1 large egg, lightly beaten

Kosher salt and freshly ground black pepper

6–8 tablespoons clarified butter (see Pantry, page 279)

1. Preheat the oven to 300°F.

2. Peel the potatoes and finely grate them on a box grater or the grating disk of a food processor. Wrap in a kitchen towel and twist it tightly to squeeze out as much liquid as possible. Put the potatoes in a large bowl and add the onion and egg, mixing well. Season with salt and pepper. Divide the potato mixture into 4 parts.

3. Heat 1½ to 2 tablespoons of the clarified butter in an 8-inch skillet over medium heat (if you have two 8-inch skillets, cook 2 pancakes at a time). Add one quarter of the potato mixture, pressing it into a flat cake with a spatula, and cook for 10 minutes, or until golden brown on the bottom. Turn the cake and cook for about 10 minutes longer, or until browned on the bottom side and cooked through. Transfer to paper towels to drain briefly, then transfer to a baking sheet and keep warm in the oven while you cook the remaining pancakes. Serve hot.

Called *raggmunkar*, these traditional Swedish potato pancakes are similar to latkes or Swiss rösti. They are usually served with crisp thick-sliced bacon and lingonberries or with bleak roe (from a European freshwater fish somewhat similar to chub — you could substitute salmon roe) and sour cream. For an elegant appetizer, serve these pancakes with Gravlax (page 18) or smoked salmon and crème fraîche.

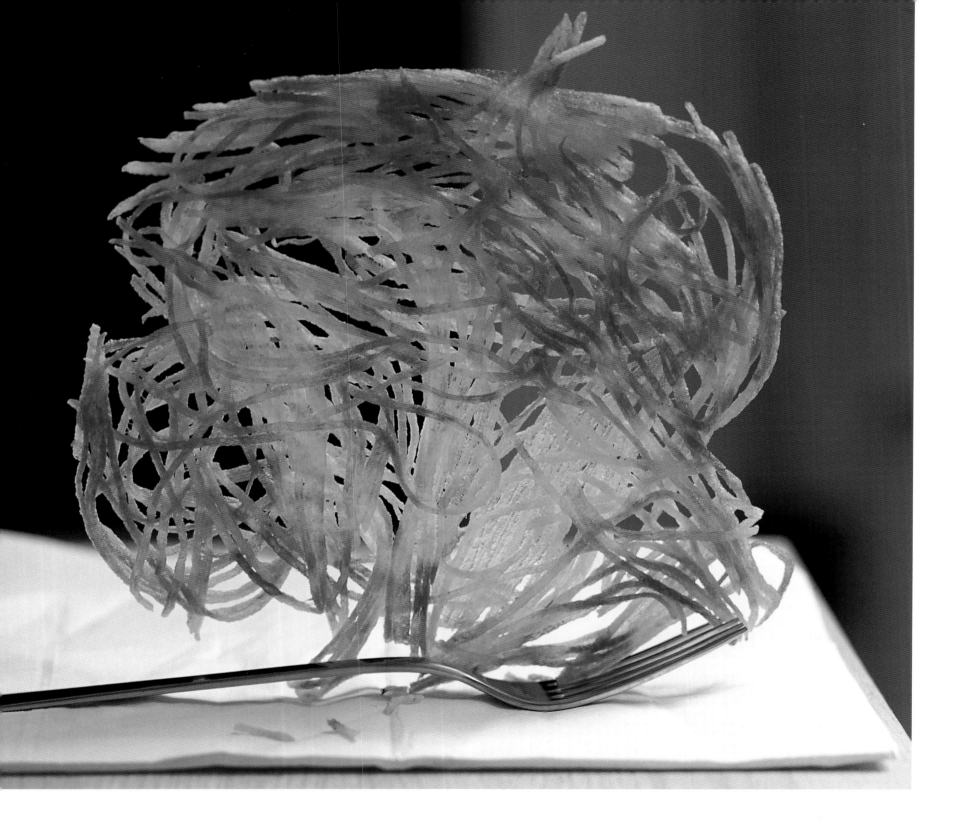

GARLIC MASHED POTATOES

SERVES 4 TO 6

1½   pounds fingerling or Yukon Gold potatoes, peeled

2   cups milk

1   cup heavy cream

8   elephant garlic cloves

2   fresh thyme sprigs

    Freshly grated nutmeg

1   tablespoon olive oil

1   tablespoon unsalted butter

1   tablespoon freshly grated Parmigiano-Reggiano

    Kosher salt and freshly ground black pepper

1.   Combine the potatoes, milk, cream, garlic, and thyme in a large saucepan and bring to a boil. Reduce the heat slightly and simmer until the potatoes are tender, 20 to 25 minutes. Drain, reserving the cooking liquid.

2.   Transfer the potatoes and garlic to a medium bowl and mash with a fork, adding the nutmeg, olive oil, butter, and Parmesan. Add about half the reserved cooking liquid, mixing well, then add additional cooking liquid as necessary until the potatoes are the consistency you like. Season with salt and pepper to taste and serve hot.

Rich and creamy garlic mashed potatoes are everybody's favorite, especially this version, which cooks the potatoes in milk and cream. I prefer to use elephant garlic here, which has a sweeter, milder flavor than ordinary garlic. The potatoes are mashed with a fork so they have an appealing rustic texture, but you can use a potato masher or pass them through a ricer or food mill for a smoother consistency.

CORN MASHED POTATOES

1 pound fingerling or Yukon Gold potatoes, peeled

2 cups milk

1 cup heavy cream

2 large egg yolks

1 tablespoon mascarpone cheese

2 tablespoons olive oil

½ teaspoon fresh thyme leaves

2 tablespoons unsalted butter, at room temperature

1 cup corn kernels, blanched in boiling salted water just until tender, about 3 minutes

Kosher salt and freshly ground black pepper

These are especially good with Glazed Salmon with Wasabi Sabayon

(page 110).

1. Combine the potatoes, milk, and cream in a large saucepan and bring just to a boil. Reduce the heat slightly and simmer for 20 to 25 minutes, or until the potatoes are tender. Drain the potatoes, reserving the cooking liquid.

2. Pass the potatoes through a food mill or potato ricer into a large bowl.

3. In a small bowl, beat the egg yolks lightly. Add the mascarpone cheese and mix well, then stir in the olive oil and thyme. Add to the potatoes, along with the butter and about half the reserved cooking liquid, and mix well, then add additional cooking liquid as necessary until the potatoes are the consistency you like. Fold in the corn kernels, season with salt and pepper to taste, and serve.

This is a great recipe for summer, whether made with fresh corn or kernels from leftover cooked ears of corn. The kernels add sweetness and a bit of crunch to the silky-smooth potato puree.

CHORIZO MASHED POTATOES
SERVES 4 TO 6

2½–3 pounds Idaho or other baking potatoes, peeled and quartered
1 Granny Smith apple, peeled, cored, and cut into small chunks
3 cups milk
1 cup heavy cream
3 garlic cloves, peeled
2 2-inch cinnamon sticks
1 tablespoon olive oil
6 ounces chorizo sausage, finely chopped
2 tablespoons unsalted butter
Kosher salt and freshly ground black pepper

Chorizo is a spicy Spanish smoked sausage. It is available in Latin markets and some specialty and gourmet markets.

Serve with Pan-Roasted Venison Chops with Fruit and Berry Chutney (page 162).

1. Combine the potatoes, apple, milk, cream, garlic, and cinnamon sticks in a large saucepan and bring just to a boil. Reduce the heat slightly and simmer for 20 to 25 minutes, or until the potatoes are tender.

2. Meanwhile, heat the olive oil in a medium skillet over medium heat. Add the chorizo and sauté for 3 to 4 minutes, until the chorizo is browned and most of the fat is rendered. Drain on paper towels.

3. When the potatoes are cooked, drain them, reserving the cooking liquid. Discard the cinnamon sticks and put the potatoes in a large bowl, along with the butter. Mash with a fork or potato masher, adding about half the reserved cooking liquid; then add additional cooking liquid as necessary until the potatoes are the consistency you like. Fold in the chorizo, season with salt and pepper to taste, and serve.

Spicy chorizo lifts ordinary mashed potatoes to another dimension. The combination is so good you might be tempted, as I often am, to serve this dish as a main course.

PEAR AND FINGERLING POTATO RAGOUT

SERVES 4 TO 6

1 cup ruby port or Madeira

1 cup dry red wine

2 tablespoons honey

2 sprigs fresh tarragon

3 ripe but firm Bosc pears, peeled, halved, and cored

1 cup heavy cream

1 cup Chicken Stock (page 263)

1 tablespoon unsalted butter

½ pound fingerling or Yukon Gold potatoes

2 endives, trimmed, cored, and cut crosswise into ¼-inch-wide strips

Slightly underripe pears are better for poaching than overripe ones, which may become too soft as they cook.

This ragout is particularly good with Coffee-Roasted Duck Breasts (page 139).

1. Combine the port or Madeira, red wine, honey, and tarragon in a medium saucepan, add the pears, and bring to a simmer over medium heat. Cook for 10 minutes, or until the pears are slightly softened. Remove from the heat and let the pears cool in the cooking liquid.

2. With a slotted spoon, remove the pears from the cooking liquid; set aside on a plate. Combine the cream, stock, butter, and 1½ cups of the pear cooking liquid in a saucepan, bring to a simmer, and simmer for 45 minutes to 1 hour, until the liquid has reduced by half.

3. Meanwhile, put the potatoes in a small saucepan, add salted water to cover, and bring to a boil. Reduce the heat slightly and cook the potatoes for 18 to 20 minutes, until just tender. Drain and let cool slightly, then peel and cut into ¼-inch-thick rounds.

4. While the potatoes are cooking, cut the pears crosswise into ¼-inch-thick slices. Set aside.

5. When the sauce has reduced, remove the tarragon, add the pears and potatoes, and heat through. Fold in the endives and serve.

For this unusual dish, sweet poached pears and tender potatoes are tossed in a rich sauce made with cream, chicken stock, and some of the port–red wine poaching liquid from the pears. The slight bitterness and crisp texture of sliced raw endives added at the last minute provide a good counterpoint to the creaminess of the ragout.

CURRY POTATOES
SERVES 6 TO 8

2½ pounds Yukon Gold potatoes

4 Granny Smith apples

Juice of ½ lemon

2 tablespoons mustard oil (see Pantry, page 282), grapeseed oil, or canola oil

1 tablespoon mustard seeds

1 tablespoon Curry Paste (page 271) or store-bought Thai yellow curry paste

½ cup white wine vinegar

1. Preheat the oven to 425°F.

2. Prick each potato with a fork and place on a baking sheet. Bake for 25 to 30 minutes, until they are almost cooked through. Remove from the oven and let sit until cool enough to handle, then peel and cut into 1-inch cubes.

3. Meanwhile, peel and core the apples. Cut into 1-inch cubes and place in a small bowl. Sprinkle the lemon juice over the apples to keep them from turning brown.

4. Combine the oil, mustard seeds, and curry paste in a large skillet and heat over medium heat, stirring, for 1 to 2 minutes, or until the mustard seeds start to pop. Add the vinegar, apples, and potatoes, reduce the heat to medium-low, and cook, stirring frequently, until the apples are very soft, about 15 minutes. Serve hot.

These spicy potatoes make a tasty side dish to Prune-Stuffed Pork Roast (page 158) and other hearty main courses. Served with a big green salad, they can stand alone as a vegetarian meal.

ORZO WITH MUSHROOMS
SERVES 4

FOR THE MUSHROOMS

- 1 tablespoon olive oil
- 1 tablespoon unsalted butter
- 1 shallot, finely chopped
- 1 garlic clove, finely chopped
- 2 cups sliced porcini mushrooms, shiitake or portobello caps, or cremini or other mushrooms, or a combination
- 1 teaspoon kosher salt
- Freshly ground black pepper

FOR THE ORZO

- 1 teaspoon kosher salt
- 1 cup orzo
- ½ cup Chicken Stock (page 263)
- 2 large egg yolks
- ½ teaspoon truffle oil (see Sources, page 290; optional)
- 1 tablespoon mascarpone cheese

For a slightly different flavor, you could substitute fresh goat cheese or crème fraîche for the mascarpone.

1. PREPARE THE MUSHROOMS: Melt the butter with the olive oil in a large skillet over medium heat. Add the shallot and garlic and sauté for 2 minutes, or until softened. Add the mushrooms, season with the salt and pepper to taste, and sauté for 8 to 10 minutes, until the juices the mushrooms release have cooked away. Remove from the heat and set aside, covered to keep warm.

2. PREPARE THE ORZO: Bring 4 cups of water to a boil in a medium saucepan. Add the salt and orzo and cook for 8 to 10 minutes, or until the orzo is al dente. Drain and transfer to a medium bowl.

3. Heat the stock to just under a boil in a small saucepan. Pour the stock into the orzo. Beat the egg yolks together with the truffle oil (if using) and mascarpone and stir into the orzo. Fold in the sautéed mushrooms and serve.

Fresh porcini mushrooms (also called cèpes) are one of the real delicacies of the Scandinavian mushroom season, and they are wonderful in this rich, creamy dish. Unfortunately, they are an expensive indulgence not often seen in markets here, but you can substitute shiitake or portobello mushroom caps or use a combination of mushrooms. Orzo, a small rice-shaped pasta now found in any supermarket, takes only minutes to cook and is very versatile.

At Aquavit, we serve this with Herb-Roasted Rack of Lamb (page 156), as a combination side dish and second sauce for the meat.

ASPARAGUS-POTATO "RISOTTO"

SERVES 4 TO 6

¾ pound medium green asparagus spears (about 12)

¾ pound thick white asparagus spears (about 8)

1 tablespoon unsalted butter

1 tablespoon olive oil

2 shallots, finely chopped

2 garlic cloves, finely chopped

2 Idaho or other baking potatoes (about 1½ pounds), peeled and cut into ¼-inch dice

½ cup dry white wine

3 cups Chicken Stock (page 263)

Kosher salt and freshly ground black pepper

1 cup heavy cream

2 tablespoons mascarpone cheese

6 large arugula or basil leaves, thinly slivered

If you can't find white asparagus, simply double the amount of green asparagus.

You can substitute fresh goat cheese or cream cheese for the mascarpone.

1. Snap off the tough ends of the asparagus. Peel the stalks and cut the asparagus into ¼-inch pieces. (You should have about 3 cups.)

2. Melt the butter with the olive oil in a large skillet over medium-high heat. Add the shallots, garlic, and potatoes, and sauté for about 5 minutes, or until the shallots start to color. Add the asparagus and white wine and simmer until the wine cooks away. Add enough stock to just cover the vegetables and cook until most of the liquid has been absorbed. Continue cooking, adding more stock as it is absorbed, until the potatoes are tender. Season to taste with salt and pepper and remove from the heat.

3. In a medium bowl, whip the cream until it holds soft peaks. Fold in the mascarpone. Fold the cream mixture into the potatoes, then fold in the arugula and serve.

In this "risotto," finely diced potatoes take the place of the rice; the diced green and white asparagus make for a fancy dish (you can use all green asparagus if white is not in season). Cutting the potatoes and asparagus into small cubes produces different textures than cutting the same vegetables into large pieces; it even brings out their flavors in a different way.

LIME RISOTTO

SERVES 4 TO 6

4 cups Chicken Stock (page 263)
4 medium limes
½ cup heavy cream
1 tablespoon unsalted butter
1 tablespoon olive oil
1 shallot, finely chopped
1 cup Arborio or Carnaroli rice
½ cup dry white wine
2 large egg yolks
1 tablespoon mascarpone cheese
Juice of 2–4 limes (to taste)
Kosher salt and freshly ground black pepper

We use this tart, creamy risotto as a base for Marinated Tuna with Parmesan Broth (page 30). You could also serve it with any simple fish or seafood main course.

1. Put the stock in a medium saucepan. Grate the zest from the limes and add to the stock; set aside the limes. Bring the stock to a simmer over medium-high heat. Reduce the heat to very low to keep the stock at the barest simmer.

2. Meanwhile, slice off both ends of the limes right down to the flesh. Stand each one on a cutting board and, using a serrated or other sharp knife, cut away the peel and white pith from top to bottom in strips, following the curve of the lime. Use a sharp paring knife to cut between the membranes to release the segments. Set the lime segments aside.

3. In a small bowl, whip the cream until it holds soft peaks. Cover and refrigerate.

4. Melt the butter with the olive oil in a large heavy saucepan over medium-high heat. Add the shallot and sauté for about 2 minutes, until softened. Add the rice and cook, stirring, until all the grains are coated. Add the white wine, stir, and cook until it has evaporated.

5. Add about ½ cup of the stock, reduce the heat, and cook, stirring, until almost all of it has been absorbed. The stock should bubble gently as you stir; adjust the heat as necessary. Continue cooking, stirring and adding the stock ½ cup at a time once each previous addition has been absorbed, until the rice is al dente and the risotto is creamy, 18 to 20 minutes from the time you first added stock (if you run out of stock, add hot water as necessary). Remove from the heat.

6. Whisk the egg yolks and mascarpone cheese together in a small bowl. Stir the lime juice into the risotto, then fold in the lime segments. Fold in the mascarpone mixture and then the whipped cream, season with salt and pepper to taste, and serve immediately.

MANGO RISOTTO

SERVES 4

The sweetness of a perfectly ripe mango is delicious in this creamy risotto, which I like to serve with Salt-Cured Duck Breasts (page 32) as a counterpoint to the saltiness of the duck. It's also good with Coffee-Roasted Duck Breasts (page 139), Marjoram-Stuffed Venison Rolls (page 161), and other duck or game dishes.

1   mango, peeled, pitted, and cut into ½-inch dice
1   cup Swedish 1-2-3 Vinegar (page 262)
4   cups Chicken Stock (page 263)
1   tablespoon olive oil
1   shallot, finely chopped
1   garlic clove, finely chopped
1   cup Arborio or Carnaroli rice
½   cup dry white wine
1   scallion, trimmed and thinly sliced
2   tablespoons freshly grated Parmigiano-Reggiano
    Kosher salt and freshly ground black pepper

The easiest way to cut up a mango is to stand it up on a cutting board and slice off the flesh from one side of the large flat pit in one large piece. Then turn the mango around and slice off the flesh from the other side. Lay each piece skin side down and score the flesh lengthwise into strips, being careful not to cut through the skin, then score it crosswise. Turn the mango "inside out," and slice off the cubes of flesh. Slice off the two narrow strips of flesh remaining on the pit, and score them as directed (or just nibble on them for a cook's treat).

1. Put the mango in a small bowl and cover with the vinegar. Cover and refrigerate for 6 to 8 hours, or overnight.

2. Put the stock in a medium saucepan and bring to a simmer over medium-high heat. Reduce the heat to very low to keep the stock at the barest simmer.

3. Heat the oil in a large heavy saucepan over medium-high heat. Add the shallot and garlic and sauté for about 2 minutes, until softened. Add the rice and cook, stirring, until all the grains are coated with oil. Add the white wine, stir, and cook until it has evaporated.

4. Add about ½ cup of the stock, reduce the heat, and cook, stirring, until almost all of it has been absorbed. The stock should bubble gently as you stir; adjust the heat as necessary. Continue cooking, stirring and adding the stock ½ cup at a time once each previous addition has been absorbed, until the rice is al dente and the risotto is creamy, 18 to 20 minutes from the time you first added stock (if you run out of stock, add hot water as necessary). Remove from the heat.

5. Drain the mango and stir it into the risotto, along with the scallion and Parmesan. Season with salt and pepper to taste and serve immediately.

DUCK CONFIT RISOTTO
SERVES 4 TO 6

4 cups Chicken Stock (page 263)
1 tablespoon olive oil
1 shallot, finely chopped
1 cup Arborio or Carnaroli rice
1/2 cup dry white wine
2 large egg yolks
1 tablespoon mascarpone cheese
3/4 cup finely chopped duck confit (see Sources, page 289)
Kosher salt and freshly ground black pepper

I use this as a base for Hot-Smoked Char with Spicy Lemon Broth (page 28), but it's satisfying enough to serve as a main course, perhaps with a salad of crisp greens on the side. It also makes a good appetizer on a cold winter night. The meat from braised oxtails is a delicious alternative to the duck confit, or substitute another meaty ingredient, such as sautéed diced chorizo or even Chinese duck sausages.

1. Put the stock in a medium saucepan and bring to a simmer over medium-high heat. Reduce the heat to very low to keep the stock at the barest simmer.

2. Heat the olive oil in a large heavy saucepan over medium-high heat. Add the shallot and sauté for about 2 minutes, until softened. Add the rice and cook, stirring, until all the grains are coated with oil. Add the white wine, stir, and cook until it has evaporated.

3. Add about 1/2 cup of the stock, reduce the heat, and cook, stirring, until almost all of it has been absorbed. The stock should bubble gently as you stir; adjust the heat as necessary. Continue cooking, stirring and adding the stock 1/2 cup at a time once each previous addition has been absorbed, until the rice is al dente and the risotto is creamy, 18 to 20 minutes from the time you first added stock (if you run out of stock, add hot water as necessary). Remove from the heat.

4. Whisk the egg yolks and mascarpone cheese together in a small bowl, then fold into the risotto. Fold in the duck confit. Season with salt and pepper to taste and serve immediately.

MUSHROOM DUMPLINGS

SERVES 4 ~~or 2~~ *pigs for a meal or 1 hopeless glutton*
easy to double

2 tablespoons olive oil

1 shallot, finely chopped

2 garlic cloves, minced

3 medium portobello mushroom caps, finely chopped

1/2 teaspoon fresh thyme leaves

1/2 teaspoon kosher salt

Freshly ground black pepper

16 wonton wrappers

1 large egg white, whisked with 1 teaspoon water for egg wash

1–2 tablespoons unsalted butter, at room temperature

Wonton wrappers, or wonton skins, are available in the freezer or refrigerated section of Asian markets and some supermarkets or specialty markets (see Sources, page 289). Most packages contain 80 or more wrappers, but they freeze well; wrap the leftovers well and freeze for another use.

To steam the dumplings, place them on a steamer rack over boiling water, without touching one another (or they will stick together), and steam for 5 to 10 minutes, until the wrappers are al dente.

To serve the dumplings in the consommé, cook the dumplings as directed; drain (omit the butter). Meanwhile, reheat the consommé over medium-low heat. Ladle the hot broth into four bowls, add 4 dumplings to each bowl, and serve.

after cook:
drain on cookie sheet lined + paper towels
can cook 2 hr. ahead/eat
reheat in light panfry
to freeze: spread on plastic lined tray cover loose.
+ freeze 1 hr. + transfer to ziplock – freeze up >3 mo.

1. Heat 1 tablespoon of the olive oil in a large skillet over high heat. Add the shallot, garlic, mushrooms, thyme, and salt, and cook, stirring occasionally, for about 10 minutes, until the juices released by the mushrooms have cooked away. Season with pepper and transfer to a bowl. Let cool.

2. [*3*] Lay out 8 of the wonton wrappers on a work surface, keeping the rest covered. Put about 1 teaspoon of the mushroom filling in the center of each wrapper. Using your index finger or a pastry brush, lightly brush the edges of each wrapper with the egg wash, then fold the wrapper over to form a triangle and press the edges together to seal. Repeat with the remaining wrappers and filling.

3. [*2.*] Bring a large pot of salted water to a boil. Stir in the remaining 1 tablespoon olive oil, then add the dumplings and cook for about 3 minutes, or until the dumplings float to the surface. Using a slotted spoon or a wire skimmer, transfer the *drain + then* ^ dumplings to a bowl. Toss with the butter and serve. [*4.*]

These dumplings are highly versatile. Serve them as a side dish for any salmon, bass, or chicken dish, or in Mushroom Consommé (page 92), or as an appetizer on their own. In place of the portobellos, you can substitute whatever flavorful mushrooms are available, such as shiitake or cremini.

can dip in Tamari / serve + chopsticks
or make Sauce
soy — 1/2 c
H₂O — 1/4 c
sugar — 2 t
rice vin. – 3 T
(scall. – 2 T thin sliced.)
add last or ready to sv.

x x sesame oil
alternative filling
gnd. meat
scallions
water chestnuts
cabbage
chives
ginger

CRACKERS

AND

BREADS

CRISPY FLATBREAD

3 cups cake flour, or more as needed

3/4 cup whole wheat flour

1 1/2 teaspoons baking powder

2 teaspoons salt

1 cup water

1 teaspoon olive oil

4 teaspoons fennel seeds

You can also make the dough using a stand mixer.

Stored airtight at room temperature, the flatbread will keep for at least 2 weeks.

1. Preheat the oven to 350°F.

2. Whisk together the cake flour, whole wheat flour, baking powder, and salt in a large bowl. Add the water and oil, stirring with a wooden spoon until a dough forms. Turn the dough out onto a floured surface and knead for about 10 minutes, adding a little extra cake flour if necessary, until the dough is smooth and no longer sticky. Knead in the fennel seeds.

3. Cut the dough into 4 equal pieces. Set 2 pieces aside, covered with plastic wrap. On a lightly floured surface, roll out each of the remaining 2 pieces of dough into two large rectangles, rolling as thin as possible and adding flour to the work surface as necessary. Transfer to two large baking sheets.

4. Bake the breads for 8 to 12 minutes, until light golden and crisp. Transfer to wire racks to cool, and repeat with the remaining dough.

5. Break the flatbread into pieces and store it in airtight containers.

Crisp flatbreads have a long history in Sweden, going back to the Vikings and even earlier. It's easy to roll this dough into big sheets with a rolling pin, as in the recipe, but you could also use a pasta machine, as we do at Aquavit. In that case, roll the dough as thin as possible, and reduce the baking time as necessary. ✤ Serve with Gravlax (page 18), smoked salmon, or Salt-Cured Duck Breasts (page 32).

RICE CRACKERS OR RICE STICKS

MAKES ABOUT 60 SMALL CRACKERS OR STICKS

¾ cup leftover plain risotto or overcooked rice

1 cup water or tomato juice

1 tablespoon olive or mustard oil

1 teaspoon kosher salt

½ teaspoon freshly ground black pepper

Scant 2½ cups unbleached all-purpose flour

Because leftover risotto does not reheat well, this is a great way to use it. If you don't happen to have leftover risotto (plain or herbed) on hand, overcooked regular rice will also work: add a few extra tablespoons of water to the pan to start, and cook the rice for 5 minutes or so longer than usual, until it is very soft. (One third cup of raw long-grain white rice will make about 1 cup cooked rice.)

Store the crackers in an airtight container at room temperature for up to 1 week.

1. Combine the risotto or rice, water or tomato juice, oil, salt, and pepper in a bowl and mix well with a wooden spoon. Start adding the flour about 1 cup at a time, mixing well, until the dough starts to come together. Turn the dough out onto a lightly floured surface and continue adding the flour, kneading until the dough is firm and no longer sticky but still pliable.

2. Shape the dough into a ball, put it in a bowl, and cover with plastic wrap. Let rest for 30 minutes in a warm place.

3. Preheat the oven to 350°F. Line two baking sheets with parchment paper.

4. Turn the dough out onto a lightly floured surface and cut it in half. One piece at a time, roll out the dough ¼ inch thick or slightly thinner. Cut the dough into small square crackers, long thin sticks (about ¼ inch wide), or any other shape as desired. Transfer to the baking sheets.

5. Bake the crackers for 14 to 16 minutes, until the edges turn light brown. Transfer the crackers or sticks to a wire rack and let cool.

With my grandmother's frugality in mind, I thought of making these crackers when I had some leftover risotto. Serve them with soups, salads, or dips. ✤ You can add a pinch or so of curry powder or another spice to the dough, as you like.

POTATO MUSTARD BREAD

MAKES ONE 9X5-INCH LOAF

1 tablespoon mustard oil (see Pantry, page 282) or olive oil, plus
   more for brushing
2 tablespoons olive oil
2 tablespoons brown mustard seeds (see Pantry, page 282)
1 tablespoon dill seeds
1 ¼-ounce package active dry yeast
½ cup warm water
   Pinch of sugar
1 cup mashed Yukon Gold potatoes (about ½ pound potatoes)
1 cup chopped fresh dill
1 teaspoon kosher salt
2 cups whole wheat flour
1 cup unbleached all-purpose flour, or more as needed
   Mustard oil, for brushing loaf

This rustic loaf is bursting with beloved Scandinavian flavors —
dill, potatoes, and mustard. The potatoes give the bread a moist, chewy texture, and it goes well with a hearty soup. Or serve it for a Scandinavian-style
breakfast with an assortment of cheeses and cold meats. It's also excellent
for sandwiches. ✷ This is a wet dough that requires some kneading before
it comes together, but persevere, and you will be delighted with the results.

1. Combine the oils and mustard seeds in a small saucepan and bring to
a simmer over low heat. Reduce the heat to the lowest possible, cover,
and simmer for 20 minutes to soften the seeds slightly. Add the dill
seeds, remove from the heat, and let cool until tepid.

2. Combine the yeast, warm water, and sugar in a small bowl. Let stand
for 10 minutes, or until bubbly.

3. Combine the potatoes, fresh dill, and salt in a large bowl and mix
well with a wooden spoon. Add the oil, mustard, and dill seed mixture,
then add the yeast mixture and mix well. Gradually add the flours, mixing well, until a moist dough forms.

4. Turn the dough out on a lightly floured surface and knead for 10 to
15 minutes, until smooth and elastic. The dough will seem very wet at
first, but then it will come together. Shape the dough into a ball and put
it in a large lightly oiled bowl, turning to coat. Cover with a kitchen
towel and let rise in a warm place for 45 minutes, or until doubled in
bulk.

5. Preheat the oven to 375°F. Grease a 9x5-inch loaf pan.

6. Punch down the dough and transfer it to a lightly floured surface.
Flatten the dough into a rectangle, fold the sides over into the middle,
and press to seal the seam. Place the dough seam side down in the prepared pan.

7. Bake for 35 minutes, or until golden brown on top and the bottom of
the loaf makes a hollow sound when rapped with your knuckles. Turn the
loaf out onto a rack, brush the top with mustard or olive oil, and let cool
before slicing.

BLUEBERRY BREAD

1   ¼-ounce package active dry yeast
    Pinch of sugar
½   cup warm water
1   cup hot water
½   cup dark molasses
1   cup crème fraîche or sour cream
3   cups unbleached all-purpose flour
2   cups whole wheat flour
1½ cups dried blueberries
½   cup chopped walnuts

The dough can also be made using a stand mixer.

In Sweden, we like our breads a little on the sweet side, and fruit breads are served in many restaurants. Here dried blueberries add their sweet-tart flavor. But depending on what is at hand, other alternatives are possible: chopped prunes or dried apricots, dried sour cherries, or raisins all work well in this recipe. With no kneading and only one rising, this moist, dense bread is very simple to make. It's delicious sliced and slathered with butter, and it makes great toast.

1.   Combine the yeast, sugar, and warm water in a small bowl and let sit for 10 minutes, or until bubbly.

2.   Meanwhile, combine the hot water and molasses in another small bowl, stirring to dissolve the molasses. Stir in the crème fraîche or sour cream.

3.   Whisk the flours together in a large bowl. Make a well in the center and pour in the molasses and crème fraîche mixture, then add the yeast mixture and mix well with a wooden spoon until a dough forms. Stir in the blueberries and walnuts until evenly distributed.

4.   Turn the dough out onto a lightly floured surface and shape it into a ball. Put the dough in a lightly oiled bowl, turn to coat, and cover with a kitchen towel. Let rise in a warm place for 45 minutes to 1 hour, or until doubled in bulk.

5.   Preheat the oven to 350°F. Grease two 9x5-inch loaf pans.

6.   Punch down the dough and transfer it to a lightly floured surface. Divide it in half. Flatten each piece of dough into a rectangle, fold the sides over, and press into the middle to seal the seam. Place the loaves seam side down in the prepared pans.

7.   Bake for 40 minutes, or until the bottom of a loaf makes a hollow sound when rapped with your knuckles. Remove the loaves from the pans and let cool on a rack before slicing.

ST. LUCIA BUNS

2 cups milk

1 ¼-ounce package active dry yeast

½ cup sugar

2 tablespoons brandy

1 teaspoon powdered saffron

4–5 cups unbleached all-purpose flour, or more as needed

½–1 teaspoon ground cardamom

½ teaspoon salt

¼ cup dark raisins

1 large egg, lightly beaten with 1 tablespoon water for egg wash

Don't brush the rolls with the egg wash before baking—it would prevent the dough from rising properly in the oven.

1. Heat the milk in a small saucepan just until warm; remove from the heat. Combine ¼ cup of the milk, the yeast, and a pinch of the sugar in a small bowl and let sit for 10 minutes, or until bubbly. Combine another 2 tablespoons of the milk, the brandy, 1 teaspoon of the sugar, and the saffron in a small bowl, stirring to dissolve the sugar. Set the remaining milk aside.

2. In a large bowl, whisk together 4 cups of the flour, the remaining sugar, the cardamom, and salt. Make a well in the center and pour in the yeast mixture, the dissolved saffron, and the remaining milk. Stir with a wooden spoon, gradually adding more flour as necessary, until a soft dough forms.

3. Turn the dough out onto a lightly floured surface and knead, adding just a little more flour if necessary, for 10 to 15 minutes, until the dough is smooth, shiny, and elastic. Knead in the raisins.

4. Shape the dough into a ball. Put it in a large, lightly oiled bowl, turning to coat, and cover with a kitchen towel. Let rise in a warm place for 30 minutes, or until doubled in bulk.

5. Line a baking sheet with parchment paper. Punch down the dough and transfer it to a lightly floured surface. Shape the dough into a log and divide it into 12 equal pieces. Shape each piece into a round roll and place the rolls about 2 inches apart on the prepared baking sheet. Cover with a kitchen towel and let rise for 30 minutes, or until almost doubled in size.

6. Preheat the oven to 375°F.

7. Bake the rolls for 30 minutes, or until the bottom of a roll sounds hollow when rapped with your knuckles. Remove from the oven and brush the tops of the rolls with the egg wash. Let cool on a rack.

In Sweden, these saffron rolls are baked only during the Christmas holidays, starting with St. Lucia's Day on December 13. According to tradition, on that day Swedish mothers are treated to a breakfast in bed that includes these buns. There's no reason to relegate them to just one month a year, however. Serve them at breakfast, brunch, or teatime, as a snack, or any time you want a slightly sweet bread. They are a fine companion to Foie Gras "Ganache" (page 62).

JAMS, SALSAS, AND CHUTNEYS

FRESH CRANBERRY RELISH

MAKES ABOUT 2 CUPS

2   cups fresh or frozen cranberries, picked over and rinsed

¾   cup sugar

Put the cranberries in a food processor and process until finely chopped.
Transfer the cranberries to a bowl and stir in the sugar. Let sit for at least
45 minutes or preferably overnight in the refrigerator, before serving.

The relish will keep for at least 1 week in the refrigerator.

Lingonberry relishes or preserves are the classic accompaniment to everything from Swedish Meatballs (page 142) to roasted chicken or duck and any game dish. Lingonberries grow wild in Scandinavia, Russia, Canada, and other northern climates, but they are rarely available fresh outside these areas. However, they are related to cranberries — they are sometimes called mountain cranberries — and this uncooked relish makes a good alternative to one made with lingonberries.

APPLE SAFFRON JAM

MAKES ABOUT 3 CUPS

1   teaspoon garam masala (see Pantry, page 281)

2   star anise

2   2-inch cinnamon sticks, broken into pieces

2   whole cloves

1   cup water

6   tablespoons freshly squeezed lime juice

1/2   cup sugar

4   fresh mint leaves

    Finely minced zest of 1 lime

    Small pinch of saffron threads

6   Granny Smith apples, peeled, cored, and cut into large chunks

Be sure to remove the lime zest from one of the limes before you juice it. Use a zester (or the rasp-type grater called a Microplane) to remove the zest and finely chop. Or use a vegetable peeler to remove the zest in long strips, then slice into thin strips and finely chop.

The jam will keep for at least 1 week in the refrigerator.

1.   Preheat the oven to 400°F.

2.   Toast the garam masala in a small dry skillet over medium heat, stirring, for about 30 seconds, or until fragrant. Set aside.

3.   With a mortar and pestle, grind the star anise, cinnamon, and cloves into a powder. Or combine in a spice grinder (or clean coffee grinder) and grind to a powder. Combine the water and lime juice in a glass measuring cup.

4.   Combine the sugar, garam masala, ground spices, mint, lime zest, 1/2 cup of the water-lime juice mixture, and the saffron in a baking pan large enough to hold the apples in one layer, and mix well. Add the apples, stirring to coat with the spice mixture.

5.   Cover the pan with foil and roast for 10 minutes. Add another 1/2 cup of the lime juice mixture, cover, and roast for another 10 minutes. Add the remaining lime juice mixture, cover, and roast for 10 minutes longer, or until the apples are very tender.

6.   Transfer the apple mixture to a food processor and process to a jam-like consistency. Transfer the jam to several jars or a tightly sealed container and refrigerate until ready to use.

My grandmother always served a version of this simple spiced apple jam with her roast chicken (page 136). Rather than simmering the apples as she did, however, I roast them, which slightly caramelizes them and intensifies their flavor.

TOMATO MUSTARD JAM

MAKES ABOUT 2 CUPS

¼ cup olive oil

3 tablespoons mustard oil (see Pantry, page 282; optional)

1 tablespoon mustard seeds

8 ripe tomatoes, peeled, halved, seeded, and coarsely chopped

3 shallots, thinly sliced

3 garlic cloves, thinly sliced

1 tablespoon honey

6 fresh basil leaves

1 teaspoon finely chopped fresh tarragon

2 bird's-eye or other small dried chiles

5 white peppercorns, crushed

1 teaspoon kosher salt

Grated zest of 1 lime

Covered and refrigerated, the jam will keep for at least a week.

1. Heat the oil in a medium saucepan over medium heat. Add the mustard oil (if using) and mustard seeds, reduce the heat to very low, and cook for 45 minutes, or until the mustard seeds are softened and the oil is fragrant.

2. Add the tomatoes, shallots, garlic, honey, basil, tarragon, chile peppers, peppercorns, salt, and lime zest to the pan. Increase the heat to medium-low and cook, stirring occasionally, for 45 minutes, or until the tomatoes have cooked down to a jam-like consistency. Remove from the heat and let cool completely. Remove the chile peppers from the jam before serving.

Serve this versatile sweet-spicy jam with Steamed Crab Rolls (page 48), grilled salmon or another simple seafood dish, or roast chicken or other poultry. ✢ Mustard oil is a hot spicy oil used in Indian cooking, but if you don't have it on hand, the chiles and mustard seeds, which are slowly simmered in olive oil until slightly softened and fragrant, add plenty of heat to the tomatoes and honey in the jam.

HORSERADISH APPLESAUCE

MAKES ABOUT 1 CUP

2   shallots, finely chopped

2   cups Chicken Stock (page 263)

2   Granny Smith apples, peeled, cored, and coarsely chopped

1   3-inch piece horseradish (see Pantry, page 281), peeled and finely grated, or 2 tablespoons bottled horseradish

1   teaspoon wasabi powder (see Pantry, page 285)

1   teaspoon Dijon mustard

Kosher salt

1. Combine the shallots and stock in a medium saucepan, bring to a boil, and cook until most of the liquid has evaporated. Add the apples, reduce the heat to low, cover, and cook for 10 to 12 minutes, or until the apples are soft enough to mash.

2. Use an immersion blender to puree the apples, or pass them through a food mill into a bowl. Stir in the horseradish, wasabi, and mustard. Season with salt to taste, and serve at room temperature.

The applesauce will keep in the refrigerator for up to 3 days.

Applesauce is a traditional accompaniment to many classic Swedish dishes, including Salt-Cured Brisket (page 150), Prune-Stuffed Pork Roast (page 158), and Potato Pancakes (page 186). I particularly like this non-traditional version, with its sharp bite of horseradish and wasabi. If you have pan juices on hand from roasted poultry or roasted meat, substitute them for some or all of the stock.

MANGO KETCHUP

MAKES ABOUT 1 CUP

1   ripe mango, peeled, pitted, and chopped

2   tablespoons store-bought mango chutney

2   tablespoons ketchup

1   tablespoon soy sauce

1   tablespoon white wine vinegar

4   drops Tabasco sauce, or more to taste

Combine all the ingredients in a food processor or blender and process until smooth. Transfer to a small bowl, cover, and refrigerate.

The easiest way to cut up a mango is to stand it on a cutting board and slice off the flesh from one side of the large flat pit in one large piece. Then turn the mango around and slice off the flesh from the other side. Lay each half skin side down and score the flesh lengthwise into strips, being careful not to cut through the skin, then score it crosswise. Turn the mango "inside out," and slice off the cubes of flesh. Slice off the two narrow strips of flesh remaining on the pit, and score as directed (or just nibble on them for a cook's treat).

The ketchup will keep in the refrigerator for up to 5 days.

This sweet, fruity ketchup with just a bit of chile heat makes a great dip for fried foods, such as Crispy Potatoes (page 44), or serve it as an accompaniment to roasted or grilled fish or chicken.

CITRUS SALSA

MAKES ABOUT 1½ CUPS

- 1 pink grapefruit
- 1 orange
- 1 lime
- 2 tablespoons grapeseed oil or canola oil
- 1 garlic clove, finely chopped
- 1 teaspoon Dijon mustard
- 2 teaspoons sherry vinegar
- 1 tablespoon finely chopped fresh mint
- 1 tablespoon finely chopped fresh cilantro

The salsa is best when freshly made, but it will keep, covered and refrigerated, for up to 2 days.

Three types of citrus fruit combine to produce a burst of flavor, the sweetness of the orange offsetting the sweet-tart grapefruit and the tang of the lime. This salsa is particularly good with shellfish — serve it with Grilled Lobster (page 132) instead of the Grapefruit Salsa, or with pan-seared scallops — or with any meaty fish, such as monkfish. Or try it with Gravlax (page 18) instead of the traditional mustard-dill sauce. You could even fold it into a plain risotto (see Lime Risotto, page 195, for guidelines).

1. Slice off both ends of the grapefruit, orange, and lime, right down to the flesh. Stand each fruit on a cutting board and, with a serrated or other sharp knife, cut away the peel and white pith from top to bottom in long strips, following the curve of the fruit. Working over a medium bowl to catch the juices, use a sharp paring knife to cut between the membranes to release the segments, dropping them into the bowl.

2. Heat the oil in a small skillet over medium heat. Add the garlic and sauté for about 2 minutes, until it barely starts to color. Transfer the garlic and oil to a small bowl and let cool.

3. Add the mustard, vinegar, garlic oil, mint, and cilantro to the citrus segments, mixing gently. Serve at room temperature.

FRUIT AND BERRY CHUTNEY

MAKES 2½ TO 3 CUPS

2 tablespoons extra-virgin olive oil

¼ cup packed dark brown sugar

1 shallot, minced

1 garlic clove, minced

1 tablespoon ginger, peeled and finely chopped

1 2-inch cinnamon stick

1 star anise

4 dried apricots (preferably from California), chopped

4 prunes, pitted and chopped

2 dates, pitted and chopped

1 cup mixed fresh berries, such as blueberries, blackberries, and raspberries

½ cup fresh or frozen cranberries

½ teaspoon minced lime zest

1 teaspoon fresh thyme leaves

⅓ cup freshly squeezed orange juice

2 tablespoons sherry vinegar

1 tablespoon Dijon mustard

Kosher salt and freshly ground black pepper

The chutney will keep in the refrigerator, tightly covered, for several weeks.

1. Heat the oil and brown sugar in a large skillet over medium heat, stirring to dissolve the sugar. Add the shallot, garlic, ginger, cinnamon stick, and star anise, and sauté for about 2 minutes, until the shallot softens. Add the apricots, prunes, and dates, and cook, stirring, for 1 minute. Stir in the berries, cranberries, lime zest, thyme, orange juice, and vinegar, and bring to a simmer. Reduce the heat to low and simmer gently for about 5 minutes, until most of the liquid has been absorbed.

2. Stir in the mustard, season with salt and pepper to taste, and remove from the heat. Serve the chutney warm, at room temperature, or chilled. Remove the cinnamon stick and star anise before serving.

Perhaps because the climate in Scandinavia is so severe — the winters so long and the summers so short — we yearn for the sweetness of fruits and berries in savory dishes. Berry picking is a favorite activity during their brief season. Cloudberries, a tart-sweet relative of the raspberry, are especially prized because of both their delicate flavor and their scarcity — they are in season for only a week or so in June. ✣ This chutney is made with a delicious mix of dried and fresh fruit and berries, which you can vary according to personal taste and whatever is available in the market. Serve it with game, meat, or pork — or the Thanksgiving turkey.

SORBETS AND GRANITAS

Sorbet tastes best and has the best texture when it is freshly made. Ideally, you should freeze it just before you start dinner, then pack it into an airtight freezer container. However, it can be made ahead and will keep well in the coldest part of the freezer for a day or two.

CUCUMBER SORBET

SERVES 6 TO 8

½ teaspoon powdered gelatin

¼ cup cold water

½ cup Simple Syrup (page 274)

2 cups fresh cucumber juice (from about 2 cucumbers; see Note)

3 tablespoons freshly squeezed lemon juice

3 tablespoons vodka

1½ teaspoons salt

1. Sprinkle the gelatin over the water in a small cup and let stand for 5 minutes to soften the gelatin.

2. Bring the syrup to a simmer in a small saucepan. Remove from the heat and add the gelatin, stirring until it is completely dissolved. Pour the mixture into a bowl and add the cucumber juice, lemon juice, vodka, and salt, stirring to dissolve the salt. Let cool.

3. Pour the sorbet base into an ice cream maker and freeze according to the manufacturer's instructions. Transfer to an airtight container and freeze until ready to serve.

This refreshing sweet and savory sorbet goes well with spicy food, especially curried dishes. It is delicious alongside smoked salmon, gravlax, or rare seared or grilled tuna. Or serve it as a garnish for a simple ceviche or oysters on the half shell — put a tiny spoonful on top of each oyster, and for a special indulgence, add a dollop of caviar.

If you don't have a vegetable juicer, coarsely chop the cucumbers and puree in a blender or food processor, then strain through a sieve lined with cheesecloth, pressing against the solids with a wooden spoon to release as much liquid as possible. Or look for fresh cucumber juice at health food stores and juice bars.

CURRY SORBET

SERVES 4 TO 6

2 teaspoons curry powder

1 14-ounce can unsweetened coconut milk

1/4 teaspoon saffron threads

1 vanilla bean, split lengthwise

2 3-inch pieces ginger, peeled and coarsely chopped

2 tablespoons light brown sugar

3/4 cup Simple Syrup (page 274)

1 8-ounce container whole-milk yogurt

1/4 cup freshly squeezed lime juice

If you have a small ice cream machine that can make only 1 quart, you will need to freeze this in two batches.

1. Toast the curry powder in a small saucepan over medium-high heat, stirring constantly with a wooden spoon, for 1 minute, or until fragrant. Add the coconut milk and saffron. Scrape the seeds from the vanilla bean and add them to the saucepan. Bring to a simmer, then remove from the heat and let stand for 1 hour to infuse.

2. Add the ginger and brown sugar to the coconut milk mixture, bring to a gentle simmer, and simmer for 5 minutes. Remove from the heat and let stand for 30 minutes.

3. Strain the coconut milk mixture into a medium bowl and whisk in the syrup, yogurt, and lime juice. Pour into an ice cream maker and freeze according to the manufacturer's instructions. Transfer to an airtight container and freeze until ready to serve.

The idea of curry sorbet might seem unusual at first, but its sweet and spicy flavors are reminiscent of combinations typical of Swedish food. Likewise, the sorbet itself is good with both savory and sweet dishes. I like to serve it as a garnish for oysters on the half shell (top each one with a very small spoonful) or for Tandoori-Smoked Salmon (page 26), where the curry flavors are a natural fit with the tandoori spices. It's also good with desserts, such as Chocolate Ganache Cakes (page 241) or Chocolate "Blini" (page 235).

GOLDEN BELL PEPPER SORBET
SERVES 6 TO 8

  1 pound (3 medium) yellow bell peppers, cored, seeded, and coarsely chopped
  ¾ cup Simple Syrup (page 274)
  2 tablespoons freshly squeezed lemon juice

1. Puree the bell peppers in a food processor. Strain the puree through a fine strainer into a bowl, pressing against the solids to release as much liquid as possible. Stir in the syrup and lemon juice.

2. Pour the mixture into an ice cream maker and freeze according to the manufacturer's instructions. Transfer to an airtight container and freeze until ready to serve.

3. To serve, transfer to the refrigerator for about 15 minutes to soften slightly. Place one or two scoops of sorbet in each dessert bowl or wineglass and serve immediately.

For a dessert with great contrasting flavors, serve alongside Chocolate Ganache Cakes (page 241) or Chocolate "Blini" (page 235).

Made with red bell peppers, Golden Bell Pepper Sorbet pairs well with Apple Sorbet (facing page)—swirl them together, or serve a few tiny scoops of each one in each bowl.

RASPBERRY SORBET
SERVES 4 TO 6

  2 pints raspberries
  1 cup Simple Syrup (page 274)
  ¼ cup freshly squeezed lime juice

1. Puree the raspberries in a food processor or blender. Strain through a fine sieve into a bowl, pressing against the solids to release as much liquid as possible. Stir in the syrup and lime juice.

2. Pour the mixture into an ice cream maker and freeze according to the manufacturer's instructions. Transfer to an airtight container and freeze until ready to serve.

3. To serve, transfer to the refrigerator for about 15 minutes to soften slightly. Place one or two scoops of sorbet in each dessert bowl or wineglass and serve immediately.

Swirl these sorbets together for a spectacular and unusual combination of flavors or serve singly. To combine, place both sorbets in a large bowl and stir with a large wooden spoon, then place in individual dishes. ✣ On its own, Golden Bell Pepper Sorbet makes a fine palate cleanser between courses.

APPLE SORBET

SERVES 4 TO 6

5 Granny Smith apples, peeled, cored, and coarsely chopped
1/3 cup freshly squeezed lemon juice
1 tablespoon honey
3/4 cup Simple Syrup (page 274)

1.   Spread the apples out in a baking pan. Sprinkle them with some of the lemon juice, tossing to mix. Freeze the apples for about 1 hour, until just firm but not rock-hard.

2.   Transfer the apples to a food processor and puree them with the remaining lemon juice, the honey, and syrup. Pour into an ice cream maker and freeze according to the manufacturer's instructions. Transfer to an airtight container and freeze until ready to serve.

3.   For a palate cleanser, serve one small scoop of sorbet in each cocktail glass. For dessert, serve two scoops in each bowl or wineglass.

The pure, tart, clean taste of this sorbet, apple accentuated by fresh lemon juice, reminds me of the fruity frozen pops I ate as a child in Sweden. Serve it between courses or as a tangy accompaniment to Black Pepper Cheesecake (page 244) or Apple Brioche "Tarts" (page 245).

BALSAMIC YOGURT SORBET

SERVES 6 TO 8

1 cup high-quality aged balsamic vinegar
1 cup fresh apple juice or apple cider
1/4 cup freshly squeezed lime juice
1 vanilla bean, split lengthwise
1 quart low-fat yogurt
3/4 cup Simple Syrup (page 274)

1.   Combine the balsamic vinegar, apple juice, and lime juice in a medium saucepan. Scrape the seeds from the vanilla bean and add them to the pan. Bring to a boil over medium-high heat, reduce the heat slightly, and simmer until the liquid has reduced by half. Transfer to a bowl and set in an ice bath to cool, or refrigerate until cold.

2.   Stir the yogurt and syrup into the apple juice mixture, mixing well. Pour into an ice cream maker and freeze according to the manufacturer's instructions. Transfer to an airtight container and freeze until ready to serve.

High-quality balsamic vinegar is aged for at least twelve years, and some artisan vinegars are aged for much longer. Good balsamic vinegar is available in gourmet markets and some supermarkets. If you can't find it, even a supermarket brand will make a good sorbet. To intensify the flavor of a commercial balsamic vinegar, boil it until reduced by half or more, then let cool completely before using.

If you have a small ice cream machine that can make only 1 quart, you will need to freeze this in two batches.

The intense flavor of aged balsamic vinegar is mellowed by the yogurt in this unusual, tangy, sweet sorbet. It makes a perfect ending to a rich meal.

VANILLA YOGURT SORBET

1 quart low-fat yogurt
1 cup Simple Syrup (page 274)
1 vanilla bean, split lengthwise

VARIATIONS

Omit the vanilla and add the finely grated zest and juice of 1 lemon.

Omit the vanilla and add ½ cup thawed frozen concentrated cranberry juice and 1 cup dried cranberries, soaked in ruby port until softened and drained.

Fold ½ cup Candied Beets (page 248) into the sorbet once it's been frozen.

1. Whisk the yogurt and syrup together in a large bowl. Scrape the seeds from the vanilla bean and stir them into the yogurt.

2. Pour the mixture into an ice cream maker and freeze according to the manufacturer's instructions. Transfer to an airtight container and freeze until ready to serve.

Yogurt sorbets turn down the heat after a spicy meal, and they can provide a welcome counterpoint to the flavors of other sweet desserts as well. Serve a scoop of this vanilla bean–scented sorbet in bowls of Strawberry Mint Soup (page 228), Blueberry Soup (page 229), or alongside Rhubarb Compote (page 230). Or, for a great light-dark combination, serve this with Balsamic Yogurt Sorbet (page 221).

CHAMPAGNE GRANITA

SERVES 4 TO 6

2 cups pineapple juice

Juice of ½ orange

½ stalk fresh lemongrass, tough outer leaves removed, tender inner
stalk lightly crushed and finely chopped

1 tablespoon sugar

1 orange pekoe tea bag

2 cups Champagne or other sparkling wine, plus more for topping
off, if desired

¼ cup freshly squeezed lime juice

The granita can be frozen, tightly covered, for up to 2 weeks.

Freeze the granita in ice cube trays and use the cubes for cocktails or

other summer drinks.

1. Combine the pineapple juice, orange juice, lemongrass, sugar, and tea bag in a medium saucepan and bring to a boil, stirring to dissolve the sugar. Remove from the heat and let cool to room temperature.

2. Strain the cooled liquid into a bowl and stir in the Champagne or sparkling wine and lime juice. Pour into a shallow metal baking pan and freeze for 30 minutes, or until ice crystals have started forming around the edges of the pan. Stir the crystals into the center of the mixture and continue to freeze until solid, stirring the granita every 20 minutes or so.

3. To serve, use a metal spoon to scrape up shavings of the granita and divide among six martini or other stemmed glasses or four wineglasses. Add a splash of Champagne or sparkling wine to each glass, if desired, and serve immediately.

This wonderfully bracing granita can be served as a palate cleanser between courses or as a light dessert after a heavy meal—try it after Thanksgiving dinner, before the pies come out. Or serve a scoop as a garnish for Blueberry Soup (page 229). Combined with a good but inexpensive sparkling wine, the granita also makes a great party drink. Simply scrape some of the granita into champagne flutes or wineglasses and fill the glasses with sparkling wine.

One of my favorite frozen treats is this sweet and savory granita. A study in contrasts, it combines icy temperatures with heat from Tabasco, ginger, and a bit of strong alcohol. At Aquavit, we serve this in shot glasses alongside Lobster Rolls with Pickled Asian Pears (page 50). But it can also be a palate cleanser between courses or a light, not too sweet dessert.

GINGER ALE GRANITA

SERVES 6 TO 8 (OR 16 IF SERVED IN SHOT GLASSES)

1 stalk fresh lemongrass, tough outer leaves removed, tender inner stalk lightly crushed and cut into 1-inch pieces

2 cups ginger ale

1/3 cup freshly squeezed lime juice

1 3-inch piece ginger, peeled and coarsely chopped

1/2 teaspoon Tabasco sauce

2 kaffir lime leaves (see Pantry, page 281)

4 black peppercorns

2 tablespoons ice-cold Lime Aquavit (page 255) or Absolut Mandarin vodka (plus more for topping off if serving as a palate cleanser)

The granita can be kept frozen, tightly covered, for up to 2 weeks.

If serving the granita as a dessert, you could place a handful of fresh strawberries, blueberries, or raspberries in each glass and top with the granita.

Freeze the granita in ice cube trays and use the cubes for cocktails or other summer drinks.

1. Combine the lemongrass, ginger ale, lime juice, ginger, Tabasco, kaffir lime leaves, and peppercorns in a small saucepan and bring to a boil. Remove from the heat and let cool to room temperature.

2. Strain the ginger ale mixture into a bowl and stir in the aquavit. Pour into a shallow metal pan and freeze for 30 minutes, or until ice crystals have started forming around the edges of the pan. Stir the crystals into the center of the mixture and continue to freeze until solid, stirring the granita every 20 minutes or so.

3. When ready to serve, use a metal spoon to scrape up shavings of the granita. To serve as a palate cleanser, spoon the shavings into shot glasses or champagne flutes and top off each with about 1 tablespoon of ice-cold aquavit. To serve as a light dessert, spoon the shavings into martini or other stemmed glasses and serve immediately.

DESSERTS

STRAWBERRY MINT SOUP
SERVES 6 TO 8

3 pints strawberries, hulled

6 cups water

1 cup freshly squeezed orange juice (from about 4 oranges)

2 3-inch pieces ginger, peeled and thinly sliced

4–5 stalks fresh lemongrass, tough outer leaves removed, tender inner stalks lightly smashed and sliced into 1/4-inch-thick rounds

1 bunch fresh mint, coarsely chopped, including stalks (about 2 cups)

1 cup sugar

You can, if you wish, top this soup with a scoop of vanilla ice cream.

Use only ripe, fragrant strawberries for this soup. Smaller berries often have a more intense flavor than larger ones.

For a delicious summer cocktail or refreshing drink, combine 1/2 cup of the soup with 1/2 cup Champagne or sparkling water and serve over ice.

1. Set aside 1/2 pint of the strawberries, and thinly slice the rest.

2. Put the sliced strawberries in a large saucepan, add the water, orange juice, ginger, lemongrass, mint, and sugar, and bring to a boil, stirring occasionally. Reduce the heat to low and simmer for 5 minutes. Remove from the heat and set aside to steep for 1 hour.

3. Strain the strawberry soup into a bowl. Cover and refrigerate until chilled, at least 2 hours.

4. Meanwhile, cut the reserved strawberries into 1/4-inch dice. Transfer to a small bowl, cover, and refrigerate.

5. Place a small mound of diced strawberries in the center of each soup plate or bowl, pour the chilled soup around the berries, and serve.

In June, people in Sweden eagerly forage for wild strawberries; their flavor and fragrance are unparalleled. Traditionally this soup would have been prepared with the wild berries, but because they have only a very short season and are not easily available, I use regular strawberries. Serve this only when strawberries are in season and plentiful; if you are lucky enough to come across wild berries, add a few to the mix. You could also make this soup with other berries, such as raspberries or blackberries, or, for a red fruit soup, a combination of strawberries and raspberries.

BLUEBERRY SOUP

SERVES 4 TO 6

3 pints blueberries, picked over to remove stems

3/4 cup sugar

2 cups water

Juice of 1/2 lemon

1 teaspoon ground cardamom

1 cup muscatel or ice wine

3/4 cup thawed frozen mango puree or 1 ripe mango, peeled, pitted, and pureed (in a blender or food processor)

Ice wine, or *Eiswein*, is a dessert wine made from grapes, usually Riesling, that are left on the vine until the first frost hits. The grapes are then immediately picked and gently crushed while still frozen, to extract only the drops of juice that have not frozen. The result is a wine that is honey sweet, comparable to nectar.

Frozen mango pulp is available in Latin markets and some supermarkets; or puree a ripe mango, as suggested above.

For a more elaborate dessert, garnish the soup with Vanilla Yogurt Sorbet (page 222) or vanilla ice cream, placing a small scoop in the center of each bowl.

1. Combine the blueberries, sugar, water, lemon juice, and cardamom in a large saucepan and bring to a boil over medium-high heat, stirring occasionally. Cook, stirring, until the sugar is completely dissolved. Remove from the heat.

2. Using an immersion blender, puree the soup. Or transfer the soup, in batches if necessary, to a regular blender and blend to a smooth puree. Transfer to a large bowl and stir in the wine and mango puree.

3. Serve the soup hot, or cover and refrigerate until chilled before serving.

This is a very popular soup in Sweden. In the summer, we make it with fresh blueberries and serve it cold, either on its own or ladled over other fruit. In the winter, we serve the soup hot as a first course, or pack it in a thermos and take it along to the ski slopes or on other outdoor excursions. When fresh berries are not in season, you can use frozen berries; in Sweden, we save some of summer's crop for the winter by macerating the fresh berries overnight with a little sugar, then freezing them.

POPPY SEED PARFAIT WITH RHUBARB COMPOTE
SERVES 8

When we were opening Aquavit Minneapolis, Adrienne Odom was one of many candidates we interviewed for the position of pastry chef. She prepared a dessert tasting for us, and as soon as I tried her Poppy Seed Parfait, I knew she was the one for the job. We've used the parfait in many different ways since then, pairing it with Chocolate "Blini" (page 235), among other combinations, or serving it as a garnish for Blueberry Soup (page 229). In this springtime dessert, the luscious creaminess of the parfait, with a delicate crunch from the poppy seeds, is a lovely complement to the sweet and tart flavors of the rhubarb compote.

FOR THE POPPY SEED PARFAIT

- 1   cup poppy seeds (about 5 ounces)
- ¼   cup pine nuts, lightly toasted
-      Scant 1/4 cup honey
- 3   cups heavy cream
- 5   large egg yolks
- ⅔   cup sugar
- 2   tablespoons dark rum
- 1   vanilla bean, split lengthwise in half

FOR THE RHUBARB COMPOTE

- 1½   pounds trimmed rhubarb stalks
- 2   cups sugar
- 1½   cups water
- 2   stalks fresh lemongrass, tough outer leaves removed, tender inner stalks lightly smashed and cut into 2-inch lengths
- 1   3-inch piece ginger, peeled and coarsely chopped
- 1   vanilla bean, split lengthwise in half

Toast the pine nuts in a small skillet over medium heat, stirring and tossing frequently, for about 3 minutes, or until beginning to turn golden brown. Transfer to a small bowl to cool before using.

The compote can be made up to 1 day ahead, covered, and refrigerated. Bring to room temperature or reheat over low heat until warm before serving.

Serve the compote alongside any duck or game main course.

1.   PREPARE THE PARFAIT: Combine the poppy seeds, pine nuts, and honey in a small saucepan and heat over low heat for about 5 minutes, until the honey is liquefied. Remove from the heat and let cool.

2.   In a large bowl, whip the cream until it holds soft peaks. Set aside.

3.   Combine the egg yolks, sugar, and rum in the top of a double boiler or a heatproof bowl. Scrape the seeds from the vanilla bean and add the seeds to the pan. Set over simmering water and heat, whisking constantly, until hot to the touch. Remove from the heat and continue to whisk until thick, pale yellow, and cool. Fold in the poppy seed mixture, then fold in the whipped cream.

4.   Divide the parfait among eight glasses. Cover and freeze for at least 6 hours, or overnight.

5.   PREPARE THE COMPOTE: Peel the rhubarb and cut it into 2-inch lengths. Slice each piece into ¼-inch julienne.

6.   Combine the sugar, water, lemongrass, and ginger in a medium saucepan. Scrape the seeds from the vanilla bean and add the seeds and pod to the pan. Bring to a boil, turn off the heat, and let stand for 20 minutes to infuse the liquid with flavor.

7.   Strain the infused liquid and return it to the saucepan. Add the rhubarb and simmer for 15 minutes, or until tender. Remove from the heat. Let cool slightly, or let cool to room temperature.

8.   Spoon about 2 tablespoons of the compote over each parfait and serve immediately.

GLÖGG-POACHED PEARS WITH ENDIVE, WALNUT, AND STILTON RAGOUT

SERVES 6

FOR THE POACHED PEARS

- 3 large ripe but firm Bartlett pears
- 2 cups ruby port or Madeira
- 2 cups dry red wine
- 1½ cups sugar
- Zest of 2 oranges — removed in strips with a vegetable peeler
- Zest of 1 lemon — removed in strips with a vegetable peeler
- 2 cinnamon sticks
- 4 whole cloves
- 6 cardamom pods
- 3 allspice berries
- 10 black peppercorns
- 1 bay leaf

FOR THE RAGOUT

- 2 endives, trimmed, cores removed, and cut crosswise into ¼-inch-wide strips
- 1 tablespoon unsalted butter
- 1 tablespoon light brown sugar
- ¼ cup walnut pieces
- Pinch of kosher salt
- 1½ ounces Stilton or other blue cheese, crumbled (about ⅓ cup)

1. PREPARE THE PEARS: Peel the pears. Cut them lengthwise in half, leaving the stems attached, and core them.

2. Combine the port or Madeira, red wine, sugar, citrus zest, cinnamon sticks, cloves, cardamom, allspice, peppercorns, and bay leaf in a large saucepan and heat over medium heat, stirring, until the sugar dissolves. Add the pears and bring to a simmer, then reduce the heat to low and simmer gently for 45 minutes to 1 hour, until the pears are tender. Remove from the heat and let the pears cool to room temperature in the poaching liquid.

3. Transfer the pears and poaching liquid to a bowl, cover, and refrigerate until chilled. (If time allows, refrigerate the pears for up to 3 days to infuse them with more flavor.)

4. JUST BEFORE SERVING, PREPARE THE RAGOUT: Cook the endives in a small dry skillet over medium heat for 2 to 3 minutes, until it has wilted slightly. Add the butter. When it has melted, add the brown sugar, walnuts, and salt, and cook, stirring, for about 2 minutes, until the sugar has dissolved. Remove from the heat and stir in the blue cheese.

5. To serve, put a poached pear half on each plate and spoon some of the poaching liquid over it. Place a small mound of the ragout on top of each pear.

A melon baller makes it easy to remove the core from the pear halves; then use a sharp paring knife to remove the tough fibers that run lengthwise down the center of the pear half.

Cooking the pears slowly infuses them with greater flavor.

If you like, strain the extra poaching liquid, heat it, and serve in small cups alongside the poached pears.

This is a traditional dessert updated with a sophisticated savory twist. I use glögg, the spiced red wine served throughout Sweden at Christmastime, for poaching the pears, then serve a ragout of endive, walnuts, and Stilton alongside to play off their spicy sweetness. Ideally the pears should be cooked two to three days before you intend to serve them so that the flavors have time to ripen.

I call these "blini" because they are so luxurious. Sprinkling the delicate pancakes with just a few grains of the fragrant sea salt both emphasizes the chocolate flavor and adds an unexpected textural note. ✤ You might serve these at brunch or on a buffet table, arranged on a platter with a chilled bowl of the sorbet alongside. The recipe doubles easily for a larger group.

CHOCOLATE "BLINI"

MAKES ABOUT 15 PANCAKES; SERVES 5 TO 8

¼ pound bittersweet chocolate, coarsely chopped

8 tablespoons (1 stick) unsalted butter, cut into chunks

2 large eggs

2 large eggs, separated

2 tablespoons sugar

2 tablespoons cake flour

2 tablespoons almond flour (see Pantry, page 279)

About 2 tablespoons clarified butter (see Pantry, page 279), for cooking the pancakes

2 tablespoons unsalted butter, melted

Fleur de sel (see Pantry, page 283), for garnish

Vanilla Yogurt Sorbet (page 222)

For this recipe, use high-quality bittersweet chocolate, such as Valhrona or Callebaut, available at gourmet and specialty shops, or Lindt, which can be found in most supermarkets.

1. Melt the chocolate and butter in the top of a double boiler or in a heatproof bowl over barely simmering water, stirring occasionally until smooth. Remove from the heat and let cool slightly.

2. In a large bowl, beat the eggs, egg yolks, and sugar with an electric mixer on medium speed for about 5 minutes, until thick, pale, and doubled in volume. Stir in the melted chocolate, then stir in both flours.

3. In a large bowl, beat the egg whites with an electric mixer until they form stiff peaks. Fold the egg whites into the batter. Cover and let rest in the refrigerator for 30 minutes.

4. Preheat the oven to 450°F.

5. To cook the blini, heat about 1½ teaspoons of the clarified butter in a large ovenproof skillet over medium-high heat until sizzling hot. (If you have two skillets, you can cook two batches of blini at a time.) Add about 2 tablespoons batter to the pan for each blini, without crowding, and cook for about 30 seconds, until bubbles begin to appear on top. Transfer the skillet to the oven for 30 seconds to set the blini, then return to medium-high heat, turn the blini over, and cook for 20 seconds longer. Remove from the heat and let stand for 1 minute—the blini should be slightly crisp on the outside and still rather moist inside. Transfer to a platter and cover to keep warm. Repeat with the remaining batter.

6. Brush the blini with the melted butter and sprinkle a few grains of fleur de sel over each one. Arrange 2 or 3 blini on each plate, place a scoop of sorbet alongside, and serve immediately.

SWEDISH PANCAKES WITH LINGONBERRY WHIPPED CREAM

FOR THE PANCAKES

- ³/₄ cup plus 1 tablespoon all-purpose flour
- 1 cup milk
- ½ cup heavy cream
- 1 tablespoon sugar
- ¼ teaspoon salt
  Grated zest of ½ orange
- 3 large eggs, lightly beaten
- 1 tablespoon unsalted butter, melted and cooled, plus additional butter for cooking the pancakes

FOR THE LINGONBERRY WHIPPED CREAM

- 1 cup heavy cream
- 1 tablespoon sugar
- 2 tablespoons lingonberry preserves (see Sources, page 289)

Although lingonberry preserves are traditional in Sweden, you can use any other preserves in the whipped cream. Fresh Cranberry Relish (page 210) is also delicious.

Undoubtedly the most famous Swedish dessert, these pancakes instantly conjure up childhood memories. We ate them every Thursday night, following the equally traditional split pea soup (page 95). You can make this batter ahead, as my grandmother and mother did, but you could also just whip it up 30 minutes in advance and it will work fine. These pancakes can be served warm or at room temperature.

1. MAKE THE PANCAKE BATTER: Combine the flour, milk, heavy cream, sugar, salt, and orange zest in a large bowl and whisk to blend. Whisk in the eggs, then stir in the melted butter. Cover and refrigerate for 30 minutes (or up to 24 hours).

2. SHORTLY BEFORE SERVING, MAKE THE WHIPPED CREAM: In a medium bowl, beat the cream and sugar until soft peaks form. Fold in the lingonberry preserves. Cover and refrigerate.

3. To cook the pancakes, heat a small nonstick crepe pan or skillet with sloping sides over medium-high heat. Add ½ teaspoon butter and heat until it melts and the bubbles subside. Whisk the batter once more to blend well, then add a scant ¼ cup batter to the pan, swirling the pan so it covers the bottom in a thin layer. Watch the pancake carefully, and as soon as the surface is dry, in less than a minute, turn it over and cook for about 30 seconds longer. (As with crepes, the first pancake is usually a "practice" one — don't worry if it doesn't come out perfectly, you can save it for a cook's treat.) Transfer the pancake to a plate and repeat the process with the remaining batter, adding more butter to the pan as needed and stacking the pancakes on the plate. The pancakes can be served warm or at room temperature.

4. Spread some of the whipped cream filling across the lower third of each pancake and roll it up, or spread a thin layer of whipped cream over each pancake and fold it into quarters. Arrange on plates and serve.

COCONUT COOKIES

MAKES ABOUT 2½ DOZEN COOKIES

2 tablespoons unsalted butter

2½ cups unsweetened shredded coconut

2 large eggs

¾ cup sugar

Stored in an airtight container, the cookies will keep

for at least a week.

1. Preheat the oven to 350°F. Line two baking sheets with parchment paper.

2. Melt the butter in a medium saucepan. Remove from the heat and add the shredded coconut, mixing well with a rubber spatula.

3. In a large bowl, beat the eggs with an electric mixer on medium speed just to blend. Beat in the sugar, then increase the speed to medium-high and beat until light and fluffy. Stir in the coconut until thoroughly mixed.

4. Drop rounded teaspoons of the batter onto the prepared baking sheets, spacing them about 1½ inches apart. Bake for 8 to 10 minutes, until the tips of the cookies are pale gold. Slide the parchment paper, with the cookies on it, onto wire cooling racks and let cool completely.

In Sweden, three o'clock in the afternoon is coffee hour, and every traditional household has a jar of homemade cookies in the pantry, ready to serve with steaming cups of freshly brewed coffee. Easy to make, chewy, and delicious, these are just the thing.

GINGER CITRUS COOKIES

MAKES ABOUT 5 DOZEN COOKIES

x3

3	1 teaspoon	ground ginger
¾	¼ teaspoon	ground cloves
1½	½ teaspoon	ground cinnamon
1½	½ teaspoon	ground cardamom
10½	3½ cups	sifted all-purpose flour
3	1 tablespoon	baking soda
3	1 teaspoon	salt
1½	½ teaspoon	freshly ground white pepper *blk or*
30	10 tablespoons (1¼ sticks)	unsalted butter, at room temperature
3	1 cup	sugar
1½	½ cup	packed light brown sugar
6	2	large eggs
2¼	¾ cup	molasses
3	1 cup	finely chopped Candied Citrus Peel (page 246)

You can substitute high-quality candied citrus peel for the homemade. Avoid supermarket candied peel; good candied orange peel is available at gourmet markets and by mail order (see Sources, page 289).

To make perfectly shaped cookies that are all the same size, use a small (#30) ice cream scoop to drop the dough onto the baking sheets.

Stored in an airtight container, the cookies will keep for up to 1 month.

1. Preheat the oven to 350°F. Line two baking sheets with parchment paper.

2. Toast the ginger, cloves, cinnamon, and cardamom in a small skillet over medium heat, stirring with a wooden spoon, for 2 to 3 minutes, until fragrant. Remove from the heat.

3. Sift the flour, toasted spices, baking soda, salt, and white pepper into a bowl or onto a sheet of wax paper.

4. In a large bowl, beat the butter and both sugars with an electric mixer until light and fluffy. Add the eggs, one at a time, beating well after each addition and scraping down the sides of the bowl as necessary. Beat in the molasses. Gradually beat in the flour mixture. Stir in the candied citrus peel.

5. Drop rounded tablespoons of the dough onto the prepared baking sheets, spacing the cookies *a wide or* 2 inches apart. Bake for 10 to 12 minutes, until the tops feel firm when lightly touched. Cool on the baking sheets for about 2 *5* minutes, then transfer the cookies to a wire rack to cool completely.

x2 = fills 8 wilton favor bags of 10 each (+ extras).

x3 = fills 6 13oz coffee cans lined plastic gallon bag + tie + leftovers or oatmeal tins (24oz.)

These cookies are similar to ginger-snaps but moister and chewier; the secret ingredient is chopped Candied Citrus Peel. The recipe is another one that was inspired by my grandmother's cooking. We often baked cookies together, and she used to add the zest of bitter oranges to one of her doughs. ✣ At Aquavit, we give these cookies as Christmas gifts, but they are delicious year-round. They also keep extremely well.

CARROT PARSNIP CAKE
SERVES 6 TO 8

10 tablespoons (1¼ sticks) unsalted butter, at room temperature
1 cup all-purpose flour
1 teaspoon baking powder
½ teaspoon baking soda
½ teaspoon ground cinnamon
2 large eggs
1 cup sugar
1¼ cups shredded parsnips (about 3 medium parsnips—remove any tough inner cores before shredding)
1 cup shredded carrots (about 2 medium carrots)
Confectioners' sugar, for dusting (optional)

Serve the cake with a scoop of vanilla ice cream alongside each slice.

My introduction to carrot cake came in Switzerland, where I sampled *rübli kuche*, and it was love at first bite. The idea of a cake made with a root vegetable intrigued me, and it made me think of using parsnips, a close relative of carrots, as well. The result of my experiments is a moist, subtly sweet cake with a pleasant, slightly chewy texture. Be sure to use only young, tender parsnips.

1. Preheat the oven to 350°F. Butter an 8-inch round cake pan and line the bottom with a round of parchment paper. Butter the parchment paper, dust the parchment paper and the sides of the pan with flour, and tap out the excess flour.

2. Melt the butter in a small saucepan over medium-low heat, then continue cooking until it is pale brown and has a warm nutty smell. Remove from the heat and let cool until barely warm.

3. Meanwhile, whisk the flour, baking powder, baking soda, and cinnamon together in a small bowl.

4. In a large bowl, beat the eggs with an electric mixer on medium speed for 3 to 5 minutes, until thick and fluffy. Gradually beat in the sugar, increase the speed to medium-high, and beat until very thick and pale. Gradually beat in the browned butter. Stir in the parsnips and carrots. Fold in half of the flour mixture, then fold in the remaining flour mixture.

5. Scrape the batter into the cake pan and smooth the top with a spatula. Put the cake pan on a baking sheet and bake for 30 to 35 minutes, or until a toothpick inserted into the center comes out clean.

6. Let the cake cool in the pan for 10 minutes, then invert onto a wire rack and peel off the parchment. Invert onto another rack to cool right side up, and serve warm or at room temperature.

7. Just before serving, dust the top of the cake with confectioners' sugar, if desired.

CHOCOLATE GANACHE CAKES

SERVES 12

Cocoa powder, for dusting

2 tablespoons unsalted butter, at room temperature

1/2 pound bittersweet chocolate, coarsely chopped

1/2 pound (2 sticks) unsalted butter, cut into chunks

4 large eggs

4 large egg yolks

5 tablespoons sugar

1/2 cup plus 2 tablespoons sifted cake flour

Use high-quality bittersweet chocolate for this recipe, such as Valhrona or Callebaut, available at gourmet and specialty shops, or Lindt, which can be found in most supermarkets.

The batter can be prepared ahead and the unbaked cakes frozen, well wrapped, for a few hours, or as long as overnight. Bake the frozen cakes for 9 minutes, turn the baking sheet around, and bake for another 9 minutes, or until the edges of the cakes look set and have pulled slightly away from the sides of the ramekins but the centers are still slightly liquid; do not overbake.

This recipe makes a lot of little cakes, but if 12 servings are too much for one occasion, you can freeze the extra unbaked cakes for up to 1 month. Bake following the timing in the note above. If you don't want to make 12 cakes, the recipe is easily halved.

1. Preheat the oven to 350°F. Grease twelve 4-ounce ramekins or aluminum foil molds with the softened butter. Dust with cocoa powder and tap out the excess.

2. Melt the chocolate and butter in the top of a double boiler or in a heatproof bowl over barely simmering water, stirring occasionally until smooth. Remove from the heat.

3. In a large bowl, whisk together the eggs, egg yolks, and sugar until well mixed. Whisk in the melted chocolate and butter. Sift the cake flour over the top and fold it in.

4. Divide the batter among the ramekins, filling them no more than three quarters full. Arrange them on a baking sheet and bake for 5 to 6 minutes. Turn the baking sheet around and bake for another 4 to 6 minutes, just until the edges of the cakes look set and have pulled slightly away from the sides of the ramekins but the centers are still slightly liquid; do not overbake.

5. Turn each cake out on a plate and serve immediately.

Individual hot chocolate cakes with an oozing, liquid center have a seductive simplicity. Pair them with anything from vanilla ice cream to Curry Sorbet (page 219). Or serve with my favorite accompaniment, Candied Beets (page 248).

SOFT GINGER CAKE WITH MASCARPONE MOUSSE

SERVES 6 TO 8

FOR THE MASCARPONE MOUSSE

- ½ teaspoon powdered gelatin
- 2 tablespoons cold espresso
- 2 large egg yolks
- ¼ cup sugar
- ½ vanilla bean, split lengthwise in half
- ¼ pound mascarpone cheese
- ¾ cup heavy cream

FOR THE GINGER CAKE

- 1½ cups all-purpose flour
- 2 teaspoons baking powder
- 1 teaspoon ground cinnamon
- ½ teaspoon ground cloves
- ¼ teaspoon salt
- 8 tablespoons (1 stick) unsalted butter
- ½ cup packed light brown sugar
- ½ cup maple syrup
- 1½ teaspoons finely chopped peeled ginger
- 1 teaspoon grated lemon zest
- 1 large egg, lightly beaten
- ½ cup cold espresso

- ¼ cup espresso
- 2 teaspoons Kahlúa
- 1 teaspoon Bailey's Irish Cream
- ¼ cup sugar

You can make the espresso using a good-quality instant espresso powder, such as Medaglia d'Oro, which is sold in most supermarkets.

1. **PREPARE THE MOUSSE:** Sprinkle the gelatin over the espresso in a small cup. Let stand for 5 minutes to soften the gelatin.

2. Combine the egg yolks and sugar in the top of a double boiler or a heatproof bowl. Scrape the seeds from the vanilla bean and add the seeds to the egg yolks. Set the pan or bowl over simmering water and whisk until the mixture is very light and fluffy. Add the gelatin mixture and whisk until the gelatin is dissolved. Transfer to a medium bowl and fold in the mascarpone. Let cool completely.

3. Beat the heavy cream in a medium bowl until it forms soft peaks. Fold into the mascarpone mixture. Cover and refrigerate until ready to serve. (The mousse can be made up to 1 day ahead.)

4. **PREPARE THE CAKE:** Preheat the oven to 350°F. Butter an 8-inch square baking pan. Line the bottom with a square of parchment and butter the parchment.

5. Whisk the flour, baking powder, cinnamon, cloves, and salt together in a large bowl.

6. Heat the butter, brown sugar, and maple syrup in a medium saucepan over medium-low heat, stirring occasionally, until the butter has melted and the sugar has dissolved. Add the ginger and lemon zest and cook, stirring, for 1 minute. Remove from the heat and add to the flour mixture, stirring to mix well. Stir in the egg, then stir in the espresso.

7. Scrape the batter into the baking pan and smooth the top with a spatula. Bake for 18 to 20 minutes, or until a toothpick inserted into the center comes out clean. Cool in the pan on a wire rack for 5 minutes.

8. While the cake is cooling, combine the espresso, Kahlúa, Bailey's Cream, and sugar in a small saucepan and bring to a simmer over low heat, stirring to dissolve the sugar. Remove from the heat and brush the warm cake generously with the syrup. Invert it onto a rack, peel off the paper, and brush generously with syrup. Invert onto a serving plate.

9. To serve, cut the cake into squares or rectangles. Transfer to dessert plates and top each slice with a large dollop of the mascarpone mousse. Pass any remaining mousse at the table.

The best tiramisù, which means "pick me up" in Italian, lives up to its name. But for the most part, the dessert has become a cliché, disappointing more often than not. I wanted an alternative that would be as good as the original. I replaced the traditional ladyfingers or sponge cake with a Swedish ginger cake and topped it with a mousse made with mascarpone to provide lightness and lift.

BLACK PEPPER CHEESECAKE

SERVES 6 TO 8

1½ teaspoons black peppercorns

¾ pound Philadelphia cream cheese, at room temperature

⅓ cup sugar

1 vanilla bean, split lengthwise in half ✳

¾ cup crème fraîche, sour cream, or whole-milk yogurt

2 tablespoons freshly squeezed lemon juice

2 large eggs

1½ cups heavy cream

If you use a springform pan for the cake, wrap the pan in a double layer of foil before adding the batter, to keep it watertight.

The cheesecake will keep in the refrigerator for up to 1 week. (Cheesecakes don't freeze well—their texture turns grainy.)

Swedish cheesecake is very different from American cheesecake. Made with rennet, it has almost a curdy texture. American-style cheesecake has recently become trendy in Sweden as well, and for my version, I add spices, a typical Swedish touch, to the creamy batter. Tamed by blanching, black peppercorns contribute bite and just a little heat. Serve with Apple Sorbet (page 221); its tart coolness offers a nice contrast to the sweet, rich, spicy cake. ✳ We also use the batter for this cake as a mousse. It's versatile: pipe it into glasses and serve it as a dessert on its own, garnish Blueberry Soup (page 229) with a dollop or two, or serve it with fresh fruit such as pineapple.

Samuelson sez: or 2 T vanilla

✳ ✳ 1 hr —1 hr 15 min: longer better —than shorter → = done in center

1. Preheat the oven to 250°F. Spray an 8-inch round cake pan with nonstick cooking spray. Line the bottom with a round of parchment paper and spray the parchment paper.

2. Blanch the peppercorns in a small saucepan of boiling water for 1 minute; drain. Repeat two more times. Drain and pat the peppercorns dry with paper towels.

3. Spread the peppercorns out in a small baking pan and dry them in the oven for 15 to 20 minutes, until thoroughly dry. Remove from the oven and let cool. Turn the oven temperature up to 350°F.

4. Grind the peppercorns medium-fine in a spice grinder (or a clean coffee grinder), or use a mortar and pestle; set aside.

5. In a large bowl, beat the cream cheese and sugar with an electric mixer on medium-high speed for about 3 minutes, until very smooth and light. Scrape the seeds from the vanilla bean and add them to the cream cheese mixture. Beat in the crème fraîche or sour cream or yogurt, and scrape down the sides of the bowl. Add the eggs one at a time, beating well after each addition and scraping down the sides of the bowl as necessary. Beat in the cream and ground peppercorns.

6. Scrape the batter into the prepared pan. Set the pan inside a large shallow baking pan and pour about 1 inch of hot water into the larger pan. Bake for 1 hour, or until the sides of the cake are set but the center is still a little loose. Transfer the cake pan to a rack to cool completely.

7. When the cheesecake is cool, cover with plastic wrap and refrigerate overnight.

8. To unmold the cheesecake, run a thin knife or spatula around the sides of the pan. Set the pan on a hot burner for about 20 seconds, shaking the pan gently from side to side to release the cake. Invert the cake onto a cake plate, peel off the parchment, and serve.

APPLE BRIOCHE "TARTS"

SERVES 4

3 large Granny Smith apples

½ lemon

¾ cup sugar

2 tablespoons Calvados or applejack

4 ¼-inch-thick slices brioche (6–8 inches long), crusts removed

4 tablespoons unsalted butter, melted

2 tablespoons vanilla sugar (see Pantry, page 284)

½ teaspoon ground cinnamon

½ cup fresh goat cheese

1 vanilla bean, split lengthwise in half

½ cup heavy cream

In place of brioche, you can use challah or another egg bread or a good firm white bread. Walnut raisin bread or even raisin fennel bread is also great with the apples and goat cheese—go ahead and experiment.

Calvados is an apple brandy from the Normandy region of France. Look for it at better liquor stores.

These simple but sophisticated tarts were inspired by apple cake, a thoroughly traditional Swedish dessert. The apples are caramelized in a skillet, then baked until tender, and arranged on the brioche over a sweetened, creamy layer of goat cheese. They are then returned to the oven just until the filling starts to melt and turn golden brown.

1. Preheat the oven to 350°F. Line a baking sheet with parchment paper.

2. Peel and core the apples. Cut each apple into 8 wedges, and squeeze the juice of the lemon over them to keep them from turning brown.

3. Heat ½ cup of the sugar in a heavy ovenproof skillet over medium-high heat, stirring with a wooden spoon, until the sugar has melted and become a dark amber caramel, about 10 minutes. Add the apples and toss them until completely coated (if any lumps of caramel form, stir gently until the caramel melts). Remove from the heat, add the Calvados or applejack to the pan, and mix well.

4. Transfer the skillet to the oven and bake for 10 minutes, or until the apples start to soften. Remove the skillet from the oven. (Leave the oven on.)

5. Cut each slice of brioche lengthwise in half. Brush each slice on both sides with the melted butter. Mix the vanilla sugar and cinnamon together and sprinkle over the top of each brioche slice. Arrange the slices on the prepared baking sheet and toast in the oven for 5 minutes, or until lightly browned. Remove them from the oven and set aside. (Leave the oven on.)

6. In a medium bowl, combine the goat cheese and the remaining ¼ cup sugar. Scrape the seeds from the vanilla bean and add them to the bowl. With an electric mixer, beat the goat cheese and sugar on medium speed until well blended and smooth. Gradually add the cream and continue beating until very smooth.

7. Spread the goat cheese mixture on the brioche, then arrange 3 apple wedges on each slice. Bake the tarts for 10 minutes, or until the goat cheese starts to turn golden brown around the edges. Serve warm.

CANDIED CITRUS PEEL

MAKES ABOUT 1 CUP

2 cups strips or slices of lemon, lime, orange, and/or grapefruit peel (remove the peel with a sharp knife, then slice off the innermost bitter white pith, leaving a ¼-inch-thick layer)

2 cups water

2 cups sugar, plus optional sugar for coating

The sugar-coated peel can be stored in an airtight container at room temperature for up to 2 weeks. Or store the uncoated peel in the syrup in the refrigerator for up to a week or so.

1. Put the citrus peels in a medium saucepan, cover with plenty of cold water, and bring to a boil; drain. Repeat two more times.

2. Combine the water and sugar in a medium saucepan and bring to a boil, stirring to dissolve the sugar. Add the citrus peels and bring just to a simmer, then reduce the heat to low and simmer very gently for 30 to 45 minutes, until the peels are translucent. Remove from the heat and let the peels cool in the syrup.

3. If you are using the candied peel for the Ginger Citrus Cookies (page 238), drain and finely chop. If you want to sugar-coat the candied peel on its own, drain well, spread a layer of sugar on a plate, and toss the citrus peel, in batches, in the sugar. Transfer to wire racks to dry.

Candied Citrus Peel, which we use in our Ginger Citrus Cookies (page 238), can also be served on its own with after-dinner espresso or coffee.

CANDIED FRUIT (OR CARROT) CHIPS

Choose 1 of the following: apple, pear, Asian pear (also called apple pear), or carrot

½ **lemon (if using fruit)**

1 **cup water**

1 **cup sugar**

Store the chips in an airtight container at room temperature. In humid weather, they may stay crisp for only a day or so; in drier weather, they will keep for 3 to 4 days.

1. Use a mandoline or other vegetable slicer to cut the unpeeled fruit into paper-thin slices: Slice the fruit lengthwise until you reach the core, then turn it over and slice the same way until you reach the core again. Squeeze some lemon juice over the cut slices as you work, to keep them from discoloring. Or peel the carrot and slice crosswise into paper-thin rounds or lengthwise into thin ribbons.

2. Bring the water and sugar to a boil in a small saucepan, stirring to dissolve the sugar. Reduce the heat to very low, add the sliced fruit or carrot, and cook at the barest simmer for 10 to 15 minutes, until the slices are limp. Drain well.

3. Meanwhile, preheat the oven to 250°F. Line a baking sheet with parchment paper and spray with nonstick cooking spray. (Use a Silpat liner if you have one; see page 287.)

4. Arrange the slices on the baking sheet and bake for 30 to 50 minutes, or until dry and crisp. Transfer to a rack to cool.

These beautiful chips can be used to garnish any dessert or served on their own as a delicate after-dinner sweet with coffee — or with a glass of Champagne as an aperitif. Make carrot chips to garnish the Carrot Parsnip Cake (page 240) — your guests will be very impressed. Or add some fruit chips to a fruit salad, for sweetness and crunch. They are also a pretty garnish for ice cream or sorbet.

CANDIED BEETS

MAKES ABOUT 2 CUPS

2   large or 3–4 small beets, trimmed and peeled
1   stalk fresh lemongrass, tough outer leaves removed, tender inner
    stalk lightly smashed and cut into $1/2$-inch pieces
1   cup sugar
$1/2$ cup packed light brown sugar
$3/4$ cup freshly squeezed orange juice
$2^1/2$ tablespoons honey

You could also serve these with Black Pepper Cheesecake (page 244) or vanilla ice cream. Or serve the beets as a garnish for any venison or pork dish.

1.   Slice the beets into $1/2$-inch-thick rounds, then cut into $1/2$-inch dice. Tie up the lemongrass in a piece of cheesecloth.

2.   Combine the beets, cheesecloth bag, sugar, brown sugar, orange juice, and honey in a medium saucepan. Bring to a simmer, stirring to dissolve the sugar, then reduce the heat and simmer gently for 45 minutes to 1 hour, until the beets are soft.

3.   Transfer the beets and cooking liquid to a bowl or other container; discard the cheesecloth bag. Let the beets cool in the liquid, then refrigerate until needed.

Since much of the world's sugar supply has traditionally come from beets, it should be no surprise to find that they make a perfect dessert ingredient. These candied beets are a great accompaniment to Chocolate Ganache Cakes (page 241), underlining the sweetness of the chocolate. They are also quite beautiful — and delicious — stirred into Vanilla Yogurt Sorbet (page 222).

DRINKS

HOMEMADE AQUAVIT

I use potato-based vodka for these aquavits because I think it has the clearest, cleanest flavor, but you could use any vodka.

When making any of the aquavits, save the vodka bottle and its cap. (If you like, soak the label to remove it and replace it with your own.) Once the vodka has steeped, strain it and return it to the bottle. Seal the bottle and store in the freezer.

If the jar you use for infusing the vodka is attractive, it can serve as a centerpiece on your table or on a sideboard while the vodka steeps.

BERRY AQUAVIT

MAKES ABOUT 1 QUART

1 cup raspberries, blueberries, lingonberries, or black currants
1 1-liter bottle potato-based vodka
2 tablespoons Simple Syrup (page 274)

FOR GARNISH

A few fresh berries

1. Put the berries in a wide-mouthed lidded jar that is large enough to hold the vodka and berries, and pour in the vodka. Add the vodka and seal the jar. Let stand at room temperature for 6 to 8 weeks, until the full flavor has developed.

2. Strain the vodka into a pitcher or bowl, and stir in the syrup. Transfer to a 1-liter bottle and add the fresh berries. Seal the bottle and store in the freezer.

3. Serve the aquavit ice-cold in shot glasses.

This is a slightly sweet aquavit with a beautiful berry color. Serve it straight as an accompaniment to almost any dessert, or use it to make a berry-flavored martini or in a cosmopolitan.

LEMON, PEPPER, AND DILL AQUAVIT

MAKES ABOUT 1 QUART

3 lemons, scrubbed

1 1-liter bottle potato-based vodka

½ cup chopped fresh dill, including stems

FOR GARNISH

3 sprigs fresh dill

2 long strips lemon peel

A few black peppercorns

1. With a vegetable peeler, remove the zest from 2 of the lemons in long strips; set the zest aside. Cut all of the lemons (including the peel) into small cubes.

2. Put the lemons, lemon zest, dill, and peppercorns into a wide-mouthed lidded jar that is large enough to hold the vodka and all the flavoring ingredients. Add the vodka and seal the jar. Let stand at room temperature for 6 to 8 weeks, until the full flavor has developed.

3. Strain the vodka into a pitcher or bowl, and pour it into a 1-liter bottle. Add the dill sprigs, the 2 strips lemon peel, and the peppercorns. Seal the bottle and store in the freezer.

4. Serve the aquavit ice-cold in shot glasses.

This is one of our most popular aquavits. With its very traditional Scandinavian flavors, it goes extremely well with any herring or cured fish dish. Not sweet, like the other aquavits in this chapter, it also makes a great marinade for meat and game, such as Pan-Roasted Venison Chops (page 162).

LIME AQUAVIT

MAKES ABOUT 1 QUART

4   limes, scrubbed
2   kaffir lime leaves (see Pantry, page 281)
1   3-inch piece ginger, peeled and coarsely chopped
1   1-liter bottle potato-based vodka

1.   Using a zester, remove the zest from 2 of the limes (or remove the zest with a vegetable peeler, then slice it into strips). Thinly slice the limes. Put the zest, sliced limes, and ginger into a wide-mouthed lidded jar that is large enough to hold the vodka and flavorings. Add the vodka and seal the jar. Let stand at room temperature for 6 to 8 weeks, until the full flavor has developed.

2.   Strain the vodka into a pitcher or bowl, and pour it into a 1-liter bottle. Seal the bottle and store in the freezer.

3.   Serve the aquavit ice-cold in shot glasses.

Infused with Asian flavors, this contemporary aquavit goes particularly well with fish dishes.

RICE TEA AQUAVIT

MAKES ABOUT 1 QUART

½   cup jasmine rice
2   jasmine tea bags
2   sprigs fresh mint, leaves only
1   1-liter bottle potato-based vodka

1.   Put the rice and ¼ cup water in a small saucepan and bring to a simmer over medium-low heat. Cover tightly, reduce the heat to low, and steam the rice for 5 minutes. Add the tea bags, replace the lid, and steam for 8 minutes longer, or until the rice has absorbed most of the water.

2.   Transfer the rice and tea bags to a wide-mouthed lidded jar that is large enough to hold the vodka and flavorings. Add the mint leaves and vodka and seal the jar. Let stand at room temperature for 6 to 8 weeks, until the full flavor has developed.

3.   Strain the vodka into a pitcher or bowl, and pour it into a 1-liter bottle. Seal the bottle and store in the freezer.

4.   Serve the aquavit ice-cold in shot glasses.

You can use this aquavit as a marinade for chicken.

Inspired by my love of sake, this aquavit has a delicate, unusual flavor that goes well with almost any fish, chicken, or game dish. Or serve it as an aperitif on its own.

YELLOW MARY MIX

MAKES ABOUT 2 QUARTS

FOR THE MIX

- 2 celery stalks (optional)
- 12 pounds yellow tomatoes
- 1/2 cup frozen mango puree, thawed, or 1/2 ripe mango, peeled and seeded
  Juice from 2 limes
- 2 tablespoons grated horseradish (see Pantry, page 281)
- 10 drops Worcestershire sauce
- 6 drops Tabasco sauce

  Lemon, Pepper, and Dill Aquavit (page 254) or Citron vodka
  Celery stalks for garnish (if not making the celery juice ice cubes)

Frozen mango puree is available in some supermarkets and in Latin and

other ethnic markets; or use a mango, as suggested above.

1. If you have a vegetable juicer, juice the celery. Pour the juice into an ice cube tray and freeze (if using).

2. Juice the tomatoes and, if using, the ripe mango, and transfer to a large pitcher or other container. Or, if you don't have a juicer, core the tomatoes and coarsely chop them, reserving the juices. Chop the ripe mango, if using. Combine the tomatoes, with their juices, and the chopped mango in a food processor, in batches if necessary, and puree. Strain the puree through a sieve set over a large bowl, pressing against the solids with the back of a wooden spoon to extract as much liquid as possible, and transfer to a pitcher or other container.

3. If using frozen mango puree, stir it into the tomato juice. Stir in the lime juice, horseradish, Worcestershire sauce, and Tabasco. Cover and refrigerate until ready to use.

4. For each drink, pour about 5 ounces of the mix into a tall glass half filled with ice, add vodka, and stir to mix. Add, if using, a celery ice cube or garnish with a celery stalk.

Make this golden version of Bloody Mary mix in the summer months, when ripe, sweet yellow tomatoes are available.

BERRY LIQUEUR

MAKES ABOUT 1½ QUARTS

2   pints strawberries, rinsed and hulled
1   1-liter bottle potato-based vodka
2   cups sugar
2   cups water

1.   Combine the strawberries and vodka in a wide-mouthed lidded jar that is large enough to also hold about 2 cups of sugar syrup. Cover and let sit for 6 days.

2.   Bring the sugar and water to a boil in a medium saucepan, stirring to dissolve the sugar. Remove from the heat and let cool completely.

3.   Pour the sugar syrup into the vodka and berry mixture. Seal the jar and let sit for 6 weeks, until the full flavor has developed.

4.   Strain the vodka into a pitcher or bowl, and pour into a bottle (you will need a bottle that is larger than the original vodka bottle, because of the sugar syrup). Store the liqueur in the refrigerator.

5.   Serve the liqueur very cold in shot glasses.

Use this beautiful berry liqueur to make a Champagne or white wine cocktail, like a kir, or simply sip it as an after-dinner drink. It's also a fabulous ice cream topping — or pour it over Champagne Granita (page 223).

GLÖGG

MAKES ABOUT 1½ QUARTS

2 cinnamon sticks, broken into pieces
1 teaspoon cardamom pods
1 small piece ginger, peeled
   Grated zest of ½ orange
6 whole cloves
½ cup vodka
1 750-ml bottle dry red wine
1 cup ruby port or Madeira
1 cup sugar
1 tablespoon vanilla sugar (see Pantry, page 284)
½ cup blanched whole almonds
½ cup dark raisins

1. Crush the cinnamon and cardamom using a mortar and pestle (or put them on a cutting board and crush them with the bottom of a heavy pot). Put them in a small glass jar and add the ginger, orange zest, cloves, and vodka. Let stand for 24 hours.

2. Strain the vodka through a fine sieve into a large saucepan; discard the spices. Add the red wine, port or Madeira, sugar, vanilla sugar, almonds, and raisins, and heat over medium heat just until bubbles start to form around the edges.

3. Serve the glögg hot in mugs, with a few almonds and raisins in each one; keep any remaining glögg warm over very low heat until ready to serve (do not let boil).

From the beginning of December on through the New Year, glögg is served in Swedish homes on every festive occasion or when visitors drop by. A plate of St. Lucia Buns (page 206) is typically offered with the hot spiced wine. ✤ Many families also like to serve glögg after the evening meal, when everyone is sitting around the fire—a plate of Ginger Citrus Cookies (page 238) makes a great accompaniment.

BASICS

SWEDISH 1-2-3 VINEGAR
MAKES ABOUT 5 CUPS

3 cups water

2 cups sugar

1 cup white wine vinegar

1 carrot, peeled and sliced

1 onion, sliced

5 white peppercorns

2 bay leaves

2 allspice berries

You can use this vinegar as a flavorful marinade for beef tenderloin. Let it marinate for at least 6 hours, or overnight.

1. Combine all the ingredients in a saucepan and bring to a boil over medium heat, stirring to dissolve the sugar. Remove from the heat and let cool.

2. Pour the vinegar into a jar, seal the jar, and store in the refrigerator.

Many cultures have their own versions of a pickling solution. The name of this Swedish one comes from the proportions of vinegar, sugar, and water used. Unlike some of our other pickling or curing solutions, this one contains a high proportion of sugar. (In Sweden the vinegar is traditionally made with *ättika*, which has a higher alcohol content than ordinary white wine vinegar.) It's extremely versatile and can be used to pickle or flavor vegetables, fruit, fish, or meat — anything from berries to herring.

CHICKEN STOCK

3–4 pounds chicken parts (such as wings) and/or bones

2 medium onions, coarsely chopped

2 carrots, coarsely chopped

6 white peppercorns

2 bay leaves

2 sprigs fresh thyme

If you are freezing the stock, divide it among half-pint or other small containers for ease of use.

When a recipe calls for chicken stock, I often use some Fish Stock (page 264) in addition, for greater depth of flavor.

1. Put all the ingredients in a stockpot, add cold water to cover, and bring to just under a boil. Skim away the scum and foam from the surface, reduce the heat to low, and simmer, skimming occasionally, for 1 hour. Remove from the heat and let stand for 40 minutes.

2. Strain the stock through a fine sieve set over a large bowl, pressing against the solids with a wooden spoon to extract as much liquid as possible. Cover and refrigerate overnight.

3. Remove the hardened fat from the surface of the stock. It can now be refrigerated for up to 3 days or frozen for up to 3 months.

No kitchen can function without a good chicken stock. I keep my version plain and simple, so it is extremely easy to make—and, unlike most classic stocks, it needs to simmer for only 1 hour.

FISH STOCK

MAKES 2 QUARTS

- 1 pound fish bones from non-oily, white-fleshed fish
- 1 tablespoon olive oil
- 1 leek, white part only, halved lengthwise and sliced
- 1 onion, diced
- 2 shallots, finely chopped
- 2 quarts water
- 1 cup dry white wine
- 2 sprigs fresh thyme
- 2 sheets kombu (see Pantry, page 281)

To intensify the flavor of the stock, add ½ cup diced celery root, ½ cup diced fennel, and/or 1 small parsnip, diced, along with the leek, onion, and shallots.

Many fish markets make and sell their own fish stock. Taste before using to make sure you like the flavor — if necessary, you can improve the flavor of most store-bought stock by bringing it to a boil, adding 1 sheet of kombu for each quart of stock, and simmering it for 5 minutes. Then remove it from the heat and let stand for 20 minutes before straining.

1. Wash the fish bones under cold running water to remove any traces of blood. Drain the bones thoroughly, pat dry, and chop them into pieces so they will fit easily into the pot.

2. Heat the olive oil in a stockpot over medium-high heat. Add the leek, onion, and shallots, and sauté for about 2 minutes, until beginning to soften. Add the fish bones and cook, stirring frequently, for 2 minutes. Add the water, wine, thyme, and kombu, and bring to just under a boil. Skim the scum and foam from the surface, reduce the heat, and simmer, skimming a few times, for 5 minutes. Remove from the heat and let sit for 1 hour.

3. Strain the stock through a sieve lined with cheesecloth into a bowl or other container. Cover and refrigerate for up to 2 days. Or transfer the stock to half-pint containers and freeze for up to 3 months.

In Sweden, with its abundance of fish, we had the luxury of making stock only with sole or turbot bones, but you can use bones from almost any non-oily fish with good results. Ask your fish market for the bones; they'll usually sell them for just a few pennies a pound. ✣ Making stock is quick, and the rewards are tremendous. The secret ingredient in this stock is kombu, or kelp, which adds that indefinable flavor the Japanese call *umami*.

LOBSTER STOCK

MAKES 1½ QUARTS

1 tablespoon olive oil

2 carrots, coarsely chopped

2 shallots, coarsely chopped

2 garlic cloves, coarsely chopped

1 3-inch piece ginger, peeled and coarsely chopped

2 tablespoons tomato paste

   Shells from 4–6 lobsters, coarsely chopped

½ cup ruby port or Madeira

½ cup cognac

2 quarts Fish Stock (page 264) or water

For a quick and delicious consommé, strain the Lobster Stock again through a paper coffee filter. Reheat, stir in ½ cup port and ½ cup cognac or other brandy, and heat through. Serves 6 to 8.

1. Heat the olive oil in a stockpot over medium-high heat. Add the carrots, shallots, garlic, and ginger, and sauté for 2 to 3 minutes, until slightly softened. Stir in the tomato paste, then add the lobster shells and sauté for another 2 minutes, stirring frequently. Add the port and cognac, increase the heat to high, and cook until most of the liquid has evaporated.

2. Add the stock and bring to just under a boil. Skim off the scum and foam from the surface, remove from the heat, and let sit for 40 minutes.

3. Strain the stock through a fine sieve into a bowl or other container. Cover and refrigerate for up to 2 days. Or transfer the stock to half-pint containers and freeze for up to 3 months.

Making lobster stock turns something you would normally throw away into a totally luxurious ingredient. Whenever you cook lobsters, save the shells, and freeze them until you have enough to make this stock. I like to use Lobster Stock in all my fish and seafood soups, and it also makes an elegant consommé on its own (see Note).

My grandmother always made her own sharp, spicy mustard with a lot of mustard seeds in it. Years later, when I visited Indian stores, I discovered that mustard seeds come in a range of colors, from yellow and brown to purple and black. At Aquavit, we use a variety of different mustards, not only as a way of adding a sharp-sweet flavor to a dish, but also to paint the plate for a dramatic presentation.

BLACK MUSTARD

MAKES ABOUT ⅓ CUP

- 2 teaspoons black mustard seeds (see Pantry, page 282)
- 2 tablespoons Dijon mustard
- 1 tablespoon Colman's mustard powder
- 1 teaspoon squid ink (optional; see Note)
- 1 tablespoon mustard oil (see Pantry, page 282)
- 1 tablespoon olive oil

1. Grind the mustard seeds to a powder in a spice grinder (or a clean coffee grinder), or use a mortar and pestle. Transfer to a small bowl.

2. Add the mustard and mustard powder, then whisk in the squid ink (if using), mustard oil, and olive oil. Store in a tightly sealed jar in the refrigerator for up to 2 weeks.

Squid ink is used in Italian, Spanish, and some Asian cuisines; it is available at some fish markets and at ethnic groceries.

PURPLE MUSTARD

MAKES ABOUT 2 CUPS

- 2 cups dry red wine
- 1 cup ruby port or Madeira
- 2 shallots, finely chopped
- 2 tablespoons purple mustard seeds (see Sources, page 282) or other mustard seeds
- 4 white peppercorns
- 2 sprigs fresh tarragon, leaves only
- 1 cup Dijon mustard
- 1 teaspoon Colman's mustard powder

1. Combine the red wine, port, shallots, mustard seeds, peppercorns, and tarragon in a medium saucepan, bring to a boil over medium-high heat, and boil until reduced to ½ cup.

2. Transfer to a blender. Add the mustard and mustard powder and blend until smooth. Store in a tightly sealed jar in the refrigerator for up to 2 months.

PASTRAMI SPICES

MAKES ABOUT ½ CUP

¼ cup pink peppercorns (see Sources, page 289)
3 tablespoons dry-packed green peppercorns
2 tablespoons black peppercorns
1 tablespoon coriander seeds
¼ cup mild paprika
2 tablespoons five-spice powder

Use the spice mixture (and kosher salt to taste) to season pork tenderloins, pork chops, or lamb chops, or even steaks, before grilling them.

1. Put all the spices into a small skillet and toast over medium-high heat, stirring with a wooden spoon, for 3 to 4 minutes, until very fragrant. Transfer to a small bowl and let cool.

2. Grind the spices to a fine powder in a spice grinder (or a clean coffee grinder), or use a mortar and pestle. Store in an airtight jar in a cool, dark place for up to 6 months.

I fell in love with this spice mixture the first time I was introduced to pastrami sandwiches at one of New York City's many Jewish delis. The coriander seeds in the spice mix evoked memories of Sweden. I use this mixture to season the Spice-Rubbed Wild Boar Tenderloin (page 164) or whenever I want to give a quick flavor lift to almost any meat.

ROASTED GARLIC PASTE

MAKES $\frac{1}{2}$ TO $\frac{3}{4}$ CUP

4 heads garlic
1 tablespoon olive oil
1 teaspoon fresh thyme leaves
1½ teaspoons kosher salt

When whole heads of garlic (or individual cloves left in the skin) are roasted slowly, the pulp softens and caramelizes into a buttery puree with a sweet, delicate taste. Just squeeze the pulp out of the skins, and use it to add flavor to sauces, dressings, and many other dishes. You can also season the puree with salt and pepper, and serve it as a condiment or dip — it's great with Root Vegetable Chips (page 43).

1. Preheat the oven to 350°F.

2. Remove just the papery outer layers of the garlic heads. Rub them with olive oil and cut them horizontally in half.

3. Brush a small baking dish with olive oil. Sprinkle the thyme and salt over the bottom. Put the garlic cut side down in the dish and roast for 25 to 35 minutes, until the garlic is very soft. Let cool.

4. Squeeze out the garlic puree from the skins. Store the puree in a covered container in the refrigerator for up to 1 week.

CURRY OIL

MAKES ABOUT 5 CUPS

1 tablespoon coriander seeds

1 tablespoon ground cardamom

3 tablespoons ground turmeric

4 cups grapeseed oil or canola oil

2 shallots, sliced in half

4 garlic cloves, finely chopped

3 3-inch pieces ginger, peeled and coarsely chopped

2 stalks fresh lemongrass, tough outer leaves removed, tender inner stalks lightly smashed and finely chopped

1 tablespoon Asian shrimp paste (see Note, opposite page)

1 cup mustard oil (see Pantry, page 282)

4 bird's-eye or other dried chiles

6 kaffir lime leaves (see Pantry, page 281), shredded

VARIATION

For Halibut Fillets Poached in Curry Oil, put the fish, without crowding, in a deep, heavy skillet and add enough oil to cover it. Heat the oil over low heat to just below the simmering point. Reduce the heat slightly and cook the halibut for 20 minutes; do not let the oil reach a simmer. Lift out the fish with a slotted spatula and serve.

1. Toast the coriander seeds, cardamom, and turmeric in a medium skillet over medium-high heat, stirring with a wooden spoon, for 2 to 3 minutes, until aromatic. Reduce the heat to medium, add 2 tablespoons of the oil, the shallots, garlic, ginger, and lemongrass, and sauté, stirring, for 5 minutes, or until the shallots start to turn golden brown.

2. Stir in the shrimp paste, then add the remaining oil, the mustard oil, chiles, and kaffir lime leaves. Reduce the heat to very low, and simmer for 2 hours.

3. Remove from the heat, pour the oil and spices into a bowl, and let stand for at least 8 hours, or overnight, at room temperature to further infuse the oil.

4. Strain the oil through a strainer lined with several layers of cheesecloth. Store in a tightly sealed jar in the refrigerator for up to 2 weeks. Bring to room temperature before using.

We use this oil for both marinating and cooking Slow-Cooked Squab (page 138). Try it as a marinade for other poultry or for meat or game — or poach halibut or other meaty fish fillets or steaks in it (see Variation). I also use it as the base for a vinaigrette.

CURRY PASTE

MAKES ABOUT 1 CUP

1/2 cup grapeseed oil or canola oil

1 stalk fresh lemongrass, tough outer leaves removed, tender inner stalk lightly smashed and cut into 2-inch pieces

5 kaffir lime leaves (see Pantry, page 281), shredded

4 garlic cloves, coarsely chopped

1 3-inch piece ginger, peeled and diced

1 tablespoon Asian shrimp paste (see Note)

4 bird's-eye or other small dried chiles

1 tablespoon coriander seeds

1 tablespoon cumin seeds

1 tablespoon fennel seeds

1 1/2 teaspoons yellow mustard seeds

1 1/2 teaspoons brown mustard seeds

2 cardamom pods

1 3-inch cinnamon stick

1 tablespoon ground turmeric

2 whole cloves

Used in many Asian cuisines, shrimp paste is made from ground salted and fermented shrimp. Like Asian fish sauce, it has a strong, pungent aroma, which becomes less strong when it is cooked. It is used sparingly to add flavor to many dishes. Sold in small grayish pink or brownish cakes, it is available in Asian markets.

1. Heat the oil in a medium skillet over medium-low heat. Add the lemongrass, kaffir lime leaves, garlic, and ginger, and sauté for 1 minute, or until fragrant. Add all the remaining ingredients, reduce the heat to low (use a flame diffuser if you have one), and cook, stirring occasionally, for at least 40 minutes (the longer the paste cooks, the darker and spicier it will become). Remove from the heat.

2. Transfer the mixture to a blender and blend to a puree. Stored in a tightly sealed container in the refrigerator, the paste will keep for months.

Curry is one of the world's most versatile spice mixtures. At Aquavit, we've fine-tuned our own combination over the years. Use this paste as a spice rub on its own, as the base for curries, or to add flavor to other spicy dishes. The paste keeps almost indefinitely in the refrigerator.

HOMEMADE DILL BUTTER
MAKES ABOUT 2 CUPS

1 quart heavy cream, at room temperature
½ cup chopped fresh dill
Salt

1.   In a large bowl, preferably the bowl of a stand mixer, beat the cream on medium-low speed until the liquid (whey) starts to separate from the solids (curds), 10 to 15 minutes. Drain the solids in a strainer, and discard the liquid.

2.   Return the solids to the bowl, add the dill and salt (to taste), and beat on low speed until the dill is uniformly distributed.

3.   Transfer the butter to a sheet of parchment paper or plastic wrap, and shape it into a log about 1 inch in diameter. Roll it up in the paper or plastic wrap and store in the refrigerator or freezer.

Making your own butter at home is very simple and satisfying. The butter has a light and fresh taste, and it is easy to flavor it by adding herbs, such as dill (my favorite) or chives, tarragon, parsley, or chervil, or a combination. ✤ Serve the herb butter on its own as a delicious spread for bread, add it to sauces, or use a slice or two as the finishing touch on grilled fish, chicken, or steak or other meat.

DRIED GARLIC CHIPS
MAKES ABOUT ½ CUP

1 large head garlic, separated into cloves but not peeled

1.   Bring a small saucepan of water to a boil. Drop the garlic cloves into the boiling water and blanch for 1 to 2 minutes; drain and let cool.

2.   Peel the garlic cloves. Slice them into paper-thin slices with a garlic slicer or a very sharp knife. Spread the slices in a single layer on a sheet of parchment paper.

3.   Let the garlic dry overnight in a turned-off oven with a pilot light, or another warm, dry place, until completely dry.

4.   Store the chips in an airtight container at room temperature. In humid weather, they may stay crisp for only a day or so; in drier weather, they will keep for 3 to 4 days.

These chips are delicious sprinkled with amchoor, or green mango powder (see Pantry, page 279) and tossed with a bowl of Root Vegetable Chips (page 43).

These versatile chips are simple to prepare and an easy way to add a light garlic flavor to salads or a vegetable dish.

CORN FLAKE, PINE NUT, AND BACON CRUMBS

MAKES ABOUT 3½ CUPS

10 slices bacon

2 cups corn flakes

2 cups pine nuts

Once you've tasted this crunchy, nutty, sweet-salty mixture, you will come up with a million uses for it. It makes a great crust or topping for chicken, fish, meat, or vegetables, and it can be used to coat fried shrimp or other shellfish for deep-frying. Sprinkle it over a salad. You may even be tempted to simply put some in a small bowl and eat it as a snack.

1. Preheat the oven to 375°F.

2. Lay the bacon on a baking sheet and bake for 10 to 15 minutes, until golden brown and crispy. Transfer to paper towels to drain and cool.

3. Spread the pine nuts on a baking sheet and toast them in the oven until they just start to color, 4 to 5 minutes. Be careful not to burn them — once they start to color, this can happen very quickly. Transfer to a plate to cool. Meanwhile, spread the corn flakes on another baking sheet and bake them for 4 to 5 minutes, or until lightly toasted. Let cool.

4. Crumble the bacon into small pieces. Combine the bacon, pine nuts, and corn flakes in a food processor and process until coarsely ground.

5. Store the crumbs in a tightly sealed container in the refrigerator for up to 2 weeks.

SIMPLE SYRUP

MAKES ABOUT 3½ CUPS

2 cups water

1 cup corn syrup

3¾ cups sugar

Simple Syrup is convenient to have on hand to sweeten cold drinks like iced tea or coffee. At the restaurant, we always serve a small pitcher of it with these drinks.

1. Combine the water, corn syrup, and sugar in a large saucepan and bring to a boil over medium heat, stirring to dissolve the sugar. Reduce the heat slightly and simmer, stirring, until the sugar is completely dissolved. Remove from the heat and let cool.

2. Store the syrup in a covered jar or other container in the refrigerator. It will keep almost indefinitely.

Simple Syrup, which is sugar and water heated until the sugar dissolves, is used for making sorbets and many cocktails. The addition of corn syrup prevents the sugar from crystallizing.

BUTTERY TART SHELL
MAKES ONE 10-INCH TART SHELL

1¼ cups unbleached all-purpose flour

¼ teaspoon salt

8 tablespoons (1 stick) cold unsalted butter

2 tablespoons ice water, or more as needed

1½ teaspoons chopped fresh herbs, such as thyme, tarragon, dill, or flat-leaf parsley (optional)

The dough can be frozen for at least 2 weeks; thaw it, still wrapped, in the refrigerator.

The tart shell can be baked up to 1 day ahead. Let cool completely, then cover with plastic wrap and store at room temperature.

For a sweet dough, add 1 teaspoon sugar and 1 tablespoon grated orange or lemon zest to the flour (omit the herbs).

1. TO MAKE THE DOUGH BY HAND: Combine the flour and salt in a large bowl. Using your fingertips, a pastry cutter, or two knives, cut the butter into the flour until the mixture resembles coarse meal. Add the water, stirring with a fork just until the dough starts to come together; if necessary, add a little more water about 1 teaspoon at a time.

TO MAKE THE DOUGH IN A FOOD PROCESSOR: Combine the flour and salt in the processor and pulse once or twice to mix. Cut the butter into 1-inch pieces, scatter over the flour, and pulse just until the mixture resembles coarse meal. Add the water, pulsing just until the dough starts to come together; if necessary, add a little more water, about 1 teaspoon at a time.

2. Turn the dough out onto a sheet of plastic wrap and shape it into a disk. Wrap it in plastic and refrigerate for at least 1 hour before rolling.

3. On a lightly floured surface, roll out the dough to a 12½-inch round. Fit it into a 10-inch fluted tart shell with a removable bottom, without stretching the dough. Trim the edges of the dough. Refrigerate for 30 minutes before filling or baking.

4. TO PREBAKE THE TART SHELL: Preheat the oven to 375°F. Line the tart shell with foil and fill it with dried beans, rice, or pie weights. Bake it for 15 minutes, then remove the foil and weights. Bake for 8 to 10 minutes longer, or until golden brown. Let cool on a wire rack.

Easily made in the food processor, this is a great herbed pastry crust. We use it for the Goat Cheese and Artichoke Tart (page 56). You can omit the herbs for a plain crust. To make a sweet crust, see the Note.

RESOURCES

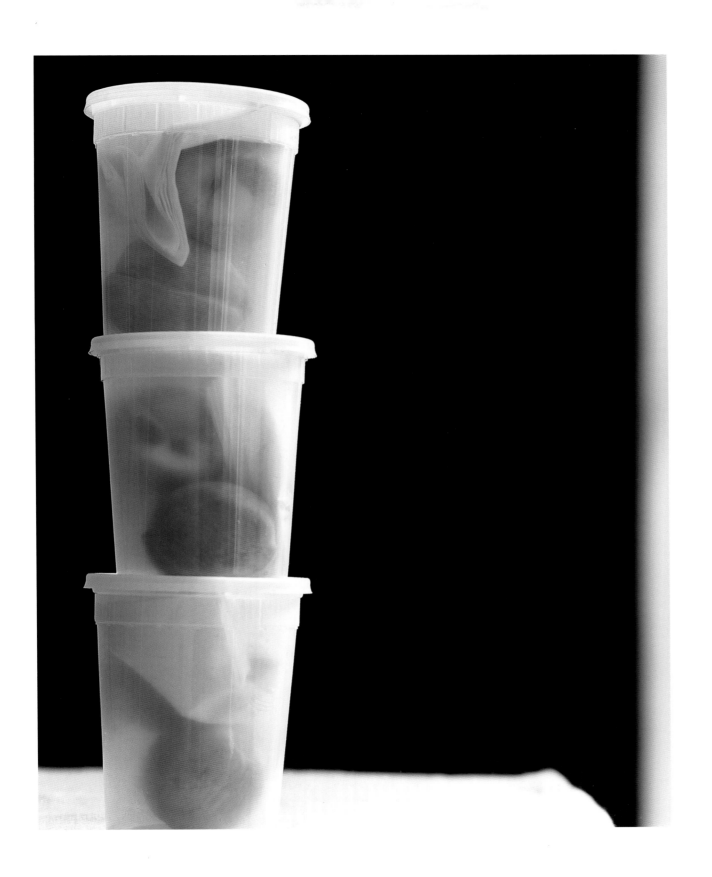

ALMOND FLOUR: Almond flour is very finely ground almonds. You can grind almonds yourself in a food processor, but be careful not to turn the ground nuts into a paste (if you are using the almonds in a dessert recipe, adding a little of the recipe's sugar while grinding the almonds will help prevent this). Commercial almond flour tends to be much finer and less oily than the homemade version. Almond flour is available from specialty markets and through mail order (see Sources, page 289).

AMCHOOR, AMCHUR: Also called mango powder, this pale brown or pale gray Indian seasoning is ground dried green (unripe) mangos. Tangy and sour, it is used in many Indian dishes such as dals, soups, chutneys, and, especially, pickles. Amchoor is also sprinkled over meats to tenderize them, and it makes an excellent addition to a batter or other coating for fried fish. It can be found in Indian and other Asian markets and through mail order (see Sources, page 290).

AQUAVIT: A strong, clear, colorless Scandinavian liquor, aquavit may be distilled from potato or grain mash. It is traditionally flavored with caraway or dill, but other flavorings may also be used. Aquavit is drunk as an aperitif (or to accompany a celebratory toast), often served icy cold. Look for aquavit at better liquor stores; for the recipes in this book, a flavored vodka (the flavor depending on the recipe) can be substituted, or see the recipes on pages 252–255 to make your own aquavits.

BERBERÉ: An Ethiopian staple, this hot spice mixture is made with chile peppers and as many as a dozen other spices, including cumin, coriander, fenugreek, ginger, cloves, and black pepper. At outdoor markets in Ethiopia, vendors sell different berberé mixes, and each cook has her own favorite blend. Use berberé to rub grilled meats or fish, or in stews and other dishes. Berberé mixes are available from specialty spice markets (see Sources, page 290).

CILANTRO: Cilantro is also called fresh coriander or, misleadingly, Chinese parsley. Although it does somewhat resemble flat-leaf parsley, it is not related to that herb. Used widely in Southeast Asian and Latin American cooking, cilantro has a pungent flavor and aroma. It is available in many supermarkets as well as at produce and other specialty markets. Look for bunches that still have their roots attached, as the herb stays fresh longer that way. Place cilantro in a tall glass of water, like a bouquet of flowers, and loosely cover it with a plastic bag. Store it in the refrigerator, and use it within a few days.

CLARIFIED BUTTER: Clarifying butter means removing the milk solids from it. Once these solids have been removed, the butter has a much higher smoking point than regular butter and can be used for sautéing without fear of its burning. It also stays fresh far longer than unclarified butter—up to a month or more in a sealed container in the refrigerator. Clarified butter is a staple in India, where it is called ghee, and in other countries with hot climates, including Ethiopia, where it is known as *qibe*.

TO CLARIFY BUTTER: It's best to start with at least $1/2$ pound butter (any extra can be refrigerated for another use). Cut the butter into tablespoon-sized pieces. Melt it slowly in a heavy saucepan over medium-low heat, then continue to cook, without stirring, until the milk solids accumulate on the bottom of the pan. Carefully skim off the foam from the surface, and slowly pour the clear butter into a container, leaving the milk solids in the pan (discard the solids). Clarifying butter reduces it by about one quarter in volume; $1/2$ pound, for example, will make 6 ounces, or $3/4$ cup, clarified butter.

COCONUT MILK: Coconut milk is not the liquid inside a ripe coconut, which is called coconut water, but shredded fresh coconut that has been blended with water and then strained. Good-quality canned unsweetened coconut milk is available in many supermarkets, as well as in most Asian markets. As it sits, the coconut milk separates into the thinner milk and a top layer of thicker cream. Shake the can and/or stir coconut milk well before measuring or using it. Don't confuse coconut milk with the canned sweet coconut cream used for Caribbean drinks.

CRÈME FRAÎCHE: Crème fraîche is a delicious thickened French cream with a slightly tangy flavor. Similar to sour cream in consistency, its flavor is richer, and, unlike sour cream, it can be simmered or boiled without curdling. Imported crème fraîche is available at gourmet markets and specialty cheese shops as well as upscale supermarkets. Recently some American artisan cheese makers have been producing crème fraîche, and domestic versions can be found in good supermarkets and in gourmet and cheese shops. Sour cream (full-fat, that is) can be substituted for crème fraîche, if necessary, in most recipes, although the flavor will not be as rich.

CURRY PASTE: Thai curry pastes are pungent seasoning mixtures that usually contain chiles, lemongrass, cilantro, and shrimp paste, among other ingredients. Green and red are the hottest; yellow is milder. They are sold in Asian grocery stores (see Sources, page 289).

CURRY POWDER: Curry powder, the quintessential Indian spice mix, has long been a staple of Swedish cooking. The spices vary, but they typically include cardamom, chiles, cloves, coriander, cumin, fennel seeds, fenugreek, ginger, mace, black pepper, and/or turmeric. Of the standard store-bought curry powders, there are two basic types; those labeled "Madras-style" are hotter. Many spice merchants and other specialty markets offer their own blends (see Sources, pages 289–290).

DRIED SHIITAKE MUSHROOMS: Also called Chinese dried mushrooms or dried black mushrooms, dried shiitakes have a much more intense flavor than the fresh kind. They can be used to make a broth. They can also be ground to an aromatic powder in a spice grinder (or a clean coffee grinder) and used as a rub, or to finish pan-seared or grilled meat. To reconstitute the dried mushrooms, soak them in hot water to cover for 20 to 30 minutes, or until softened. Lift them out of the water and trim off the stems, which tend to be tough, then slice or chop them as directed in the recipe. In most cases, you will want to strain the flavorful soaking liquid through cheesecloth or a coffee filter to remove any grit.

FLEUR DE SEL: See *Salt*.

FOIE GRAS: A specialty of France's Gascogne and Périgord regions, foie gras is the liver of a specially fattened goose or duck. Until the late 1980s, fresh foie gras was unavailable in this country, but now there are two foie gras producers in the United States, both of which raise ducks on their farms, and several in Canada. In addition, federal regulations, which used to forbid the import of the fresh product, were recently eased. For the recipes in this book, use duck foie gras (available at specialty butchers and through mail order; see Sources, page 289).

Grade A livers are the largest and the best — and the most expensive; Grade B foies gras are smaller and somewhat veinier than Grade A's, but they are also good. Fresh foie gras is usually sold whole (Grade A livers weigh around $1\frac{1}{4}$ pounds; Grade B's range from $\frac{3}{4}$ to 1 pound), but some specialty purveyors sell vacuum-packed slices.

TO PREPARE FOIE GRAS: If using a whole liver, carefully separate the two lobes (each liver consists of a large and a small lobe), cutting the connective vein if necessary. Peel off any thin membranes and remove any white fat on the inner part of the lobes; trim away any greenish spots (these can taste bitter). A

large vein runs lengthwise through each lobe, with a network of smaller veins; unless you are cooking the foie gras whole, it's easiest to remove the veins after slicing the foie gras or cutting it into smaller pieces — simply pull out any noticeable veins with your fingers, or use a small, sharp knife if necessary. (Don't worry if a slice cracks or breaks; in most cases, you can press the foie gras back into shape.) Keep refrigerated until just before cooking.

GARAM MASALA: Garam masala (literally, "hot spices"), another cornerstone of Indian cooking, is, like curry powder, a longtime staple of the Swedish pantry. It's often used in the favorite holiday drink, glögg. And, like curry powder, the makeup of garam masala varies from cook to cook and from dish to dish, but in general the aromatic mixture tends to be sweeter and less hot than curry spices. Garam masala usually includes bay leaves, cardamom, cinnamon, cloves, cumin, coriander seeds, mace, and black peppercorns. It can be found in Indian and other Asian markets, as well as through mail order (see Sources, pages 289–290).

HORSERADISH: Fresh horseradish root is available at specialty produce markets and in some supermarkets. Look for firm, smooth roots without wrinkles or blemishes, and refrigerate them in a plastic bag. Peel and grate the horseradish just before using, as its flavor can fade fast. The nose-stinging aroma can be powerful.

KAFFIR LIME LEAVES: Kaffir limes and their leaves are widely used in Thai, Vietnamese, and Cambodian cooking. Sometimes called wild limes, the fruits are small with bumpy, wrinkled skin; they yield very little juice, and only the fragrant rinds and leaves are used. The limes are rarely seen in the United States, but the leaves are becoming more widely available. Dark green, smooth, and shiny, the double-lobed leaves are used to flavor soups, salads, curries, and other dishes. The leaves freeze well, and frozen leaves can be substituted for the fresh in any recipe. Look for fresh or frozen leaves in Southeast Asian markets (you might want to buy extra fresh ones when you see them and freeze them yourself) or through mail order (see Sources, page 289). Avoid dried kaffir lime leaves, which have little flavor.

KETJAP MANIS: Also called kecap manis, ketjap manis (the English word *ketchup* comes from *ketjap*) is a sweet, syrupy Indonesian sauce/condiment based on soybeans; it is usually sweetened with palm sugar and includes garlic, star anise, and galangal (a relative of ginger). You can find it at most Asian markets or through mail order (see Sources, page 289).

TO MAKE A GOOD SUBSTITUTE FOR KETJAP MANIS: Combine 1 cup soy sauce, $1/3$ cup molasses, 3 tablespoons dark brown sugar, $1/4$ teaspoon ground coriander, and $1/4$ teaspoon cayenne pepper. The mixture will keep almost indefinitely in an airtight container in the refrigerator.

KOMBU: Also called konbu or kelp, kombu is dried giant sea kelp. Greenish black folded sheets of kombu, sealed in plastic packages, are sold in Asian markets and health food stores. Kombu adds great flavor to fish stock and many other broths (it's an essential ingredient in the Japanese stock called dashi and so may be labeled "dashi kombu"). The sheets have a whitish coating of dried salt; don't rinse this off, or you will lose some of the flavor — simply wipe them clean with a damp cloth or paper towel.

LEMONGRASS: A staple of Southeast Asian cooking, fresh lemongrass is increasingly available in markets here, its long stalks looking something like woody scallions. Fresh lemongrass can be stored, well wrapped, in the refrigerator for up to 2 weeks; it also freezes very well. To use lemongrass, remove the tough outer layers and trim the root end. Smashing or crushing the stalks slightly will tenderize them and bring out more flavor.

Then halve or quarter them to add to stocks and broths, or thinly slice or finely mince them, depending on the recipe. If the lemongrass will be served in the dish rather than strained out, use only the tender lower part of the inner stalks. Fresh lemongrass is available in Asian markets as well as many produce markets and some supermarkets. Avoid dried or powdered lemongrass, which has little flavor.

LINGONBERRY PRESERVES: Lingonberries are sometimes called cowberries or mountain cranberries, and these small, tart red berries are in a fact a relative of the cranberry. They grow wild in Scandinavia, Russia, Canada, and other northern regions, including parts of Alaska and Maine. Because of a short growing season in the late summer, they are rarely available fresh outside these areas. However, they make delicious preserves, jam, and syrup. The preserves form a traditional accompaniment to many Swedish specialties, from meatballs to pancakes. Lingonberry preserves are available in gourmet markets and some supermarkets.

MASCARPONE: A rich Italian cream cheese, mascarpone has a silky-smooth texture and a delicate flavor. It is used in both savory and sweet dishes. Sold in plastic tubs, it can be found in gourmet markets and specialty cheese shops, as well as some supermarkets; the American versions now available can be very good.

MISO: A staple of Japanese cooking, miso is fermented soybean paste. It's made by combining crushed cooked soybeans with a special mold, salt, and a grain, usually barley or rice. The mixture is aged for at least three months or for as long as three years. Different types of miso vary in color, flavor, and texture, depending on the grain used and the aging period. The most common are white (also called pale miso) and red (or brown) miso;

hatcho miso, or mamemiso, is a high-quality, more expensive miso made from only soybeans. Some misos, usually the paler types, are mellow and almost sweet; others are quite salty and strong flavored. Miso is used in soups, sauces (including dipping sauces), and dressings; it's great as a marinade for fish and many grilled foods. Miso is available in Japanese markets and health food stores, as well as some supermarkets. It should be kept tightly sealed or wrapped in the refrigerator.

MUSTARD OIL: Mustard oil is a spicy oil made from mustard seeds. It is used for cooking in northern and northeastern India and as an ingredient in making many different kinds of pickles throughout the country. Mustard oil is golden yellow and has a pungent aroma and taste. Mustard and mustard seeds are common ingredients in Scandinavian cooking; I like to use the oil in small quantities to add a sharp mustard flavor to a dish. Mustard oil can be found in Indian markets and through mail order (see Sources, page 289). If you do not have it on hand, you can substitute whole-grain mustard as a flavoring.

MUSTARD SEEDS: Mustard seeds may be yellow (or white), brown, or black. Yellow mustard seeds are the most commonly available; they are also the mildest and are the basis for "American-style" mustards. Brown and black (or purple) mustard seeds are hotter, with black being the most pungent. Yellow mustard seeds are available in any supermarket; brown mustard seeds can be found in some supermarkets, and in Asian and specialty markets or through mail order (see Sources, pages 289–290). Black mustard seeds are relatively rare; brown mustard seeds can be substituted for them in most recipes.

NUT OILS: Some of the recipes in this book call for nut oils, including hazelnut and almond oils. These fragrant oils can turn rancid very quickly, so it's important to buy them from a reliable

source with good turnover and to choose smaller bottles rather than large. Store them in the refrigerator or a cool, dark place, and use within 6 months (or sooner) after opening. (If refrigerated, the oils will thicken; bring to room temperature before using.)

PANKO: These Japanese-style bread crumbs are coarser and more irregular in shape than ordinary dried bread crumbs. When panko are used for breading fried foods, they absorb very little oil and produce a light, crisp crust. They are available in cellophane bags and in boxes in Japanese and other Asian markets.

PICKLED GINGER: Thinly sliced ginger pickled in vinegar, sugar, and salt is a Japanese condiment, called *gari*, most often served as a garnish with sushi. Jars of pink-hued pickled ginger are available in many supermarkets as well as in Asian markets.

PORT: Port is a fortified wine produced in Portugal's Douro Valley. There are three main types: white, ruby, and tawny. White port (from white grapes) may be dry or extra-dry; in Portugal, it is often served as an aperitif rather than after the meal, as other ports are. Ruby port is fruity and sweeter. The color (and hence the name) of tawny port is a result of aging; tawny ports are made from a blend of red grapes or, occasionally, from a combination of red and white grapes. For the recipes in this book, a dry sherry can be substituted when white port is called for; a medium-sweet Madeira (another fortified wine, from the Portuguese island of Madeira) can be substituted for ruby port.

SAFFRON: The most expensive spice in the world (it's actually the stigma of a type of crocus and must be painstakingly gathered by hand), saffron is used in a variety of Scandinavian dishes and baked goods, most notably St. Lucia Buns (page 206), to which it contributes a distinct flavor and a golden yellow hue. Saffron may be purchased as whole threads or ground; if buying ground saffron, which loses its flavor more quickly, choose a high-quality brand from a spice purveyor or a specialty spice market. Saffron is available in many supermarkets and most gourmet markets, as well as through mail order (see Sources, pages 289–290).

SALT: I always use kosher salt for cooking because of its pure flavor and flaky texture. Ordinary table salt has been treated with anti-caking agents and other additives, which are noticeable when you taste it; kosher salt doesn't contain any additives. Teaspoon per teaspoon, it is less salty than table salt because it is coarser. Thus, if substituting table salt in the recipes in this book, you may want to use a bit less than specified.

For garnishing certain dishes, I use fleur de sel, an aromatic sea salt from France's Brittany. Rarer than ordinary sea salt, it has large flaky crystals and a pure briny flavor and aroma. Fleur de sel is not used for cooking but rather as a finishing touch. It is expensive, but a little goes a long way. It is available at specialty markets and through mail order (see Sources, page 289).

SAMBAL OELEK: Sambals are Indonesian chile sauces and pastes used both in cooking and as table condiments. Sambal oelek is made primarily from ground red chiles, vinegar, and garlic. It has a good amount of heat and a nice tartness from the vinegar. It's available in Asian markets and some gourmet shops, as well as through mail order (see Sources, pages 289–290).

TANDOORI SPICES: Tandoori spices, also known as tandoori masala (*masala* is the Hindu word for "spices"), are the fragrant spice mixtures used in the Punjab region of India for seasoning foods to be cooked in the clay ovens called tandoors. The mix can be used as a dry rub, added to a marinade, or heated in oil for sautéing. As with other spice mixes, there are many versions,

but typical ingredients include cumin and coriander seeds, cayenne, cinnamon, cloves, ginger, turmeric, and garlic. Commercial versions (and many homemade ones as well) often contain red food color powder, giving the marinated food its characteristic coloring, but paprika may also be used to similar effect. Tandoori spice mixes are available in Indian and some other Asian markets and through mail order (see Sources, pages 289–290).

TARO ROOT: A starchy tuber, also known as dasheen, malanga, and eddo, among many other names, taro is a staple ingredient throughout the Caribbean, as well as in the Polynesian Islands, Hawaii, China, and Japan. Though similar to potatoes when cooked, it has a unique nutty flavor. Taro has rough light brown to dark brown skin and dense white, creamy, or slightly pink flesh. Choose roots that are firm with no signs of shriveling, and store them at room temperature for no more than a few days. Taro should never be eaten raw, as some types can be toxic if not thoroughly cooked, and it must be peeled before cooking. (The root can sometimes irritate skin; wear disposable plastic gloves if you notice this — and don't rub your eyes while preparing it.) Look for taro in ethnic and specialty produce markets.

THAI CURRY PASTE: See *Curry Paste* (page 280).

THAI RED CHILE SAUCE/SWEET CHILE SAUCE: Made from red chiles, garlic, sugar, vinegar, and salt, these delicious thin sauces are both hot and sweet. They are served as dipping sauces, especially for grilled foods, and used as glazes, in dressings, or as condiments. They are usually sold in glass bottles in Asian markets and specialty markets and through mail order (see Sources, pages 289–290).

TRUFFLE OIL: Truffle oil is olive oil or another oil, such as grapeseed, that has been infused with the flavor of truffles, either white or black. The best of these oils are incredibly fragrant, and just a few drops can flavor a whole dish. Black and white truffle oil can be used more or less interchangeably, although the black tends to be more compatible with beef and other meats, the white with fish and vegetables — but it's often a matter of personal taste. Truffle oil is relatively inexpensive, especially since a little goes a long way; it is sold in small bottles at gourmet markets and through mail order (see Sources, page 290). Once the bottle is opened, the oil should be kept in a cool, dark place; do not refrigerate it, as chilling will cause the oil to congeal and allow the fragrance to escape. Unopened bottles of truffle oil can be kept for a year or more (most have sell-by dates on the label); once opened, however, the oil should be used within a month or two.

VANILLA BEANS: Vanilla beans are the seed pods of a climbing orchid native to Latin America. The best vanilla beans come from Madagascar (these are sometimes called Bourbon vanilla beans), from Mexico, and from Tahiti; high-quality vanilla beans are also now being grown in Hawaii. Vanilla beans are relatively expensive, but they have a stronger, purer flavor than vanilla extract. (But if you do use extract, buy only pure extract.) Vanilla beans can be found at gourmet markets and some supermarkets and through mail order (see Sources, page 289).

TO USE A VANILLA BEAN: Split the bean lengthwise with a sharp paring knife, then scrape out the mass of tiny seeds with the back of the knife. Depending on the recipe, just the seeds or both the seeds and the pod may be added to other ingredients (then the pod is strained out or removed after it has infused its flavor).

TO MAKE VANILLA SUGAR: When you are using only the vanilla seeds in a recipe, save the pod for vanilla sugar. One or

two are enough to flavor a pound of sugar; freeze extra pods to use later if you like. Simply bury the pod (or pods) in a canister of granulated sugar and let stand for a few days before using. Replenish the sugar as you use it — buried in sugar, the vanilla pod will remain aromatic for a few months or longer. Use the sugar in desserts and sweets, or stir it into hot coffee or chocolate.

WASABI: Often called Japanese horseradish, this Asian root is not actually a relative of horseradish, but it is similarly pungent. The fresh root is rarely, if ever, available in the United States. However, wasabi powder makes an excellent stand-in. It is mixed with a little water to make the condiment served with sushi. It is sold in small tins in Japanese and other Asian markets, as well as in some supermarkets. Avoid the wasabi paste that comes in tubes, since it loses its flavor and bite rather rapidly.

NOTES ABOUT EQUIPMENT

IMMERSION BLENDER

A hand-held immersion blender, also called a wand blender, allows you to puree soups and other foods right in the cooking pot; it is also handy for making vinaigrettes and other emulsified sauces. Immersion blenders are sold in most housewares departments and in kitchenware shops.

MANDOLINES AND OTHER SLICERS

A mandoline is a classic French metal slicer that has several adjustable blades for cutting food into thin or thick slices, julienne strips, and even waffle-cuts. Now made of stainless steel, mandolines are quite pricey. Several types of inexpensive plastic vegetable slicers make good alternatives. The Japanese slicer called a Benriner comes with a set of razor-sharp blades and can slice ingredients paper-thin. This type is sturdy enough even for restaurant kitchens, and many restaurant chefs now use them. Benriner-type slicers are available at Asian supermarkets, many kitchenware shops, and through mail order (see Sources, page 289). Other plastic slicers are sold in kitchenware shops, including various German brands that come with several different blades. Most plastic slicers come with hand guards, as do mandolines.

STOVETOP SMOKER

At the restaurant we make our own stovetop smoker using a large roasting pan, a wire rack, and heavy-duty aluminum foil. For home smoking, you might consider the Camerons Stovetop Smoker. It is inexpensive, easy to use, and versatile, as it can also be used as a steamer. For more information, go to www.camersonssmoker.com.

SILPAT

Silpats are reusable silicone baking liners that turn any baking sheet into a nonstick pan. They are perfect for baking Candied Fruit (or Carrot) Chips (page 247), certain cookies, and anything that might otherwise stick to the baking pan. Although Silpats, which come in various sizes, are fairly expensive, they can be used hundreds of times, and they are easy to clean. They can be found in kitchenware and some gourmet shops, as well as through mail order (see Sources, page 289).

SOURCES

AQUAVIT

www.aquavit.org

LINGONBERRY SPREAD.

THE BAKER'S CATALOGUE

P.O. Box 876

Norwich, VT 05055-0876

Tel: 800-827-6836

www.bakerscatalogue.com

ALMOND FLOUR, FLEUR DE SEL, VANILLA BEANS, AND OTHER INGREDIENTS FOR BAKING, AS WELL AS MANDOLINES AND BENRINER SLICERS, SILPATS, AND OTHER EQUIPMENT.

CUZINS MARKET

520 Ninth Avenue

New York, NY 10018

Tel: 212-736-5737

HIGH-QUALITY MEAT, INCLUDING SPECIALTY CUTS AND GAME OF ALL KINDS.

D'ARTAGNAN

280 Wilson Avenue

Newark, NJ 07105

Tel: 800-DARTAGN (327-8246); 973-344-0456

www.dartagnan.com

FRESH DUCK FOIE GRAS AND DUCK CONFIT; SQUAB, PHEASANT, VENISON, AND OTHER POULTRY AND GAME.

KALUSTYAN'S

123 Lexington Avenue

New York, NY 10016

Tel: 212-685-3451

www.kalustyans.com

MIDDLE EASTERN, ASIAN, AND MEDITERRANEAN SPICES AND OTHER INGREDIENTS, AS WELL AS AN ARRAY OF OTHER INTERNATIONAL FOODS AND PRODUCTS, INCLUDING AMCHOOR, KAFFIR LIME LEAVES, KETJAP MANIS, MUSTARD OIL, SAMBAL OELEK, AND WONTON WRAPPERS.

PENZEYS SPICES

19300 Janacek Court

Brookfield, WI 53045

Tel: 800-741-7787

www.penzeys.com

SPICES OF ALL KINDS, INCLUDING JUNIPER BERRIES, PINK PEPPERCORNS, AND VARIOUS SPICE MIXES.

The Sausage Maker

1500 Clinton Street

Buffalo, NY 14206

Tel: 716-824-6510

www.sausagemaker.com

Sausage casings.

Tsar Nicoulai Caviar

144 King Street

San Francisco, CA 94107

Tel: 800-952-2842

www.tsarnicoulai.com

Farm-raised California sturgeon caviar.

Urbani Truffles USA

29-24 40th Avenue

Long Island City, NY 11101

Tel: 800-281-2330; 718-392-5050

www.urbani.com

Fresh and canned truffles and truffle products of all kinds, including truffle oils, truffle juice, and truffle peelings.

World Merchants

1509 Western Avenue

Seattle, WA 98101

Tel: 206-682-7274

www.worldspice.com

A wide variety of spices and spice mixes, including amchoor, berberé, and kaffir lime leaves.

INDEX